OUR DAILY WAR

Andrey Kurkov

OUR DAILY WAR

OPEN BORDERS PRESS
LONDON

First published in Great Britain in 2024 by
Open Borders Press
an imprint of
Orenda Books
London
www.orendabooks.co.uk/openborderspress

9 8 7 6 5 4 3 2 1

A CIP catalogue record for this book is available from the British Library

ISBN (HB) 978-1-916788-68-8

The publisher acknowledges with gratitude the editorial contribution
to this text of Elizabeth Kurkov

The publisher acknowledges the original use of the author's speeches and
texts to the Financial Times, the Haldór Laxness International Literature
Prize, the Geneva Conference, the Munich Security Conference 2023
and the American Academy of Arts and Letters

Map © Emily Faccini

Designed and typeset in Sabon by Libanus Press Ltd
Printed and bound in Great Britain by
CPI Group (UK) Ltd, Croydon, CR0 4YY

CONTENTS

For the soldiers of the Ukrainian army

BELARUS

POLAND

UKRAINE

VOLYN

RIVNE

Lutsk

ZHYTOMYR

Chernobyl

Irpin

Bucha

K

Radekhiv

Stavishche

Vorzel

Kostivtsi

Makariv

Yavoriv

Lviv

LVIV

TERNO
-PIL

KHMELNY
-TSKYI

Bila
Tserk

Slavske

Ternopil

Khmelnytskyi

Vinnytsia

SK.

IVANO
FRANKIVS'K

VINNYTSIA

Uman

Uzhhorod

ZAKARPATTIA

Mukacheve

CHERNIV
-TSI

Dniester River

TRANSNISTRIA

HU.

ROMANIA

Carpathian
Mountains

MOLDOVA

ODES

Odesa

KYIV

① Andrii's Descent
② Baikove cemetery
③ House of Teachers
④ Kyiv University
⑤ Mariinsky Park
⑥ Opera House
⑦ Parliament
⑧ Podil District

Bilgorod

Zat

ODESA

Reni

Kiliya

⑨ Pechersk Lavra Mon.
⑩ Sophia Square
⑪ Circus
⑫ Volodymyrska St

⑬ Taras Shevchenko Blv.
⑭ National Museum
of the
History of Medicine

01.08.2022

Do You Know Your Bedroom's G.P.S. Coordinates?
They do!

When, many years ago, I first read that the Internet was invented for military purposes, I did not really believe it. I was a humanities student, and I did not really understand the technological sciences. Only this can explain my naivety. Later I remembered that nuclear bombs appeared much before the first nuclear power plants.

Now that the "military Internet" is playing as crucial a role in Ukraine as the "peaceful Internet", I no longer have any doubts about the priority of military scientific developments. Moreover, I understand that from a military point of view, everything and everyone in the world is a potential target and that everything in the world has G.P.S. coordinates that enable destructive forces to hit their chosen target with precision. The same G.P.S. coordinates that help me to find a prehistoric cave on the island of Crete can be fed into a missile launched from a Russian submarine in the Black Sea in order to destroy or, in modern Russian terms, to "de-Nazify" this cave.

It seems that at least one of the 40 rockets sent to blow up the Ukrainian city of Mykolaiv on the night of July 31 was programmed to hit the master bedroom of a private house. It was this rocket that killed the owner of the largest Ukrainian grain trading company, Nibulon, Oleksiy Vadatursky, and his wife Raisa.

The editor-in-chief of the Russia Today television channel, Margarita Simonyan, immediately commented on this murder, stating that Vadatursky was included in Russia's sanctions list for allegedly financing "punitive detachments". It is not clear what kind of "punitive detachments" she was talking about, but Simonyan tweeted confidently: "He can now be crossed off the list."

I am almost sure that Vadatursky, as the fifteenth richest man in Ukraine according to *Forbes* magazine, was helping his country and the Ukrainian army. He must have been confident about Ukraine's victory. Otherwise, he surely would have left Mykolaiv, subject to daily missile attacks, for somewhere safer. The *Le Monde* journalist Olivier Truc, who had met Vadatursky a few days before his death, reported that the millionaire was aware that he was a target.

A key figure in the Ukrainian grain export business, Vadatursky was involved in the preparation of shipping routes for the export of grain under the Turkish U.N.-brokered agreement. The first test ship, with 26,000 tons of corn under the flag of Sierra Leone, set sail from the Odesa seaport on Sunday, August 3 without his blessing.

The grain corridor from Odesa through the Bosphorus and beyond has started working and Ukraine has resumed exporting agricultural products during the full-scale war with Russia. It is hard to imagine the cost of insuring the cargo ships, but the fact that export routes have reopened is extremely valuable. Ukraine needs to earn money to support the war effort and will do so mostly in Africa and Asia. Russia can earn money to support its aggression almost anywhere, including in Europe, since it is still selling gas and oil to E.U. countries.

In Kyiv, there have been no shortages of gas yet. There were problems with petrol and salt for a few days, but they have already been resolved. The ongoing issue is the constant need for blood donors. Kyiv residents, like other Ukrainians, are already accustomed to donating blood. No-one is surprised by the queues outside the blood donor department at the Central Children's Hospital, which since the very beginning of the war has been treating wounded servicemen, but eyebrows were raised when, recently, monks from the Kyiv-Pechersk monastery, as well as students of the theological schools and colleges of the Moscow Patriarchate, decided to donate blood for wounded Ukrainian soldiers.

Not so long ago, the leaders of the Ukrainian Orthodox Church of the Moscow Patriarchate refused to stand up to honour the memory of Ukraine's dead soldiers. Now the monks of the same Moscow-controlled church are donating blood for the Ukrainian wounded. Perhaps they want to prove their loyalty to Kyiv, not Moscow. Or maybe they do so in memory of the monks and nuns of the Svyatogorsk monastery of the Moscow Patriarchate in Donbas, who were killed by Russian artillery shelling. Whatever has brought about this change of heart, the main thing is the result – better-stocked blood banks.

One thing that is now missing in Kyiv are notice boards outside money exchange points and banks announcing the rates on offer. Until recently, the exchange rates had changed very little since the start of the Russian invasion. These exchange rate boards were a reassuring sight around Ukrainian towns and cities. Now, after sharp falls in the value of the hryvnias, the National Bank has forbidden the public display of exchange rates. If you want to know the latest rate you must go into the bank or currency exchange office and, putting on your glasses, peer up at the table of exchange rates behind the glass of the cashier's window. The print size used in these notices is often so small that you might need a magnifying glass to read them. Of course, if they prove friendly and do not mind answering the same question for the hundredth time, the easiest way is to ask the cashier.

Despite tragic news daily, Ukrainians have not lost their sense of humour. Jokes are probably the cheapest way to maintain optimism. The National Bank's instruction to keep exchange rates in a state of semi-secrecy has spawned dozens, if not hundreds, of anecdotes, jokes, and cartoons. The most popular quip is that in the coming days the Ukrainian authorities will prohibit the display of prices in supermarkets. Shoppers will only know the cost of their purchases once they get to the checkout.

Ukrainians have been greeting other innovations from local or central authorities with humour – albeit sometimes very angry humour. Since last week, many cities have introduced a rule that public transport must stop running whenever an air raid siren sounds and that passengers must be directed to the nearest bomb shelter. This rule has already been introduced in Kyiv and Vinnytsia. True, this has become reality only in part. Buses and trams do stop when the siren sounds and drivers do ask passengers to get off and proceed to a safe place; however, passengers in general remain standing close to the tram or bus – to await the end of the alert and to continue their journey. In this way, moving targets have become stationary ones and easier to hit.

You can argue about the logic of some decisions, but almost all state decisions are motivated now by only two things: security issues and the country's difficult financial situation. Owing to the lack of money for armaments, the government is discussing the introduction of a new ten per cent. tax on all imported goods. That will mean a price hike of ten per cent. on top of the inflation that Ukraine is already experiencing.

In peacetime, a tax like this might stimulate domestic production of goods, but the Ukrainian economy, as President Zelensky said the other day, is in a coma. Many factories and plants have closed, while others are in the process of moving to the relative safety of western Ukraine. For now, increased local production is a distant dream.

It has to be said that some new businesses are appearing – mainly those servicing the war effort – such as producers of clothes and reliable shoes for soldiers and manufacturers of equipment for military personnel, including body armour. These locally produced goods are purchased by volunteers and volunteer groups with money collected from citizens and foreign friends of Ukraine.

War also creates other unusual job opportunities. For example, firms have emerged that provide preparatory surveys for agricultural land that requires demining. The demining itself can only be carried out by certified sappers from private or government agencies. In Ukraine, while only three private companies have the right to clear mines, the licences of two of them are about to expire. These companies employ only between ten and fifteen sappers, while the number of farmers waiting to have their fields and orchards cleared is huge. Some farmers feel they cannot wait and so turn for help to unofficial (and therefore illegal) help. These unofficial sappers are often former military men, as well as treasure hunters who own metal detectors. The unofficial sappers charge a lot of money to do the job quickly but do not give any guarantees.

The official sappers' charges for demining from a licensed private demining company are quite high, starting from three dollars for the inspection of one square metre of land. True, the official sapper companies will sometimes demine private agricultural areas for free. Instead of a charge, they ask the farmers to make a donation towards their petrol costs and the salaries of the sappers. Today, legal sappers in Ukraine earn about $700 per month. How much the unofficial sappers earn is not known. According to stories told by farmers, unofficial sappers ask for $1000 for the survey and demining of one hectare of field (that is, 10,000 square metres).

According to the Association of Sappers of Ukraine, at least 4,800,000 hectares of Ukrainian land are mined, not counting the Chernobyl zone which was also temporarily occupied by the Russian army. Some fields in Donbas have not been demined since 2015.

It is a pity that Google Maps has not yet developed a system to warn you when you are approaching a mined area. According to Google Maps, even today you can reach occupied Donetsk from Kyiv by road in under eleven hours. Are they also trying to entertain us by joking?

08.08.2022

Poetry and Other Forms of Torture

"Posthumous journeys" are once again a sad hallmark of Ukrainian burial culture. The longest and most famous post-humous journey in Ukrainian history was made by the country's national poet, Taras Shevchenko. He died in St Petersburg in 1861, having returned there after sixteen years of penal service as a soldier in the tsar's army in the Kazakhstan desert.

Shevchenko was first buried in St Petersburg, but after

fifty-eight days, the poet's body was exhumed and, in accordance with his wishes, taken to Kyiv. For two nights, the lead coffin with the poet's body lay in the Church of the Nativity in the city's Podil district. It was then loaded onto a boat and taken down the Dnipro River to Kaniv where, on a hill above the riverbank, the poet was once more laid to rest.

The Donetsk poet Vasyl Stus died in a prison camp in 1985, when Gorbachev was already in power in the Soviet Union. In 1989, his remains were transported home by plane to Ukraine from the Urals region of Russia. It is a good thing that he was reburied at the Baikove cemetery in Kyiv and not in Donetsk, the city of his youth, otherwise his grave would by now have been destroyed by Russian special services or the military. A bas-relief memorial to him on the wall of Donetsk University was demolished by separatists in 2014.

The spirit of the nation is kept alive by the souls of dead writers and poets. Just as the Scots' pride and vision are sustained by the spirit of Robert Burns, Ukrainians still feel supported by the souls of Taras Shevchenko and Vasyl Stus. The first was a victim of the Russian Empire, the second a victim of the Soviet Union. Both lived short lives, both were punished for their free thinking and their poetry, and both died in a foreign land. That foreign land now wants to reach out and disturb their resting places.

Over the past six months, hundreds of vehicles have made the mournful journey from the front line to the homes of fallen soldiers throughout Ukraine. Dead or alive, soldiers must return home.

In Kyiv, a church funeral service was held for Oleksiy Vadatursky and his wife Raisa who were killed by a Russian missile. Their bodies were brought from Mykolaiv for the funeral mass and then taken back to their hometown of Mykolaiv, located

500 kilometres south of the capital. You might ask why the bodies of a murdered couple had to travel one thousand kilometres for the sake of a church ceremony. The answer is simple – because of the war. Mykolaiv is bombed several times a day and Russian artillery would not allow the deceased couple's loved ones to say goodbye to them in safety. The posthumous journey of the Vadaturskys allowed their Kyiv friends and State representatives to pay their respects.

After his death, it emerged that Vadatursky had played a key role in preventing the Russian army from occupying the port city of Mykolaiv. At the very beginning of the war, he gave his company's cargo vessels to the military to block the port's entrance, making it impossible for Russian ships to approach.

In Mykolaiv, as in other cities near the front line, every morning the authorities report to residents what has been destroyed during the night by shelling and Russian rockets. The city is gradually being reduced to ruins. Many villages around the city have already been completely destroyed. Their inhabitants have either died or have become refugees. At first, of course, the inhabitants of the villages nearest to Mykolaiv sought protection in the city. As in the Middle Ages, people see the city as a fortress that can protect them. The villagers from around Mariupol must have seen that city in the same way, as the inhabitants of the town of Derhachi near Kharkiv still do.

When a town or city, or what is left of it, is captured by the enemy, there begins a procedure for checking and registering residents, one decreed in the Russian army's rulebook. This is called "filtration". Filtration camps are set up near the captured cities. Section by section, the local population are told to bring their documents and mobile phones and are then driven to the camp. Only those who have no patriotic tattoos and have not made pro-Ukrainian posts on social media networks and who can prove their loyalty to Russia, "pass" the filtration process.

For a while, the Russians denied the existence of filtration camps in the occupied territory of Ukraine. Later, however, they justified their use, saying that the camps help to prevent pro-Ukrainian elements – Maidan participants or army personnel, for example – from entering Russian territory. This explanation indicates another reason why the Russians have set up eighteen filtration centres in former prison camps and purpose-built detention facilities in the occupied territories. Those who pass the filtration process are sent to Russia as refugees. They are mostly sent to depressed regions: to Murmansk in the far north and even Kamchatka, areas where the local population is particularly sparse. Those who do not pass filtration are sent to prison camps or, according to some eyewitness accounts, are killed immediately inside the filtration camps. Almost all of those who are prepared to speak about their experiences during the filtration process prefer to remain anonymous. They are afraid of intimidation.

Among those Ukrainians who have gone through filtration and have been sent to Russia, some have managed to escape to Estonia or Finland and then find their way back to Ukraine, bringing with them accounts of the filtration process. Their stories are similar. A lot has already been written about the checking procedures employed – the interrogations, finger-printing and compulsory completion of questionnaires. In fact, these procedures were invented in the 1940s by the Soviet secret police agency of the time.

For me, the most surprising thing about the shadowy activity inside the camps is the use of poetry as torture or punishment. Early on it was said that Ukrainian citizens and prisoners of war were being forced to learn the Russian anthem, a slightly modified version of the Soviet anthem. But recently, reports tell of Ukrainians being forced to memorise the poem "Forgive Us, Dear Russians".

I had assumed that this poem had been written by a Russian poet "on behalf" of the Ukrainians, but the poem's author is a Ukrainian, a pro-Russian poet from Poltava, Irina Samarina. She wrote the poem in 2014 in response to a better-known poem "We Will Never Be Brothers" by the then-Russian-speaking Ukrainian poetess Anastasia Dmitruk. Anastasia's poem, addressed to the Russians, ends with the words "You have a tsar, we have democracy. We will never be brothers." Although now for the most part forgotten, in 2014 this poem became quite a popular song. Anastasia Dmitruk continues to write poetry, but mostly now in Ukrainian. She also helps to organise protests around the world against the Russian war in Ukraine.

Irina Samarina grew up in Poltava in central Ukraine, but her work is little known. On her Facebook page, she writes, apparently without irony, that she works for the G.R.U., Russia's military secret service. She also reposts the anti-Ukrainian video monologues of the pro-Russian propagandist Anatoliy Shariy, who probably does work for the G.R.U. He is suspected of receiving money from the Russian secret services to buy a villa in Spain. Spanish authorities have taken possession of the property.

Samarina's poem states, "But there is no Ukraine without Russia, just as a lock has no use without a key . . . But they will not destroy my love for Russia, as long as we are together, God is with us!" Russian mass media and online platforms have tried to boost Samarina's popularity inside Russia, presenting her as an example of "healthy Ukraine". This strategy does not seem to have worked, possibly because of the mediocrity of her poetry. However, at least one of her poems will remain in the memory of Ukrainians who experienced Russian captivity.

For many Ukrainians trapped in the occupied territories, having to learn rotten poetry will not be their worst memory. Married couples are sometimes separated in the filtration camps: a wife passes filtration and is driven out of the camp and into Russian territory, while what happens to her husband remains unknown.

Many "filtered" Ukrainian citizens who end up in Russia are helped secretly by Russian volunteer groups to travel to Europe. This activity is co-ordinated mainly from abroad, including from Georgia and Britain. The Rubicus group, which has already helped nearly 2000 Ukrainian internees to leave Russia, operates from Britain but with help from Russian volunteers, who are monitored constantly and hunted by the Russian special services.

Russians can denounce any of their compatriots seen trying to help Ukrainian refugees. In the city of Penza, for instance, neighbours reported Irina Gurskaya, a volunteer who was collecting clothes and money for refugees who had been brought from Mariupol to a nearby village. Gurskaya was summoned to the police station and questioned for several hours, being threatened with prosecution and huge fines. When a local lawyer, Igor Zhulimov, volunteered to defend Gurskaya, his neighbours painted the words "Ukrainian Nazi" on his apartment door. Nonetheless, some Russian volunteers continue to collect money for Ukrainians and help them to reach the borders with Estonia or Finland.

The vast majority of Russians support the aggression against Ukraine. For the few people who choose to help Ukrainians, the pressure and persecution can become too much. Then they also leave for Europe, further increasing the proportion of people in Russia who support Putin.

Another factor enlarging the pro-Putin majority in Russia is migration from the occupied part of Donbas, from the two separatist republics. These migrants would probably be happy to learn Samarina's poem "Forgive Us, Dear Russians", but most likely they have yet to hear of it or of her. They prefer Pushkin, not as a poet, but as a symbol of the greatness of Russian culture. Recently in Ukraine, defenders of Russian culture have been called "Pushkinists".

The war against Russian culture has become an integral part of the Russian–Ukrainian war. Ukraine's Ministry of Culture and Information has announced a project called "Turn Russian Books into Wastepaper". The project plans to use the money raised from recycling Russian and Soviet books to support the Ukrainian army. I asked my Ukrainian publisher Oleksandr Krasovitsky how much money could be made by recycling such wastepaper. "Very little!" he said, "there are almost no factories in Ukraine that can efficiently turn wastepaper into usable paper." I wonder whether this project to recycle all Russian books will continue even if it is proven to be inefficient.

The war of words goes on.

15.08.2022

War-time Odesa

Last Saturday, "Don Quixote" was performed at the Odesa Opera and Ballet Theatre. Although it started at four o'clock, the hall was almost full. Daytime is now considered safer for theatre. The poster for "Don Quixote" still states that the ballet was staged by the Honoured Artist of Russia, Yuri Vasyuchenko. Not so long ago he was the chief choreographer of the Odesa Theatre, but he now works in Kazakhstan, at Almaty's Abai Theatre. The new chief choreographer is Armenian, Garry Sevoyan, and the guest principal conductor is Hirofumi Yoshida from Japan. Among the ballet dancers and theatre musicians there are many citizens of neighbouring Moldova.

The theatre's cosmopolitan mix reflects Odesa's origins: it is a city built by the Basques, Spaniards and French. One of the first mayors of the city was the Duke of Richelieu, whose monument stands at the top of the city's famous Potemkin Steps, above the city's presently non-functioning passenger port. Richelieu was both mayor and governor-general of Odesa. When the Bourbons regained the throne in France, he returned home to become Prime Minister in the government of Louis XVIII. It was Richelieu who gave impetus to the development of the port of Odesa, from which now, during the war, flotillas of cargo vessels loaded with wheat, corn and other food products set out to feed the world.

In the last two weeks, Odesa has not been bombed and life, especially the cultural and epicurean, has flourished, almost returning to pre-war levels of activity. Odesa's most famous market, Privoz, is open. However, the fish rows are practically empty – fishermen are forbidden to go to sea. Odesa without fresh fish is a vivid symbol of wartime life. It was the same during World War II, when Odesa was occupied by Romanian troops, Hitler's allies. On the other hand, fruit and vegetables are abundant and prices have risen very little.

Tourists, refugees from eastern Ukraine and residents have all already decided exactly where it is (relatively) safe to swim in the sea off Odesa. Officially, there is a ban on going to the beach. Mines hidden under the water have proved fatal – most recently near the beach in Zatoka where two people were killed and one wounded. Nonetheless, people still bathe along the length of the coast of Odesa region. Hotels and recreation centres are working. Local winemakers deliver wine to the beachside bars and cafés. Watermelons in the south of Odesa region are as sweet as the better-known Kherson variety. And now they must replace watermelons from Kherson because Russian troops have prohibited Kherson farmers from delivering any products to unoccupied areas of Ukraine.

Despite the holiday atmosphere in Odesa city, the region is regularly reminded of the war. Russian forces know that Odesa's coastline is protected by American Harpoon missiles. Russian intelligence would like to seek out the launch pads so that they can be destroyed. No-one knows whether Russia has managed to find and destroy even a single missile launcher, but Russian missiles frequently blow up hangars and warehouses along the Odesa coast, apparently believing that they contain the Ukrainian army's weapon stocks. Zatoka, one of the most popular Ukrainian resorts, was likewise sprayed with rockets that killed several tourists and left hotels and cafés in ruins.

In Odesa region, even internally displaced people become "holidaymakers", especially those who can pay to stay in campsites and hotels. But autumn will arrive, spelling an end to the holiday season. Once September comes, those "holidaymakers" who remain in the region will be considered internally displaced people. Many of those who now pay to stay in holiday houses will be allowed to continue to stay there for free during the winter. The only problem is heating. Most holiday homes and hotels do not have any because they are, for the most part, used exclusively in the summer season.

In their determination to find out where in Odesa region the

Ukrainian army is hiding its rocket launchers, Russia's troops and its main intelligence directorate of the Russian Ministry of Defence are actively scouring the region for potential traitors, especially among Russian citizens who have been living in Ukraine.

It is easy for them to manipulate Russian citizens – they can be blackmailed through relatives who are still in Russia. But there are also a number of pro-Russian Ukrainians. The money offered for such information may also be a factor. If you agree to collaborate, payment is sent directly to your electronic wallet. All you have to do is walk or drive around Odesa and Odesa region photographing everything related to the Ukrainian army, sending the co-ordinates over the Internet.

The Ukrainian security service continuously reminds citizens to be aware of anyone who photographs military or civilian structures and to report them to the security services or the police. All Ukrainians, including me, get reminders about this on their mobile phones.

The Ukrainian counter-intelligence officers are also keeping busy. They are especially interested in Russian citizens living in Ukraine. There are a lot of them: 175,000, according to official statistics. Most of them are on the side of Ukraine in this war, but there are plenty of exceptions. Unlike citizens of Ukraine, a citizen of another country living in Ukraine cannot be tried for treason. He or she can only be tried for aiding the enemy or for espionage. This accusation could still land a person in prison for fifteen years.

Recently, the Prymorsky Court of Odesa sentenced a Russian citizen living in Odesa to 30 months in prison for providing Russian intelligence services with information about the location of Ukrainian military facilities. He was a native of Moscow and had worked previously at the Institute for Nuclear

Research of the Russian Academy of Sciences. He moved with his Ukrainian wife to live in Odesa.

His short prison sentence angered many Ukrainians. They once more raised questions about corruption in the Ukrainian judicial system. This time, however, corruption does not seem to have played a part in the court's decision. During the judicial investigation, the Russian citizen sincerely repented of his crime. What is more, while he did not bribe the judge – a not uncommon occurrence in Ukraine – he chose to donate almost $100,000 to the Ukrainian army. I think that this case should be publicised so that those Russian agents who are caught in the future know how to get a minimum prison sentence for their crimes.

My Odesa friend Konstantin, a retired journalist, cannot now see his wife. She has been stuck in Moscow since the beginning of the war. For many years, she lived shuttling between Odesa, her home, and Moscow, where her eldest son settled. She went there last to look after her grandchildren. In Moscow, she received a Russian passport and applied for a pension, although she was born and lived most of her life in Odesa. Before the war, she regularly visited Konstantin. On the last visit she left him her Russian pension bank card as his Ukrainian pension, the equivalent of 160€ a month, was not enough for him to live on. Since the beginning of the war, all Russian bank cards have been blocked in Ukraine and Konstantin no longer has access to this additional money, meaning that he has no money for the medicines he needs for his eye treatment. He is almost blind.

More and more couples find themselves separated because of the Russian passport held by one of them. Russian citizens with temporary Ukrainian residence permits can no longer renew them and are required to leave, as are citizens of Belarus.

Those who have been living in Ukraine for a long time and have permanent residency can stay, although Ukrainian special services certainly keep an eye on such people.

Recently, they were keeping tabs on the Akivisons, a family of hotel owners in Odesa whose four popular hotels include the Mozart located near the Opera House. I was lucky enough to stay there several times. The Akivisons are all Russian citizens who live in St Petersburg. Lina Akivison, the daughter of the founder of the company, somehow managed to get a Ukrainian passport without coming to Ukraine and, as a citizen of Ukraine, she managed to re-register the hotels in her own name. In April, some investigative journalism led to the opening of a criminal case regarding her illegal acquisition of Ukrainian citizenship. Now the hotels have been transferred to the state committee for the management of confiscated assets. From the very beginning of the new phase of the war, Lina Akivison has publicly supported the actions of the Russian army in Ukraine and advocated the annexation of occupied Ukrainian territories.

We can assume that she will probably not repent of receiving a Ukrainian passport illegally – no doubt in return for a bribe. She is also unlikely to donate money to the Ukrainian army, but at least she will no longer receive income from any hotels in Odesa. According to the law adopted by the Ukrainian Parliament in early March 2022, all assets of Russian legal entities will be confiscated without compensation and the money received from their sale will be transferred to the state.

At the end of February this year, a new private museum of contemporary art was due to open in Odesa. It was supposed to be located on the premises of the recently bankrupt Odesa Champagne Winery, built in Soviet times. The war has pushed back the opening of the museum until calmer times. The contemporary art collection that was supposed to hang on the walls of the former factory has now been evacuated to western Ukraine. However, the Odesa Champagne, which this plant produced before its closure, is still on sale in Odesa, Vinnytsia, and Kyiv. This plant produced so much Champagne that there may even be enough of it for the future celebration of Ukraine's victory and the end of the war.

There is no great demand for Champagne in Ukraine at the moment. It remains, however, a tradition to drink it at theatre performances, which, thank goodness, are taking place again. So, Champagne will be drunk during the intermissions at the Odesa Opera and Ballet Theatre, in the buffet on the second floor, where theatre lovers can also obtain sandwiches filled with red caviar.

Odesa has always tried to live glamorously, and the city does its best to keep this up even during the war. Odesa's French first governor must have brought to the city a love for luxury and Champagne, and it seems natural even in today's grimmer context.

Upcoming performances at the Odesa Opera and Ballet Theatre include Rossini's "The Barber of Seville" and Verdi's "Aida", as well as the ballets "Masquerade" by Aram Khachaturian and "Giselle" by Adolphe Charles.

22.08.2022

Air Raid Sirens and Crowd Funding

As evening falls in the forests of Zhytomyr region you can often hear the blows of an axe or the sharp buzz of a chainsaw. After dark, late in the evening and sometimes in the middle of the night, you might catch the hum of old cars pulling trailers full of logs, or even the rumble of huge timber trucks carrying the trunks of freshly cut pines away from the forests. The old cars and their trailers are usually making for nearby villages.

The same thing is happening all over Ukraine. This is how the rural population is stocking up on fuel for the winter. This method of obtaining firewood is of course illegal, but the police rarely pay attention to small-time illegal lumberjacks. In the past action was sometimes taken against the large-scale night loggers, those who processed the wood and sold it to builders and furniture makers. These illegal logging operators are now also working for the winter firewood market, but the police have no time to deal with them.

Since 2014 and the beginning of the war with Russia, many residents of Ukrainian villages and towns have ceased to put their trust in gas-powered boilers. They have converted their heating systems to run on other fuel, especially wood. In every village yard and even in the yards of private houses in small towns, the piles of firewood, covered with oilcloth against rain, are steadily growing. I would not be surprised to learn that the same thing is happening in Poland, the Czech Republic, or even in Austria. In Europe, this phenomenon would be due to soaring gas prices. In Ukraine, the prices for gas and gas heating remain at pre-war levels. A decree freezing fuel prices was recently signed by President Zelensky to reassure Ukrainians as winter approaches. Nonetheless, for rural dwellers, the gas bill is the one that hurts the most. While Zelensky can freeze the price of gas, electricity and water, he cannot guarantee the supply of these amenities to Ukrainian homes this winter. That will depend on the Russian artillery. There are already several Ukrainian cities, both occupied and free, which will not have heating this winter.

While Ukraine stubbornly prepares for winter, air raid sirens sound many times a day, warning of Russian missiles flying towards military and civilian targets. The explosions kill citizens and destroy buildings and the infrastructure around them – gas, sewerage and water pipes, electrical networks, and thermal power stations. Where possible, repair teams immediately set out and begin repair work, that is, if the town or city has not been destroyed completely.

There will be no heating this year in Mariupol or Melitopol, in Sloviansk or in Soledar. While heating in Kharkiv and Mykolaiv is by no means a certainty.

Kyiv Mayor Vitali Klitschko has warned residents that the temperature in apartments this winter is not to rise above 18°C. He advises people to buy dry spirit for camp cookers, look out warm clothing, and find additional electric heaters. In our apartment in the centre of Kyiv, the temperature never rises above 18°C in winter. Quite often it drops to thirteen. We are already accustomed to the cold.

The other day, the mayor of Kharkiv, Ihor Terekhov, said, "The enemy is killing the heating system, but we will get through the winter." Repair work on the city's centralised heating systems goes on around the clock and very often under shelling. For the system to work properly this winter, all 200 kilometres of pipes, both those above ground and underground, will have to be replaced during October. Everything depends on the Russians not destroying the pipes and the thermal power plants that have already been repaired.

Oleksandr Senkevych is the mayor of another regularly shelled city, Mykolaiv. He has warned residents that the city's most difficult heating season lies ahead. "Shelling is possible. Today it is warm, but if tomorrow the heating infrastructure is shelled, it will be necessary to drain the water from the system, repair damaged pipes, and only then re-launch the system. During this time, you could be freezing," he said.

Senkevych mentioned something else that all residents of large cities are afraid of, something that is not being discussed: the evacuation of residents in the event of the absence of heating. It would be strange if this issue were not broached sooner or later. The deliberate destruction of thermal power plants by Russian missiles during sub-zero temperatures will make any city uninhabitable. Water will freeze in the buildings' pipes and sooner or later those same pipes will burst. Electric heaters will not suffice to heat an apartment through a Ukrainian winter. But how could a city's population be evacuated and to where? We are talking about hundreds of thousands of people all requiring simultaneous evacuation – no simple task.

The sirens, which warn Ukrainians about the danger of missile attacks, have recently taken on another function: they have become the signal for flash mobs fundraising in support of the Ukrainian army. This crowdfunding plan was created by Natalia Andrikanich, a young volunteer in Uzhhorod. When she found herself getting angry every time an air raid siren growled over the city, she decided to change her attitude and made the siren a reminder to herself that the Ukrainian army needed support to put an end to the need for sirens once and for all. From then on, every time the siren sounded, as well as making her way to the bomb shelter, she donated a small sum of ten to twenty hryvnias (fifteen to 30 euro cents) to the bank account in support of the army.

Other Ukrainians heard about the idea and started doing the same. Now every siren sounding in Ukraine increases the financial support for the Ukrainian armed forces. Most of the money raised this way comes from regions away from the front line. The well-known Kharkiv photographer, Dmitro Ovsyankin, told me,

"In Kharkiv, nobody's salary is large enough to allow them to donate that often!"

Indeed, there are areas and cities where the sirens never stop. It is like that in Nikopol and Derhachi and the entire area of the Donetsk, Zaporizhzhia, Odesa and Mykolaiv regions. In these places, you simply do not have time to go online to donate.

We do not know exactly how the money that goes into the bank account in support of the Ukrainian army is spent. This is definitely a "military secret", but Ukrainians can monitor how and on what the best-known and most active volunteers spend the money they collect. To date, the most successful volunteer fundraiser is the famous showman, stand-up comedian and popular T.V. presenter Serhiy Prytula.

Until 2019, Prytula was a rival of comedian Volodymyr Zelensky on T.V. comedy shows. When Zelensky became president, Prytula started to take an active interest in politics. He tried unsuccessfully to get into Parliament as a deputy from the Voice party founded by the Ukrainian rock singer Svyatoslav Vakarchuk. Prytula also used the Voice platform to put forward his candidacy in Kyiv's mayoral election. Now many Ukrainians see him as a rival to Zelensky in the next election. He has proved his popularity in the process of collecting money for the "people's Bayraktar". He planned to raise 500m. hryvnias (about thirteen million euros) for three combat drones. In just a few days, he collected 600m. hryvnias and immediately brought the fundraising project to a close.

When the Turkish manufacturer of Bayraktar drones learned about Prytula's fundraising project, they decided to donate three drones to the Ukrainian army. So Prytula announced that he would spend the money he had raised to buy a Finnish ICEYE satellite – capable of taking high-quality photographs of the earth even in bad weather. In addition to the satellite itself, he paid for an annual subscription to another group of satellites, which can also provide Ukraine with high-quality photographs of Russian army positions in Ukraine and Crimea. In short, Prytula's volunteering and popularity have reached cosmic heights. However, not all volunteers are television celebrities with political ambitions and, for those with more modest positions in Ukrainian society, it is far more difficult to raise money.

The cult poet from Kharkiv, Serhiy Zhadan, has been actively supporting both military funding campaigns and the cultural life of his much-shelled city from the very beginning of the all-out war. Recently, he announced plans to raise money for one hundred used jeeps and pickup trucks for the army. Zhadan has already sent fifteen vehicles to the military. The cult prose writer from Uzhhorod Andriy Lyubka, whom I mentioned a couple of months ago, has already delivered to the front line the 38th vehicle bought with money raised by him.

In Ukraine, they are joking that there are no used jeeps and pickups left in Europe. Soon, they say, vehicles will have to be brought in by ship all the way from Australia. Every joke has an element of truth in it. The number of jeeps and pickups already handed over to the Ukrainian army today runs into the thousands. In some cases, the military immediately installs mortars or mini-artillery systems and sends them into battle. The military regularly posts on social media networks photographs both of newly received vehicles and of vehicles destroyed by Russian artillery and tanks. The latter photos prove the continued need for further second-hand jeeps and pickups and indicates that replacements will be required for as long as the war continues. Ukrainian volunteer fundraisers could remain key customers for sellers of these versatile vehicles from the rest of Europe for a long time to come.

Traitors and Bees

Last week, volunteers arrived in Kyiv with homeless and orphaned cats from two destroyed cities on the front line in Donbas, Bakhmut and Soledar. The cats and kittens need homes.

While news about the evacuation of pets from the war zone has long ceased to be exotic, the tale of some recently internally displaced bees from the Bakhmut area did catch my attention.

Before the war, there were thousands of beekeepers in Donbas. In addition to coal, the region has always been famous for its honey. Two years ago, despite the loss of Crimea and part of Donbas, Ukraine was still exporting more than 80,000 tons of honey per year. Alas, for the next year or two and perhaps even longer, we can forget about such impressive figures in the honey trade.

We are already accustomed to the idea that pets can become homeless because of the war, but now we have to get used to the idea that tens of thousands of bee colonies have become homeless in Donbas and southern Ukraine. Usually, if a hive is damaged by shelling, the bees become wild and "return" to nature. They swarm from place to place, settling on the walls of destroyed buildings or in trees, until they find a more permanent place for themselves, such as in the hollow of an old tree or the attic of an abandoned house. While looking for a new home, the bees are also trying to fly away from the noise and destruction of war. They flee, not only because collecting pollen that smells like gunpowder is not very pleasant but chiefly because bees love silence, silence in which they can hear each other's buzzing.

At the beginning of summer, on the front line near the town of Bakhmut, a swarm of bees that had flown away from a war-damaged hive settled near some Ukrainian military positions. Among the soldiers was a beekeeper, Oleksandr Afanasyev. He had left his hives at home in Cherkasy region in the care of some volunteer beekeepers. When he saw the swarm, Oleksandr took an empty wooden shell box, made some holes in it and settled the bee colony inside. The bees put up with the cramped conditions of their new home and, having settled inside it, flew off to explore their surroundings in search of flowers.

At the end of the summer, Oleksandr was ordered to transfer to another detachment in a different sector of the front. His brothers-in-arms, who knew nothing about beekeeping, were afraid to take responsibility for the hive and asked Oleksandr to take it with him. Soldiers are not allowed to keep any pets, let alone swarms of bees. So, it was lucky that a volunteer from Cherkasy region, Ihor Ryaposhenko, who brings old pickups and jeeps to the front, arrived at Oleksandr's detachment in time to take the bees home with him, although he had no experience of beekeeping.

The bees travelled more than 700 kilometres in the ammunition box which had become their new hive. They survived the journey and are now settling in Ihor's garden. So as not to disturb them further, Ihor decided not to move them to a proper hive and has left them in their makeshift home. Fortunately, there are several beekeepers in the village, so Ihor has someone to advise him on caring for the bees. He will soon borrow a honey extractor from his neighbours to pump out the honey and will send some proportion of it to the frontline position where the bees first found their military home.

The location of these Ukrainian military positions has not changed recently, although Russian troops are approaching Bakhmut from the east and shell the town every night with artillery and rocket launchers. More than 70,000 inhabitants lived in the city before the war. There are now about 15,000. The Ukrainian military does not have much confidence in the residents. They have chosen to remain in the town or nearby villages in spite of being offered help to evacuate.

Many of these "remainers" continue to say, "We will wait. Let's see what will happen next!" Ukrainian soldiers call such people "waiters" because they seem to be waiting for the territory to be captured by Russia. Some of the "waiters" do seem to have a positive attitude towards the Ukrainian soldiers. Sometimes they give them vegetables and fruit. Nonetheless, not all are considered to be completely trustworthy. They could be coming specifically to see where military equipment is located, information they could send to the Russian artillery forces.

Of those who remained in occupied Melitopol and Mariupol, some, including certain former police officers, decided to cooperate with the Russian occupation authorities. The topic of betrayal is not very popular in Ukraine and certainly not very pleasant to discuss. But recently, more and more information has appeared about Ukrainians helping the Russian army and special services in various regions of the country, even in Kyiv. Arrests have been made among officials of the Cabinet of Ministers and the National Chamber of Commerce, leaders of the pro-Russian Opposition Bloc for Life party, prosecutors, and judges. Those arrested have been charged with treason. But these Kremlin agents are far outnumbered by collaborators inside the occupied territories. The first shock for Ukrainians was the number of judges, prosecutors, S.B.U. officers and police officers who switched to serving Russia in Crimea after the annexation in 2014. It was a mass betrayal but, as it turned out, it was also the result of long and painstaking work in Crimea by the Russian secret services.

It was also the result of a failure by Ukrainian special

services. Now, even in Donbas, betrayal is not as widespread as it was in Crimea. Most of the remaining residents do not want to cooperate with the occupiers. But Russia possesses many tools to force Ukrainians to recognise the occupation administrations, at least passively. You have to register with them to receive humanitarian aid, to have your water supply reconnected, or to access any kind of pension.

The theme of betrayal remains like a scar on the villages and towns around Kyiv that fell under Russian occupation at the beginning of the war. In every village, every town, there were Moscow supporters who offered the invaders lists of pro-Ukrainian activists, the addresses of participants in the Maidan protests and veterans of the anti-terrorist operation in Donbas.

In the village of Andriivka, not far from Borodyanka, north-west of Kyiv, a former monk from a monastery belonging to the Moscow Patriarchate turned out to be a traitor. He not only allowed several of the invaders to stay in his house but also showed them which houses in the village could be burgled and which residents could be kidnapped and exchanged for ransoms. The monk did not have time to escape when the village was liberated. He was arrested, tried and sentenced to ten years in prison. Another family, migrants from Donetsk, who settled in the village after 2014 and who had also helped the Russian occupiers, left with the Russian army as they retreated to Belarus.

More than 30 Andriivka residents are still listed as missing. Russian soldiers shot at least seventeen people and many houses are still in ruins. Mykola Horobets, a well-known Germanist and retired researcher who worked for most of his life at Ukraine's central academic library in Kyiv, went to his house in Andriivka as soon as the village had been liberated from

Russian troops. Before the war, he would have spent all summer there, but last week he visited his childhood home for only the fifth time since the village's liberation.

He has managed to plant potatoes but only in the part of the garden that is closest to the house. He is afraid to work the land further away – what if there are mines? The garden has not been checked for explosives. Despite the reduced size of his potato plot, Mykola is moderately happy with the crop. He has been able to put a good store of potatoes away in his cellar. Now he is stocking up on firewood for the winter. He, too, often thinks of the traitor monk and the traitor resettlers from Donetsk.

During the occupation, Mykola's hut was lived in by Russian soldiers. They were very surprised by all the German language books on the shelves. The soldiers asked the neighbours about the owner of the hut: is he by any chance a German? They left behind a broken sofa, several issues of the Russian Ministry of Defence newspaper *Krasnaya Zvezda* (Red Star), and many personal belongings, including a hat, powder to make an energy drink, and a camping pot for cooking food.

When Mykola arrived for the first time after the village had been liberated, Ukrainian police entered the house ahead of him. They looked around and asked Mykola to identify what had been left by the Russian soldiers. Mykola found a large canister of machine oil in the shed, probably for the engine of a tank. The police were not interested in oil but one of them took a fancy to the Russian soldier's camping pot and requisitioned it.

The canister of engine oil is still in the shed. Perhaps the local history museum in Makariv, the nearest town, will take it. The director of the museum is preparing an exhibition about the occupation of the Makariv district and has asked all residents to donate artefacts from the Russian aggression to the museum.

"I'm afraid to come to Andriivka too often," Mykola admitted to me. "In the evening, a lot of people here get drunk and then they let off guns in the dark. The Russians probably left a lot of weapons around too." It seems that the police are in no hurry to look for "trophy" weapons collected by villagers. And no-one wants to criticise alcoholics who survived the occupation. Some believe that they drink because of the psychological trauma, although this does not make the situation less frightening.

In fact, all residents of Andriivka are now deeply traumatised, including those, like Mykola, who were not there during the occupation. He remained in Kyiv with his adult daughter, who has cerebral palsy. Because of her, he did not even think of trying to evacuate from Kyiv. His village neighbour Andriy, a friend since childhood, is also an alcoholic. Sometimes Andriy steals vegetables from Mykola's garden and sells them to buy a bottle. Oddly enough, he is also a beekeeper, or rather a former beekeeper who still has bees. One swarm recently "escaped" from Andriy and settled on a cherry tree in Mykola's garden. Andriy brought a ladder around and climbed up the tree, breaking several branches in the process, although he did manage to recapture the swarm.

I have a feeling those bees will fly much farther away next time, to a place where their drunken owner will not be able to find them.

Neglect is a form of betrayal and bees, like people, cannot forgive a traitor.

Uman Gets Ready for the Jewish New Year

Every year in September, the population of the town of Uman, in Cherkasy region 190 kilometres south of Kyiv, quadruples as Hasidic Jews arrive to celebrate Rosh Hashanah, the Jewish New Year.

This pilgrimage to Uman honours one of the founding fathers of Hasidism, Rabbi Nachman of Bratslav (Breslov), who is buried there. He died in 1810 in Uman and, in accordance with his wishes, lies in the Jewish cemetery next to the graves of the victims of the Haidamack massacres of 1768. Had Rabbi Nachman not insisted on being buried in Ukraine, his ashes would have been transported to Jerusalem and today Uman would be an ordinary, quiet, provincial town. As it is, the city has long been Ukraine's main centre of religious pilgrimage and tourism.

A significant industry has developed around the celebration of the Jewish New Year involving transportation, real estate, rental accommodation and kosher cuisine. Many Hasidim have purchased real estate in Uman and are involved in the property rental business themselves. Before the war, dozens of charter flights from Israel and the United States of America flew into Kyiv at this time of year, and lines of specially reserved buses and cars could be seen waiting at the airport to whisk the pilgrims off south to Uman.

The celebration can last for over a month and security has always been an issue. In cooperation with the Ukrainian authorities, Israeli police officers used to fly to Ukraine specifically to monitor the behaviour of their fellow citizens. Local police also carefully patrolled the streets of Uman, trying to make sure that conflicts did not break out between residents and visitors. Nonetheless, every year some friction did arise – it was almost inevitable. After all, the Hasidim celebrate with a great deal of energy and noise, singing songs and dancing every night. They obviously like Uman and feel at home there, despite some tragic history and the memory of the pogroms, which are, indirectly, the reason for their coming.

This year, in view of the war, the Ukrainian and Israeli authorities have been encouraging the Hasidim to cancel the celebration of Rosh Hashanah in Uman. The threat of rocket attacks is very real. Also, there has been no civil aviation in Ukraine since the start of the war, making it impossible to fly to Kyiv. The borders in the west of the country are open, however, and trains and buses are running. Already the first thousand Hasidim have reached Uman by road. The international Flix bus company has introduced new routes to Uman, including from Kraków, Prague, and Brno.

In response to warnings about the danger, representatives of the Hasidim said that life in Israel is constantly fraught with the danger of terrorism, so they see no reason to change their traditions because of the war in Ukraine.

While Hasidim from Israel, New York, and elsewhere make their way to Uman, there are those who live in Uman permanently. They remember the early days of the war when Russian missiles fell on the city and nearby villages. At the beginning of the war, the number of Hasidim living in Uman actually increased, with many coming to help the local Jewish community, as well as the non-Jewish population, both permanent residents and refugees. A Jewish charity kitchen was set up which continues to feed everyone in need.

In late February and early March, shelling left many dead and wounded in the town. The basement of the synagogue was opened as a bomb shelter for all, whatever their faith. At the end of March, there was a real possibility that Russia would try to destroy the synagogue using rockets: the Russian Ministry of Defence announced that the Hasidim had given the synagogue to the Ukrainian army as an arms depot. "The property of the Jewish cult in Uman is deliberately being used by Kyiv's nationalist regime for military purposes," said Igor Konashenkov, Russian Defence Ministry spokesman. In response, the leaders of the Jewish community in Uman recorded a video showing the empty premises of the synagogue and other religious buildings and declared the words of the representative of the Russian Ministry of Defence to be a lie. Fortunately, no Hasidic shrines in Uman were damaged during Russian shelling.

Traditionally, some pilgrims remain in Ukraine after the celebration of the Jewish New Year to visit other places connected with Jewish history in Ukraine, including the old Jewish settlements, or shtetls, in Vinnytsia region on the border with Moldova, as well as towns in the former region of Galicia and Bukovina.

The local authorities in Uman are still hoping that there will be fewer pilgrims this year. If their attempts to dissuade people from coming are successful, the other Jewish tourist destinations will also suffer, such as those to Sharhorod. Sharhorod is located in Vinnytsia region, 347 kilometres south-west of Kyiv; before the war, many Jewish historical monuments in the city were carefully restored, including the oldest synagogue in Ukraine, built in the sixteenth century.

Even under Soviet rule, Sharhorod was an almost entirely Jewish town until World War II, with a population of about ten thousand people. Now, with the same population, only a dozen Jews live in the city, although the townspeople protect the Jewish heritage and hope very much that tourism will sooner or later bring some money to the town. This year, that is almost certainly not going to happen.

In contrast, Odesa, Lviv, and even Kyiv are benefiting from some, mostly internal, tourism. Ukrainians, tired of the war, are trying to distract themselves by taking short sightseeing trips to other cities. In towns away from the front line, the museums are open, as are almost all of Kyiv's museums – even the National Museum of the History of Medicine not far from the Opera House. Located in a former school of medicine, you can visit the anatomical theatre in this museum where, a little more than a hundred years ago, the future writer Mikhail Bulgakov attended lectures in anatomy. Fortunately for literature, he swapped the scalpel for the pen. The Bulgakov Museum, located on Andry's Descent, has always been a popular tourist attraction.

The cult of Mikhail Bulgakov arose during the Soviet era when his books were still banned. The writer was born in Kyiv and survived the civil war that began after the 1917 revolution. He wrote about what happened at that time in his novel *The White Guard*. Now, because of this novel, the Writers Union of Ukraine has demanded that the Bulgakov Museum be closed and the premises turned into a museum dedicated to the choral master Oleksandr Koshyts, who was active in the Ukrainian independence movement.

In 1919, the government of independent Ukraine sent Koshyts, together with his choir, on a tour of Europe and America with the aim of introducing Ukrainian choral music to the world. However, Ukraine remained independent for only a few months before the Bolsheviks took over and made it a Soviet republic. Koshyts and his choir never returned. It is an interesting story, but you might be wondering what Bulgakov did to deserve being turfed out of his museum. The thing is, in *The White Guard*, Bulgakov's characters talk arrogantly about the Ukrainian independence movement and the leading Ukrainian nationalists, Petliura and Skoropadskyi. It is clear from the novel that Bulgakov, an ethnic Russian and Russian speaking, adhered to a rather ironic view of the Ukrainian army and Hetman Skoropadskyi who, while determined to win recognition and some form of autonomy for Ukraine, was prepared to work with almost anyone, including the Germans, Tsarists and Slavophiles, to achieve this.

The anti-Bulgakov campaign started to gather pace five years ago, when one of Ukraine's most famous writers, Oksana Zabuzhko, declared war on the cult of Bulgakov. Recently, a memorial plaque dedicated to the writer was publicly removed from the wall near the entrance to Kyiv University, where he studied. Now a host of Ukrainian intellectuals and writers have decided to "take up arms" against his museum.

Russian-speaking Ukrainian intellectuals no doubt feel awkward about defending Bulgakov and tend to keep quiet. However, some Ukrainian-speaking activists have come out in his defence. Now the dispute over the fate of the museum is between opposing groups of Ukrainian-speaking activists. Many of my close friends have found themselves on different sides in this dispute and some have become estranged as a result. The question seems to have quite divided the Ukrainian intellectual community. Pushkin failed to do this. No-one in Ukraine spoke out in his defence. For Ukrainians, Pushkin turned out to be a stranger, especially after the Russian authorities decorated occupied towns with billboards of his portrait and quotations of his saying, "Ukraine . . . is a beautiful part of the Russian Empire".

While Russia is rewriting Ukrainian history, trying to prove that Ukraine never existed, some Ukrainian writers and intellectuals are compiling a new list of enemies of Ukrainian culture and Ukrainian independence. Mikhail Bulgakov has been added to this list. Who will be added next is unclear but we do know what Ukrainian soldiers at the front think about these campaigns. "While we are fighting here, are you out of your minds?" – this kind of comment regularly appears in the Facebook posts of Ukrainian soldiers. The comments are aimed at Ukrainians who remain at home looking for new internal enemies among the living and the long-dead. As things stand, no-one is going to close the Mikhail Bulgakov Museum. This has been stated by the Ukrainian Minister of Culture, Oleksandr Tkachenko. Having so said, he also gained enemy status with some Ukrainian intellectuals.

In the meantime, another evening of poetry was held in the museum at which two participants in the current war read from their work. They were the poets Pavlo Ritza, who is a volunteer soldier, and Irina Rypka who has become a military nurse.

07.09.2022

Dreaming of an Island

(Halldór Laxness International Literature Prize acceptance speech)

There is nothing new in dreaming of an island but this hopeful vision continues to live and enthral. The dream of an island is born in the imagination of every child who envies Robinson Crusoe and his adventures. It stirs in the thoughts of a person who is burdened by stress or failure, or the pressures of the outside world, or who is threatened by an unfriendly environment, or an enemy. The dream of an island can arise in the minds of an entire family, or even a whole nation, fermenting until the entire population wills the country to become an island. For a small country, this dream might even be realisable, if its borders are defined by rivers. It might even be possible to change the course of the rivers so that they follow the borders.

Water is the perfect boundary – the best way to separate one bit of land from another. In many cultures, water represents a cleansing power or truth, able to insulate a country from falsity and false neighbours. Water inspires a sense of stability. Looking at tranquil water calms the nerves and even the roar and the crashing of a stormy sea can inspire quiet reflection, if you are safe on your own island.

If Iceland did not exist in the real world, it would have been invented. It would have been invented by ancient philosophers and writers. In their manuscripts, the imaginary Iceland would have become synonymous with Paradise – inhabited by honest, friendly people – with a wonderful soft climate, lots of orchards, and flower gardens. It would definitely have exotic jungles and waterfalls and lots of colourful songbirds.

Iceland, as we know, does exist, with all its fabulous and real attributes, with its wild and austere beauty, its volcanoes and geysers, and its magnificent stones. Iceland exists on geopolitical maps and maps of world culture.

I have always admired the way Icelandic literature is better known in Europe than the literature of some continental European countries with much larger territories and populations. I know this has been achieved by conscious effort at a state level, but I think that the geographical status of the island has also played an important role here. The island, or rather its ocean frontiers, limit the available horizons and forces those living there to focus on themselves, on their thoughts, dreams, plans, and on their history and culture. And when all these thoughts, fuelled by love for the island, become a mission, then the most fantastic ambitions become ripe for implementation. This is how I think Icelandic culture has been built, each generation adding its layer of stones, gradually creating a mighty palace, visible from Europe, America, and Africa.

On the other hand, the curiosity of the surrounding world towards Iceland has been whipped up by its beauty and remoteness. The world became acquainted with Iceland through the pages of books by classical Icelandic writers such as Thórbergur Thórdarson and Halldór Laxness. The world loves and reads Icelandic sagas; the world follows modern Icelandic literature.

I would like the world to follow Ukrainian literature and culture with the same curiosity but, alas, Ukrainian classical literature has hardly been translated into any foreign languages. Some of our modern authors are just beginning to attract the attention of foreign readers, but the world today is following the war in Ukraine and not the achievements of Ukrainian culture.

The truth is that Ukraine was lucky with its geology but unlucky with its geography. Ukraine is a European country rich in minerals, with vast expanses of fertile land, which, until recently, made it possible to produce and export up to ten per cent of the world's wheat. Ukraine has as much agricultural land as Iceland has "fish fields" – the ocean!

Ukraine's natural wealth has bequeathed the country a history of wars, including wars for Ukrainian independence, as Germany, Russia, the Austro-Hungarian Empire, and other countries have intermittently claimed Ukrainian land, Ukrainian coal, Ukrainian oil. But there was always one aspect of Ukraine's wealth that no neighbouring power wanted to steal – rather they wanted to destroy it – that is Ukrainian culture, the Ukrainian language, the very identity of Ukraine which is impossible without culture and language.

Culture is the most obvious connection between an individual and the land on which he or she lives. People create a culture around their relationship with the land and, by extension, with their country. The connection between a people and its territory is legitimised in world history through culture. If the culture is destroyed, then it can be said that the people no longer have anything to do with the country, or with the land.

Ukrainian culture has always been an island – at times a surprisingly small island – so small that it was in danger of disappearing. For centuries, attempts have been made to force Ukrainians to forget their native language, to stop singing Ukrainian songs and to abandon their history. For almost 400 years, Russia has been fighting against Ukrainian identity, against the Ukrainian language.

In the seventeenth century, Ukrainian church books were banned and destroyed. In 1720 Peter the Great signed a decree banning the publication of any book in the Ukrainian language. In 1763, Catherine II forbade the use of Ukrainian as a language of tuition at the oldest Ukrainian university, the Kyiv-Mohyla Academy. In 1804 teaching in Ukrainian was forbidden in schools. In 1884 Tsar Alexander III banned theatrical performances in Ukrainian. Four years later, in 1888, he also banned the use of the Ukrainian language in official institutions and made it unlawful to give a Ukrainian name to a child at baptism. In 1892, a decree was signed banning the translation of books from Russian into Ukrainian. In the 300-year period when much of eastern Ukraine was part of the Russian Empire, from the early eighteenth to the early twentieth century, the various tsars signed more than 40 decrees prohibiting or restricting the use of the Ukrainian language in Ukraine.

After the revolution of 1917, Ukraine gained a short period of independence. However, in 1921 the country became part of the new Russian Empire – the Soviet Union – and the process of Russification was revived.

I remember how in Kyiv in the 1970s and '80s, anyone who spoke Ukrainian was assumed to be either an ardent nationalist or an uneducated peasant. I am glad that these times are over and the Ukrainian language has slowly begun to return to the territories from which it was once expelled. However, the threat to Ukraine and Ukrainian culture remains and, because of Russian aggression, the threat has now increased.

All the policies of tsars are now being implemented by Russian President Vladimir Putin. Teaching in Ukrainian is once more prohibited in the occupied territories of Ukraine and Ukrainian books are being withdrawn from libraries there. On the territory of Russia, camps are being created for the assimilation of Ukrainians deported from the occupied territories. In these camps, they will be forcibly taught Russian traditions and customs and "turned into" Russian people.

For me, the dream of an island, an island called Ukraine, is more relevant today than ever. I wish Ukraine was an island – although not disconnected from the whole world and living in isolation, like North Korea – certainly not! No, I would like it to be an island of security located a safe distance from a dangerous neighbour, the Russian Federation.

Today, the entire democratic world is helping Ukraine in this war, helping with weapons and humanitarian aid. There is another way to help that does not require funding. It does require a little personal time from everyone who wants to help. Ukrainian history and culture are still little known in Europe and the rest of the world. So, I ask you to find and read non-fiction books about the history of Ukraine. Those such as Anne Applebaum's *Red Famine*, Timothy Snyder's *Bloodlands*, or Serhii Plokhy's *The Gates of Europe*. Find books by Ukrainian writers, take the time to learn a little more about Ukraine than you know now, so that it becomes closer to you, despite the physical distance separating Ukraine from Iceland.

———

I am very grateful to Iceland for awarding me the Haldór Laxness International Literature prize. I am also grateful to my Icelandic publisher and my Icelandic readers for receiving Penguin Misha there, so warmly, about twenty years ago – a warm welcome in a cool climate is exactly what a penguin needs! But I am even more grateful to the Icelandic government for the generous support that the country provides to Ukrainian refugees and for Iceland's support to my country. Even tragic events can bring unexpected opportunities.

Throughout the world, Russia's aggression has generated waves of sympathy towards Ukraine, but it has also generated interest in my country. More people than ever before are willing to learn Ukrainian, which has become the language of freedom itself. Today there are several million more Ukrainian speakers outside Ukraine than there were this time last year. Ukrainian may not yet be taught at the University of Reykjavík, but I am sure that among the Ukrainian diaspora in Iceland you will find people who want to help with Ukrainian language learning – perhaps in exchange for lessons in Icelandic.

We in Ukraine have many stories to tell you and we want and need to hear your stories. This is how cultural dialogue arises. It is dialogue and exchange that forms the foundation of good relations. Genuine dialogue and exchange builds bridges between islands of democracy, allowing strangers to become close friends.

12.09.2022

Teaching and Learning

I have only visited Luhansk once in my life. It was a couple of years before the Euromaidan of 2013–4. I gave a talk to students at Vladimir Dahl University. Dahl (1801–1872) was a Russian writer and creator of the most famous explanatory dictionary of the Russian language, which took him fifty-three years to compile. Danish by origin, he was born in Luhansk and died in Moscow.

After my lecture, the rector of the university brought two students to me and said that they would show me around the city. During our short walk in the centre of Luhansk, I was surprised to learn that there was a Komsomol (Young Communist) organisation at Dahl University and that these students were Komsomol members. I thought that the Komsomol had died along with the Communist Party and it was a challenge to hide my sense of amusement at the irony of what the young people told me as we walked along. The amusement faded when we arrived at the monument to Soviet teachers killed in western Ukraine by "Ukrainian nationalists". The monument, a large black stone, was erected back in Soviet times and remained in the city after Ukraine gained independence. As far as I am aware, it is still there.

I recall this trip to Luhansk now because, during the recent retreat from the town of Kupiansk, in Kharkiv region, Russian troops "forgot" some Russian teachers who had come to work at schools in the temporarily occupied city. The teachers had come on the invitation of the Russian government and were paid very high salaries. They had planned to stay for between six months and a year, some for even longer and some were planning to remain in the occupied territories for ever. The Russian authorities had promised them a piece of Ukrainian land and a house or apartment free of charge. It is clear that no-one was building anything in the war zone, so we must assume that the promised apartments and houses would be properties belonging to Ukrainians who had fled.

A couple of months ago, Russian journalists managed to get a list of teachers from different regions who had signed up for "temporary contract work" in Ukraine. The list included about five hundred teachers from all over Russia, some even from Kamchatka and Sakhalin in the Far East. The majority were teachers of Russian language, Russian literature, and history. Often, they were happy to give interviews to Russian media about how they were going to educate Ukrainian children.

Konstantin Matyukhov, a history teacher, who was preparing to travel to Luhansk region, said in his interview, "In the Luhansk People's Republic, I will not only teach children. I'll also carry out patriotic extracurricular activities, to help our peoples to get closer to one another. After all, there can be no division between Russians and Ukrainians because we are one Russian people."

Daria Ganieva, a teacher of Russian and English, who left Siberia to teach at the Pochetnensky Educational Complex in occupied Crimea and who was considering moving to "help" the educational process in occupied Melitopol, also shared her thoughts and feelings with a Russian journalist. "I came to Crimea from Siberia and have not yet acquired a permanent place to live. Of course, I'm scared to move but I hope for housing and a decent salary. In addition, the ecological situation in Melitopol is good and there's the sea too!"

Of course, Daria Ganieva is a teacher of Russian and English, not geography. So, she may be forgiven for not knowing that

Melitopol is a long way from the sea. Not being a history teacher, she may also be unaware of how the local Ukrainian population received Soviet teachers who were sent to work in schools in western Ukraine after the annexation of the area by the Soviet Union during and after World War II. About two thousand Soviet teachers and doctors died at the hands of Ukrainian anti-Soviet rebels. On the other hand, Daria Ganieva admits that she is afraid to move. So, maybe she does suspect something.

Today, Ukrainian collaborators who have agreed to serve the Russian occupiers have good reason to be scared. Some are no longer alive: they have been killed by Ukrainian partisans or Ukrainian special forces operating behind Russian lines. Among Ukrainian teachers in the occupied territories, there are also collaborators who, before the Ukrainian army's counter-offensive, were sent on "training courses" in annexed Crimea or inside the Russian Federation. I suspect that some of the Ukrainian teachers on these courses are finding it hard to concentrate on the Russian school curriculum. After all, their home towns have been liberated from Russian troops. What should they do now? Go back home and go to jail? They probably do not want to do that. Most likely, they will remain on Russian territory and become Russian teachers. Or are they still hoping that Russia will strike again and retake Kupiansk, Izyum, and other liberated towns and villages?

Trying to predict the course of a war is a thankless task, especially when even the official mass media channels sometimes throw out disinformation designed to confuse the enemy. Of course, it also confuses ordinary Ukrainians. Disinformation or fake news can be very effective and useful but it leaves a bitter aftertaste for Ukrainians. We understand that during a war no news can be trusted.

The entire country watched the Ukrainian army preparing

to liberate Kherson. Residents of Kherson and Nova Kakhovka were also anxiously waiting to be freed from occupation. They are still waiting because it turned out that the news of an imminent push to liberate Kherson region was a red herring. The Ministry of Defence and the General Staff of the Ukrainian army were actually preparing an operation to liberate Kharkiv region.

Even when you cannot have total faith in any information, you may still allow yourself to hope for some truth in the rumours. On Sunday evening, my friends and I were on our way to a restaurant when an English journalist friend messaged me, "Have you heard something about a possible military coup in Moscow? The centre of Moscow is closed!" My mood improved immediately. I found myself walking with a lighter step. I checked the news feed but could find no confirmation of a coup. I did come across reports that Putin had once more changed the command of his troops and, it seemed, arrested several generals who were considered responsible for the Russian army's failures. There was not even a hint of a coup in the news. Even so, I imagined the blocked centre of Moscow and for a few hours allowed myself to believe that Putin's rule was over.

It turned out that Moscow was celebrating the city's 875th birthday. In honour of the event, the streets were taken over by fairs and theatrical performances. Russian films were shown in cinemas for free. A festive concert was held in the Zaryadye concert hall. It was attended by Putin and Moscow's Mayor Sobyanin and, during the show via a video link, President Putin launched the newly built Ferris wheel, "Europe's largest", Moscow's London Eye, the 140-metre-high Sun of Moscow.

Moscow has found a reason to be proud, and Russia without pride is impossible. This is why there is no official admission that Russian troops are retreating from the front lines of the war in Ukraine. Russia calls it the "regrouping" and "relocation" of troops. Ukrainians have suggested a new military term that the Russians might use to better describe these tactics: "advancing negatively" on the Kharkiv front.

The fact that Putin did not personally come to open the largest Ferris wheel in Moscow and did not ride on it himself also caused a surge of humour among Ukrainians: "He didn't go up in the Ferris wheel because he doesn't want to see the Ukrainian army approaching!" The Ukrainian offensive has lifted our spirits and given impetus to many new jokes and anecdotes. Soldier humour is special and good only during a war.

It is harder to make jokes about schools and teachers. Many Ukrainian children could not go to school on September 1 this year, the day traditionally celebrated as Knowledge Day. They study online because their schools have been destroyed by Russian rockets, or because their schools are not equipped with bomb shelters.

Those schools that have not been damaged and do have bomb shelters live a special wartime life. The shelters are prepared for school lessons and some even have high-speed internet. Children must be prepared to go to the bomb shelter at any moment and nobody knows how long an air raid will last.

Classes have not yet begun in the schools in the newly liberated towns and villages. Most of the schools have been destroyed and those remaining lack teachers. The situation is also still dangerous. The front line is too close and the Russian army continues to shell newly liberated territories.

In cities that are still occupied, such as Melitopol or Kherson, schools operate according to a Russian educational programme. Despite threats from the occupying authorities, many children do not attend school. Representatives of the occupation administrations have promised to take children away from the parents who do not send their children to school, although so far these threats have not been carried out. There are no known cases of "confiscation" of children from Ukrainian parents in Melitopol. It is known that the Russian textbooks promised to the occupied towns have not been delivered, at least not in sufficient quantities.

Russian teachers who agreed to help in schools in the still-occupied areas are now more likely to be preparing for a quick getaway than for their lessons. Most Ukrainian collaborators in Kharkiv region fled together with the invading army just before the towns and villages were liberated. Those who did not manage to flee are already under arrest, charged with treason.

Moscow celebrated Moscow Day with a lengthy barrage of colourful fireworks. At the same time, the website for the new Ferris wheel was hacked by Russian Nationalists who believe that celebrating Moscow Day while Russian soldiers are retreating or being killed in Ukraine is some sort of blasphemy.

These days, in schools in Kharkiv and Poltava regions, lessons are constantly disrupted by air raid sirens. In retaliation for the offensive by the Ukrainian army, Russia is firing missiles at critical infrastructure sites in those regions, attempting to deprive them of electricity, heating and water supply. Soon, electricity generators and warm sleeping bags will become the most popular goods in Ukraine. Thanks to the Russian aggression this winter promises to be at once very cold and very hot.

War, Mushrooms and Watermelons

The first snow has fallen on the mountain peaks of Pip Ivan and Drahobrat in the Carpathian Mountains. It fell and settled and will lie there now until late spring.

Below, in the valleys, the sun still shines from time to time and the temperature rises to 17°C.

Transcarpathia lives its usual life, the life of the region most remote from the front line. The mushroom season has arrived and tens of thousands of Transcarpathian folk are out in the forests. The tasty white mushroom *Boletus edulis* is plentiful in this region. Under ordinary circumstances, in addition to being a pleasurable pastime, mushroom picking can produce additional income. The region is frequented by tourists who are happy to buy dried mushrooms for soups and marinated ones for the festive table.

At present, there are almost no tourists, but the internally displaced people living in the region have joined in the search for mushrooms to bring variety to their diets and to save money. Collecting mushrooms is a lot cheaper than buying them at the market. However, the temporary residents are strangers to the forests and often get lost. Some have even had to call out rescue parties. Last weekend, rescuers went up into the mountains four times to find people who had lost their way or been injured.

The mushroom season brings other serious problems to doctors. Every autumn, dozens of people, locals and visitors alike, are poisoned by eating the wrong kind of mushroom. Sometimes this is fatal. There are popular but unscientific methods of testing to see if the mushrooms you have picked are edible, methods that have remained unchanged for centuries.

The mushrooms must first be boiled, sometimes changing the water twice, then fried or stewed with potatoes. When Ukrainians boil mushrooms, they throw a peeled onion into the water, believing that if it goes dark, then there is at least one poisonous mushroom in the pot.

Another method to check is to dip a silver spoon into the water in which the mushrooms are boiling. If the spoon goes dark that means there is a poisonous mushroom in the pot. Not many families can boast of owning a solid silver spoon, so this method is less commonly used. The truth is that neither method is reliable.

There are a lot of mushrooms in the forests along the front line in the south and east of Ukraine, especially after the recent rains, but no-one picks them – neither the residents who have chosen not to evacuate nor the Ukrainian soldiers. The forests are littered with mines and unexploded ordnance.

Soon snow will fall there and the carpets of mushrooms on the forest floor will be covered over and rot into the soil. During a war, snow creates additional problems. Against a white background, it is easy to see things of a slightly different colour. Ukrainian soldiers are now focused on making themselves invisible.

Throughout Ukraine, volunteers have been weaving hundreds of thousands of camouflage nets for the army using rags, mostly from old clothing. These nets cover military positions so that they cannot be seen from above by Russian reconnaissance drones. The Ukrainian offensive means that the front line is very dynamic. The soldiers are constantly changing positions, digging trenches, and then masking these with nets. When a unit has to reposition, the camouflage nets are left behind;

there is no time to remove them from the trees and bushes. So, new nets are always in demand.

When the snow falls, the military will need white camouflage nets. People do not often wear white clothes. These nets will be made mainly from bedsheets and pillowcases. In recent years, it has become fashionable to buy coloured bed linen, so collecting enough old white fabric for tens of thousands of winter camouflage nets might prove problematic. But I am confident that the net-making volunteers will find a solution. If necessary, they will buy new white bedding to cut up. Or perhaps one of our N.A.T.O. friends will help. They must have everything, including winter camouflage nets!

While trucks with military supplies are travelling from the western borders of Ukraine towards the front line via secret routes, there is also a flow of trucks from east to west. This is the movement of equipment from factories and plants located near the war zone. The relocation of each unit is also a military operation.

One night in late August, several tarpaulin-topped trucks stopped in the centre of Chernivtsi, an ancient city on the border with Romania. The usual curfew was in place, but the police were there. Trying not to make a noise, workers unloaded the trucks and carried cupboards, ovens, refrigerators and tables into the former House of Officers at 6 Theatre Square.

By five o'clock in the morning, as the curfew was lifted, the early risers of Chernivtsi were surprised to see a new café on Theatre Square, called Kasha Maslom (a dish of porridge made with butter). The café, which originally operated in Kharkiv, had moved to Chernivtsi along with its cooks, designers and cashiers.

Before the war, there was a chain of these cafés in Kharkiv. They were popular both because the menu was what you would expect in any big city and because the prices were very reasonable. Now there is only one Kasha Maslom left in Kharkiv and it is used largely as a charity and volunteer centre.

For Chernivtsi folk, the Kasha Maslom's menu turned out to be rather exotic. People went along to the café to discover what folk in Ukraine's second city enjoyed eating. The relocation of the café turned out to be a successful experiment in the export of Kharkiv cuisine. The owner of the restaurant chain, Denis Gavrilchenko, is pleased with the café's first month of business in Chernivtsi and he plans to keep a branch in the town after the war.

Originally, he had no intention of expanding his business beyond Kharkiv. The war made him change his plans and the Ministry of Economics helped with the move. They have an assistance programme for businesses forced to relocate from a war zone. The authorities in Chernivtsi helped with the search for premises and with administrative issues. What is more, internally displaced persons from Donbas and Kherson have now found work at the café.

Transporting businesses and restaurants may be troublesome, but it is not as complex as relocating a farm. Even farmers are having to abandon thousands of hectares of leased land in the occupied territories or near the front line and move to other regions where there is agricultural land to spare. They do not find the expanses of terrain that they used to farm, but at least they can farm and grow something in peace – mostly.

This is what happened to the Ye Vse (We Have Everything) farm from Kherson region, an area famous for its watermelons. It grew enough of the fruit to supply most of Ukraine. However, in the spring of this year, the Russian occupiers banned farmers from taking their produce into the territory of free Ukraine. At that point, many farmers stopped cultivating their lands and began to think about moving. The farm Ye Vse moved to

Transcarpathia, where there is little agricultural land. Having analysed some soil samples, the farmers decided to try growing watermelons near Uzhhorod on four hectares of rented land. Their first harvest, of more than one hundred tons of watermelons, was not too bad. Of course, in Kherson region, with its better soil and climate, they could have grown two hundred and fifty tons or more.

Thanks to the Russian aggression, Transcarpathia has not had to wait for the acceleration of global warming to become a watermelon-growing region and, without the cost of transportation from Kherson region, people can now buy the fruit relatively inexpensively. The neighbouring region of Chernivtsi will no doubt also benefit from the new agricultural trends in Transcarpathia. Perhaps the Kasha Maslom café will add watermelon to its menu.

The agricultural enterprise Ye Vse remains registered in Kherson and Kakhovka, cities that are still under occupation, but, as in the case of the Kharkiv café, I think that even after the war, a section of this enterprise will remain in Transcarpathia, growing watermelons for the westernmost region of Ukraine.

Many of the occupied territories' educational institutions have gone into the cloud in Internet space. Among them is the Nova Kakhovka technical college, which is physically located at 2 Peremoha Avenue – an address that is now under the control of occupying forces and collaborators. As a result, the college now exists in two forms: one controlled by the occupying authorities, where students are being recruited to specialise in gas welding, hairdressing, tailoring and building construction under the Russian educational programme; the other is in Nova Kakhovka, under Ukrainian administration and offering the same courses but through online learning.

The Ukrainian authorities warn that colleges controlled by

occupier administrations and collaborators are operating illegally and that their diplomas will not be recognised. It is not yet known how many young people have decided to enrol in the Russian version of the Nova Kakhovka college or in the Ukrainian online one.

I cannot quite imagine how you can teach hairdressing or gas welding online. Perhaps the practical classes for these subjects will be held secretly in the occupied territory. We know that secret learning options exist because recently the Russian special services arrested two Ukrainian teachers in Kherson region for teaching covert, online lessons following the Ukrainian school curriculum. The schoolchildren whom they were teaching were also detained.

The number of pro-Ukrainian citizens in the occupied territories came as a big surprise to the Russians. In an attempt to deal with the situation, police and intelligence officers from all over the Russian Federation have been arriving in great numbers in the occupied territories. They go from home to home checking people's smartphones for photographs and messages that might reveal their owners' political views. Clearly, detecting all pro-Ukrainian citizens is beyond their capabilities.

The counter-offensive of the Ukrainian army in the east and south of the country provides hope and courage for those who are still living under occupation. Under cover of darkness, they hang out Ukrainian flags or put up pro-Ukrainian posters. The struggle for the liberation of Ukraine continues on both sides of the military front line.

27.09.2022

What Do You Know About Russia?

Russian forces are being pushed out of Kharkiv region and, amid the debris of their occupation, we find the "Russian World" packaged so that it could be force-fed to Ukrainians under occupation. Which two species of hare live in Moscow and the Moscow region? How many species of hedgehog live in the Moscow region? What is the name of the largest species of deer living in the Moscow region? Who, in September 1911, was mortally wounded in Kyiv by the anarchist and agent of the tsarist secret police, Mordka Bogrov?

You probably do not know the answers to these questions, but if the Russian occupation of Ukraine's Kharkiv region had continued, for people living under the occupation these facts and many more besides would have become their daily bread. Russia advertises the "Russian World" as a humanitarian project. So, it is no surprise that, in the form of humanitarian aid, Russia brought to the once-occupied town of Izyum, some 620 kilometres south-east of Kyiv, a large number of "What Do You Know about Russia?" card games.

I try to imagine the inhabitants of Izyum – in an apartment with broken windows and doors, with a table slashed by shell fragments – playing this "What Do You Know about Russia?" game. Dad turns over a card with a question. His wife and children watch his mouth expectantly. He reads, "What plant was called a 'damn apple' in the time of Catherine the Great?" The son asks, "Who is Catherine the Great?" While daughter thinks about an apple and licks her dry lips.

Back in early summer, the Russian occupying authorities received an order from Moscow to prepare for the introduction of the Russian school curriculum from September 1, "Knowledge Day". In Izyum, on this day, the traditional first day of the school year, despite being free of Russian forces nobody went to school, for the simple reason that there was not a single undamaged school left in the city.

After its liberation, a large number of "What Do You Know about Russia?" card sets were found in the city's Department of Education, along with other "humanitarian" supplies. Apparently, the plan was to present them to the schoolchildren of Izyum in ceremonies on September 1. What is to be done with all these games is unclear, but I am sure the displaced people of Izyum could suggest something.

In the village of Shevchenkove, not far from Izyum but liberated later on, some children did go to school on September 1. They even managed to receive some Russian textbooks before the Ukrainian troops arrived. The question is, who taught them during the occupation? The head teacher was evacuated before the town was occupied.

The Russian authorities gave the job of running the school to the deputy director, who had been previously in charge of procurement and facilities. True, it seems that there were very few children in Shevchenkove; more than 50 unopened boxes of Russian textbooks were found in the school following liberation, mostly textbooks on Russian history, Russian language, and Russian literature. Even the covers of the mathematics textbook had pictures of Russian folk heroes on them. This is how the "Russian World" arrives, with bombs and with textbooks on all things Russian.

While the Ukrainian military is wondering what to do with the Russian textbooks, mass graves continue to be found in and around Izyum. Ukrainian writers are following this gruesome process especially closely; one of the graves may contain the body of the well-known Ukrainian children's writer Volodymyr Vakulenko. He lived with his son in Izyum and decided to stay there even as the front line came ever closer to the town. Russian special services captured him immediately after the city was occupied. He must have known what awaited him, but for some reason he refused to leave. Vakulenko was a very stubborn person. As the Russian troops approached Izyum, he collected his diaries and manuscripts and took them to his mother's garden in the nearby village of Kapitolivka. There, he buried them.

Vakulenko's son now lives with his grandmother. The other day, my good friend, the writer Victoria Amelina, went to visit them. Volodymyr's mother showed her the place under the cherry tree where her son had buried the manuscripts. Victoria dug them up. Among the manuscripts, she found 30 pages of a diary – his last entries. They contain a farewell message to friends and relatives and express stout confidence in Ukraine's victory.

Ukrainian writers are now divided over Volodymyr's fate. Some are sure that he was killed. Others believe the rumours that the Russian special services moved him to Bilgorod and that he is a prisoner there. More than six months have passed since he was taken from his home. When all the victims from the mass graves of the city of Izyum and its environs are identified, the hope that he is alive will either grow or disappear for ever.

The war continues and the liberation of Kharkiv region from the Russian invaders goes on, albeit slowly. War is also a kind of school. Not only a school of survival but also of ingenuity. In this war, for the first time, drones are being used on a massive scale, both to attack and to reconnoitre. From the sky, it is easier to see the enemy, it is easier to understand what he is doing and to predict what he is going to do next. Thanks to drones, Russian forces have lost a lot of military equipment. Still, they come up with new ways to supply their troops on the front line with gasoline and ammunition.

Ukrainian intelligence officers noticed a sharp decline recently in the number of Russian fuel trucks and other military vehicles in the area around the front line. At the same time, there was a striking increase in the number of dairy trucks using the dirt tracks that traverse the fields. The farms in these areas have long been destroyed and looted by the Russian military and there are certainly no cows left in the vicinity. Drones enabled Ukrainian intelligence officers to discover that the milk trucks, which had been stolen from Ukrainian farmers, were transporting gasoline to forward positions of the Russian army, as well as military equipment to frontline storage units.

It must have been painful for Ukrainian reconnaissance-drone operators to transmit the coordinates of Ukrainian dairy trucks to their artillery units. But this is war. Even Ukrainian equipment has to be destroyed if it has fallen into enemy hands and is being used against Ukraine.

The Ukrainian military is making use of captured Russian tanks and artillery systems, but they have not yet seized any Russian dairy trucks. None have yet reached Ukrainian soil and I hope they never do.

The war continues to drive up food prices. Milk and butter, sugar and salt, eggs and meat all rose in price recently. From October 1, the Ukrainian government is raising the minimum wage, but it will be difficult for salaries to keep up with the prices.

There is no talk of a full-fledged economic crisis, but war will always exacerbate existing economic problems and fears. The Ukrainian government is fighting to prevent panic. Many people are afraid of the collapse of the banks. Perhaps because of this, the leadership of one of the largest banks, Alfa-Bank, has announced its readiness to invest one billion dollars in the Ukrainian economy.

The process of privatising state assets has also been revived. The other day, Chinese investors bought the Zbruch sanatorium, which is located in a national park in a forest not far from the border with Romania. Interestingly, the buyer, a Chinese citizen, Duan Xiao Peng, has been living in Ukraine for many years and is already the owner of several Ukrainian companies, including a construction company, an agro-complex and a factory that produces plastic goods.

Ukrainians have a positive attitude towards such news. They think that if the Chinese are buying Ukrainian businesses, then the war will end soon, or at least it will not reach the western regions of the country. In Ukraine, the Chinese still have the reputation of being wise people who do not take risks.

I wonder when this sanatorium will open and who will go there for rest and spa treatments – Ukrainian military personnel or representatives of the Chinese diaspora in Ukraine? My family once spent Christmas in a sanatorium which had been bought by Indian investors. That sanatorium was in Chernihiv region, not far from the border with Russia. I doubt it is working now.

While Putin is threatening Ukraine and the world with nuclear weapons, the Ukrainian government has revived archived plans to build a nuclear power plant in the centre of the country, near the ancient Cossack town of Chigirin, in Cherkasy region. Construction of the power plant was first considered back in the 1970s. The project was shelved after the Chernobyl disaster. Now, when so much of Ukraine's electricity infrastructure has been destroyed by the Russian army and the Zaporizhzhia nuclear power plant has become a Russian military base with every chance of repeating the fate of Chernobyl, the Ukrainian government has once more decided to consider the nuclear power option.

It seems that Russia has so often threatened Ukraine and the world with a nuclear attack that people have ceased to be afraid of atomic bombs or explosions at nuclear power plants. Or have they simply become resigned to the idea that nuclear war is a possibility? In Kyiv, young people have responded to Putin's nuclear threats with humour. Now it is said commonly that in the event of a nuclear explosion in Ukraine, guys and girls will rush to a party or possibly an orgy at Shchekavytsia, a hilltop in the centre of Kyiv associated with ancient tales of witchcraft. There are also ancient cemeteries nearby, both Orthodox and Muslim.

Ukrainians do not want to believe in the reality of a nuclear attack, just as they once did not want to believe in the threat of a Russian invasion. The latest Ukrainian anecdote speaks volumes about what people think, or wish to think, during these dramatic times: "When Ukrainians are asked whether they are preparing for the end of the world, they say that they are, indeed, getting ready for it and for the first six months after that."

Ukrainians do have plans, many plans. Among them is to learn the truth of their own story. They already know something of this and can answer at least one question from the Russian board game found in Izyum called "What do you know about Russia?" Most Ukrainians know that the person mortally wounded in Kyiv by Mordka Bogrov, the anarchist and agent of the tsarist secret police, was Pyotr Stolypin, the chairman of the Council of Ministers of the Russian Empire. However, in this Russian board game they use the Yiddish equivalent of his name, Mordka. Did the authors of the board game wish to emphasise that he was Jewish?

05.10.2022

The Value of a Man's Life

In the Republic of Tuva, the homeland of Russian Defence Minister Shoigu, the authorities are trading men for sheep. For each man who is mobilised, his family receives a live sheep and a quantity of flour, potatoes and cabbages, along with coal to heat the house in winter. Russia has not brought gas to the homes of people living in Tuva, nor to those of many other regions and autonomous republics, so coal is of great value there.

Mobilisation is slow and those who sign up complain that they are not given proper uniforms, that the food is poor and that they are forced to spend the night out in the open even if winter is already beginning in some regions. A number of recently mobilised Russians swiftly found themselves at the front and are already in Ukrainian captivity. The promised military training had not been organised for them. Judging by the interviews given to Ukrainian journalists by newly captured recruits, they are pleased that the war ended so quickly for them. Most of those mobilised had no wish to fight but did not have the money to avoid call-up by escaping to Georgia, Mongolia or Kazakhstan, as others have done.

While the Ukrainian army is advancing along several sectors of the front, the Russian army is actively preparing for defence. The combat effectiveness of the Russian armies should not be underestimated. Russia still has much more artillery and many more tanks and aircraft than the armed forces of Ukraine.

In Luhansk region, Russian troops have been told to "stand to the death". Forbidden to retreat, they are looking for buildings that can be turned into unassailable fortresses. One such place turned out to be the regional psychiatric hospital in the town of Svatovo which comprises a dozen old one- and two-storey buildings with thick brick walls and deep underground rooms.

Before the outbreak of hostilities, more than 500 patients were cared for there by 340 staff. A few days ago, the Russian military evicted the hospital's patients and the remaining staff and began to fill the buildings with ammunition and weapons. It is not clear what awaits the patients, but it is quite clear what awaits the hospital complex itself. It was overhauled, using government money, only a year ago. If the hospital becomes a military stronghold, it will be destroyed. I doubt that the patients will be rehoused in Russian hospitals, but the evacuation of Russian civilian specialist workers in occupied Lysychansk has already been announced. Electricians and builders who came to occupied Sieverodonetsk to work on infrastructure projects are already going back to Russia, not wanting to find themselves under fire from Ukrainian artillery.

In the past, many of Ukraine's ancient, massive and well-fortified castles and estates were turned into psychiatric hospitals and specialised boarding schools. This trend started in Soviet times. The communist government sought to isolate mentally ill citizens. In Russia, where there were few such castles or estates, psychiatric hospitals were located on islands in rivers or lakes. Today, most of the psychiatric hospitals in the occupied territories are either closed or have been taken over by the Russian military.

In late September, the village of Strelcha, in Kharkiv region, found itself under fire from Russian artillery. Doctors and orderlies tried to evacuate patients from the psychiatric hospital. Of the 600 patients, only 30 could be taken to safety. Four doctors were killed and two patients were injured.

As in the Middle Ages, ancient churches and monasteries have also become strongholds for the Russian military. This is not so much a sign of their faith in the church as an indication of their wish to make use of the thick stone walls of these ancient buildings. Even the St Grigorievsky Bizyukov monastery in the village of Krasny Mayak, Kherson region, seems to have become a fortress for the Russian army. It is not clear where the monks are now, but if they are still in the monastery, they will be able to add another page to their fraternity's tragic history. Founded at the end of the eighteenth century , the monastery has experienced many hard times. In 1919, during the civil war following the revolution of 1917, Red Army soldiers captured it and turned it into a fortress from which they raided neighbouring villages. They held the monks hostage, mocking and beating some and killing others. The monks secretly complained about the soldiers of the Red Army to the commander of the free Cossacks, Osaulenko, who was camped with one hundred men nearby in the town of Beryslav. The Cossacks launched a surprise attack on the 2000-strong Red Army force encamped in and around the monastery. The Cossacks won the day, driving the Red Army out of the monastery. But many of its buildings were destroyed in the process.

During World War II, the Germans removed all the treasures from the monastery, including the church silver hidden by the monks during the 1917 revolution. In the 1970s, by order of the Soviet authorities, the main cathedral of the monastery was blown up. Restoration work began in the 1990s. Just last year, with money collected by believers throughout Kherson region, the work was completed to rebuild the almost three-metre-high stone walls around the monastery. This had taken several years. If the Russian military starts firing from the territory of the monastery, then the Ukrainian army will return fire. Thick walls might survive bullets but artillery and missile fire will destroy them once more.

As well as ancient fortifications and church buildings, the Russians have shown an interest in military antiquity. In the liberated town of Izyum, Ukrainian soldiers found a box with ancient weapons stolen by the Russian military from the local historical museum. Apparently, the Russian army left the town in a hurry – it seems without enough trucks for all their loot. The antique weapons had been abandoned. Now they will be returned to the museum.

Some ancient church books will also be returned to the museum, including a gospel, published at the expense of Hetman Mazepa in the early eighteenth century. The books were hidden at home by the museum's curator, Dina Listopad. With tears in her eyes and a smile on her lips, she now gives interviews to reporters explaining how she hid these rare and very valuable books.

For some reason, in tracing the course of hostilities in the south and east of Ukraine on a map, I cannot help but recall computer war games. It seems to me that while many Russians might well perceive this terrible reality as resembling a computer game, I am afraid that many Ukrainian young people might also see it in the same way. This would explain their casual attitude to war-time rules and regulations. Yesterday, my elder brother Misha told me over the phone from Kyiv, "Young people do not pay attention to the curfew, they go to illegally operating bars and nightclubs. They get drunk and wander the streets at night. If they are stopped by police and military patrols, they are only fined two hundred hryvnias (five euros) for violating the curfew."

Kyiv has not been hit by missiles for more than two months. Perhaps this creates an illusion of security. In recent weeks, sirens have sounded regularly in the city, but only a minority of residents react to them. Perhaps to destroy this illusion of security, air raid sirens were heard wailing in Kyiv from last Tuesday to Wednesday, from late night until early morning. This time Kyiv was lucky – the city was not damaged. However, Iranian drones did strike the town of Bila Tserkva, a large industrial city only 75 kilometres from Kyiv and a centre for the production of car tyres.

As the residents of Bila Tserkva described the powerful explosions and the fires engulfing the industrial facilities and shared photographs of the town illuminated by the resulting fires, the sleepless capital followed the attack on this nearby town on social media. In the morning, the authorities appealed to residents of Bila Tserkva not to open windows until the fires could be extinguished. A complex of military buildings dating from 1900 was destroyed.

While Russia was bombing Bila Tserkva, Kharkiv enjoyed some rest, being bombed much less than usual. Ukrainian troops have pushed Russian artillery far enough away from Kharkiv that artillery shells cannot now reach the city. The Russians have now to use expensive ballistic missiles to continue the destruction of this Ukrainian city, the one closest to the Russian border.

Ironically, Soviet government policies have made the Ukrainian army's counter-offensive in the east of the country easier. In the 1930s, atheist communists made a huge effort to destroy the old churches in the area. New churches, built after independence, mainly of the Moscow Patriarchate, were built quickly and economically. Their walls are no thicker than residential buildings. Accordingly, in the Kharkiv and Donetsk regions there are fewer places for Russian soldiers to hide or to turn into strongholds.

After the collapse of the U.S.S.R., thousands of churches

were hastily built in Ukraine. Many of those in the south and east of the country are now destroyed. After this war, I think that the reconstruction of churches will proceed much more slowly than previously. Ukraine will have another priority – to build housing for those who have lost their homes. Churches can wait.

Churches can wait for another reason. Many residents who have remained in the south and east of Ukraine, or those who will soon return to the territories liberated from the Russian army, will have to make a difficult decision: whether to remain parishioners of the Ukrainian Orthodox Church of the Moscow Patriarchate – which, of course, represents Russia, whose army destroyed their own churches and monasteries – or to go over to the Ukrainian Orthodox Church. In fact, it can be problematic to convert to the Ukrainian Orthodox Church in the east or south of Ukraine, as there are almost no churches of the Ukrainian Autocephalous Orthodox Church in these regions. These too will have to be built.

One strategy might be to capture and make use of Russian military mobile churches. These churches comprise large inflatable tents with an inflatable cross on an inflatable dome. During this war, however, Russia does not seem to be making as much use as usual of these camp churches. Although they are often used in military exercises, for some reason they are not being used in combat operations in Ukraine. Could it be that Russia does not want Russian soldiers to turn to God during this war? What if God tells them to be merciful, what if He says, "Thou shalt not murder"? This would contradict the sermons of the Russian Orthodox Church's Patriarch who justifies the war and the killings of the Ukrainian military and civilians.

17.10.2022

The Persistent Pressure of Putin's Plan

I imagine the Russian President was hoping the latest bombardments of Ukrainian cities would have the same effect on the population as February's long-awaited but nonetheless unexpected all-out assault on the country. He wanted to see tens of thousands of cars racing towards the safety of the European Union, with the mayor Vitaly Klitschko, the President, his team and other Ukrainian politicians all fleeing Kyiv. When the attack came, Russian telegram channels even reported on Zelensky's "escape", saying that he was no longer in power. The reality was somewhat different. Ukraine faced the massive missile strike of October 10 steadfastly, without flinching. The attack involved nine dozen missiles fired almost simultaneously, but the country stayed on its feet.

Kyiv, which had become accustomed to a sense of relative safety over the last few months, very quickly recovered from the shock. Within an hour of the rocket explosions, public utility services had begun boarding up the broken windows of the Khanenko Museum and were clearing the roads of burned-out cars and rocket fragments.

One missile exploded near Kyiv's House of Teachers, beside which is a monument to the first chairman of the Ukrainian Parliament, Mykhailo Hrushevsky. He was elected in 1918. In that year, the Parliament sat in the building that is today known as the House of Teachers. The people of Kyiv reacted characteristically, with a joke, saying, "The Russian army seems to be using maps of Kyiv from a hundred years ago!"

Many of Kyiv's citizens are of course in no mood for jokes. Among the dead from Monday's attack was a young oncologist from the main children's hospital in Ukraine. She had just taken her daughter to kindergarten and was on her way to work. Her car was incinerated by a direct hit of a missile. The head of cyber security for Kyiv City's Police also died as his car was blown up. In total, eight people died and more than 80 were treated in hospital.

Two days after the explosions, my daughter and her fiancé went to see Irina Khazina, who lives across the road from Shevchenko Park. They helped clear her apartment of broken glass and plaster. Irina was still very upset. She was worried about leaving her home unattended with all its windows broken. It is located on the top floor of her building and with the roof damaged, water will get in if it rains and ruin her late husband's library. Petro Khazin was the first publisher of *Death and the Penguin* in Ukraine.

Irina's daughter could not find plywood with which to board up the windows, so she sealed them temporarily using plastic sheeting – which any strong wind would rip out. There is hope that the city's utility services will fix the roof soon, but it seems that at the moment it is the property owners themselves who must take care of repairs of their apartments. It is almost impossible to find builder-decorators at the moment. Many have gone into the army and those who remain have too many demands on their time because there are so many buildings in need of urgent repair throughout Kyiv region – in Bucha, Borodyanka, Hostomel.

By the beginning of October, many refugees from Kyiv region had come back to the city to start repairing their homes. Those without the resources to pay for the work have tried to raise money on Facebook. For absent homeowners, the priority is to get help to protect their properties from looters. In Bucha and Irpin, several locals have already been caught stealing from apartments and houses left open by the war. Repairs are going on everywhere, despite repeated shelling. Three days after Monday's attack, Bucha was once more the target of Iranian drones, which exploded near an electrical substation there.

On October 10, one of the missiles struck the intersection of two major Kyiv streets, Taras Shevchenko Boulevard and Volodymyrska Street, leaving a deep funnel-shaped hole. It immediately filled with water from a damaged mains pipe. Within a day, the water pipe was repaired, the pit was filled in and new asphalt laid on top. Kyivites went to photograph the site of such recent devastation. They wished to boast about how quickly Kyiv could recover from any kind of attack.

Yes, Ukraine has learned how to quickly repair missile-damaged infrastructure, but with each new attack, the problems accumulate. Local authorities have published a schedule of power cuts and residents have been asked to save energy wherever possible. Even foreign diplomats have taken up the cause to conserve electricity. British Ambassador Melinda Simmons posted how she was working on documents using a handheld torch rather than electric light. In towns and villages throughout Ukraine, the evening sees far fewer lit windows than usual. In Kyiv, there is only essential street lighting. Once dusk has fallen, the city centre's beautiful churches and Ukrainian baroque apartment buildings stand in darkness.

The capture of the Zaporizhzhia nuclear power plant by the Russian army has further complicated the electricity supply situation. As we move into winter, it will get harder. The heating systems in most Ukrainian apartment buildings are centrally controlled – a legacy of their Soviet past. In Kyiv, there is already talk of setting the room temperature at a chilly 16°C, but is it possible to guarantee any kind of heating in the city while Russia is constantly directing missiles at infrastructure facilities?

During a war, there can, of course, be no guarantees. For as long as it goes on, it is impossible to insure oneself against death or injury. It is surprising that insurance companies which refuse to insure people because of the hostilities nonetheless agree to insure pets against bullet and shrapnel wounds. True, many Ukrainians would agree that their cats and dogs deserve better treatment than they do themselves.

Irina Khazina was fortunate in being able to move in with her daughter after Monday's missile attack. However, the trauma of seeing her apartment wrecked left her unable to sleep for two nights. On the third day, she decided to go to the pharmacy for some sedatives. At the door of the chemist's, she stumbled on the step and fell badly, breaking bones above and below her elbow. The ambulance, which arrived swiftly, took her to a hospital near her daughter's apartment. One misfortune led to another.

Irina Khazina could be added to the list of victims of Russian missile attacks. She was not injured by shrapnel or flying glass, that would have been much worse, but she has suffered. In the same way, thousands of other residents of Kyiv, along with displaced people who came to the city seeking temporary shelter, can also be considered victims.

There are no published statistics, but I would assume that the number of heart attacks and strokes has increased in Kyiv since Monday, October 10. I know that Irina's neighbour, at whose kitchen table I often sat chatting about life, died that day from cardiac arrest. He was not even in Kyiv. He was in Germany, a refugee. He will be buried there, unlike my friend Dr Valentin Suslov. He too found shelter in Germany and died a couple of weeks ago in Mainz, at the home of an old friend who had offered shelter to him and his wife, Tanya. Valentin was cremated. On October 10, Tanya was going to start the journey back to Kyiv with his ashes so that he could be buried at home. Because of the missile attack, she cancelled her trip and does not yet know when she will make another attempt to return to Kyiv with her husband's ashes.

There are still many empty apartments in Kyiv. Some who fled to Europe rent out their apartments to refugees from Kharkiv and Kherson. At the start of the new phase of the war rental prices in Kyiv fell by 50 per cent., but then gradually they rose again. They have not reached pre-war levels, but rates seem to change almost daily, their volatility clearly reflecting the perceived level of danger in the city. Prices do not change for existing tenants, only for new ones. On October 10, apartment rental prices fell by 25 per cent. but within two days the rates began increasing again. New tenants who signed rental agreements after lunch last Monday will certainly be paying less than those who signed the day before, although I doubt that many people signed contracts that day as everyone was sitting in bomb shelters or underground stations.

Kyiv residents have now started reacting much more rapidly to air raid warnings. Even those who would casually finish their coffee at one of the many street cafés now carry thermos cups so that they can take their drink away to a safer place as soon as the moan of the siren rises into the air.

As the memory of October 10 recedes and its particular impact is dampened by further attacks, we can safely say that Putin's attempt to intimidate Ukrainians has failed. Permanent residents and internally displaced persons are quietly steadfast. They understand that the level of danger is now much higher than it has been for the last two or three months. They have become more demanding of the city authorities, insisting that the locks be cut off the doors of underground premises which were designed as shelters but which were earlier privatised and then closed. The city government claims that it does not have the legal authority to do this. This, of course, raises questions, as the bomb shelters are protected by law and cannot be privatised. The suspicion rests that their status was changed in violation of the law.

In general, the people of Kyiv are satisfied with the city authorities and with their mayor, boxer Vitali Klitschko. Both his words and behaviour express eloquently the militant mood of the majority of Kyivites. He is not afraid to appear at the scene of the explosions along with the firefighters and rescuers. His face always expresses determination and readiness for an instant response to each new extreme situation.

I would like to believe that Kyiv will continue to stand up to the absurd pressures that Putin continues to enforce upon its inhabitants. Kyivites know that they are not alone. They witness with awe and pride the fighting spirit of other cities, towns and villages throughout Ukraine. This weekend, Shevchenko Park was once more full of relaxed families taking selfies against the autumn colours, including photographs taken inside the deep pit next to the children's swings made last Monday by a missile. These same families might feel a bit strange looking at their photographs today as there is yet another vicious bombardment of the centre of Kyiv.

An air raid warning gave residents about ten minutes to make it to their chosen "safer place" and then the drones arrived, swooping over the roofs, hitting an historic four-storey apartment building near to the circus, as well as a high-rise office block. There are more dead and wounded.

Between Nationalism and Patriotism

Since February of this year, the question of identity has been much on my mind. The subject comes up on a daily basis during my talks and lectures in various cities of Europe. I try to explain to Europeans the difference between the Russian–Soviet mentality and the Ukrainian mentality. Once I have explained this difference, it is much easier for me to talk about the causes of this war. It also allows me to explain my own identity, which has long hindered my communication with Russia and creates many problems for me in Ukraine as well.

In fact, mine is one of the varieties of Ukrainian identity that, until recently, in no way conflicted with the main value markers of "a Ukrainian". However, there is one element in my identity that has the same effect on some of my fellow Ukrainian intellectuals as a red rag has to a bull. I am an ethnic Russian and my native language is Russian. In all other respects, I am a typical Ukrainian. I do not listen to the opinion of the majority, I value my own opinion. For me, freedom – especially freedom of speech and creativity – is more valuable than money and stability. I rarely find myself in support of an existing government's policies and I am always ready to criticise them.

In short, if I exclude from the list of my characteristics the fact of my native language and Russian origin, I come out as an ideal Ukrainian who could be enthusiastically welcomed into the fold of ideal Ukrainians. Existing members of this group spend a great deal of time on Facebook publicly determining who is and who is not a proper Ukrainian – and who is not a Ukrainian at all.

I consider myself Ukrainian – a Ukrainian of Russian origin.

And that is all there is to it. I live in a beautiful country with a complex character and complex history, where each citizen has his or her own image of the Ukrainian state in their head and everyone considers their image to be the correct one. In other words, we are a society of individualists.

This society derives from the historical experience of organised anarchy into which Ukrainian society has regularly plunged over the centuries. No wonder Europe's largest-ever army of anarchists, the revolutionary rebel army of Nestor Makhno, appeared and fought in Ukraine and not in Russia – a country with a collective mentality. Makhno's army fought successfully against all participants in the civil war of 1918–21.

Looking at present-day Ukraine, I see proof of Ukrainian individualism in the presence of more than 400 political parties registered with the Ministry of Justice. I understand and accept Ukrainian society as it is, with all its contradictions and paradoxes.

Over the last 30 years, acquaintances and strangers from among Ukrainian nationalists have from time to time approached me to request that I start writing in Ukrainian. Sometimes they have accepted my explanation that I write in my native language – in Russian – and that I have the right to my native language. Sometimes this explanation is met with incomprehension and/or dissatisfaction. However, my conversations with people on this topic have usually remained amicable. Occasionally, anonymous opponents have posted messages on social media stating that I am not a Ukrainian but a Russian writer. I do not react. Everyone in Ukraine has the right to their opinion and everyone has the right to express their opinion. And everyone has the right to disagree with the opinion of another person.

In Ukraine, by the way, there are many Russian-speaking Ukrainian nationalists. A large number of the members of the well-known radical organisation, the "Right Sector", which became influential in 2014, were Russian speaking. So, nationalism has not always been connected with the Ukrainian language. I should add, in Ukraine, there are dozens of different groups of nationalists and very often they fight with each other in their attempt to define "correct nationalism". Even the famous historical character Stepan Bandera came into conflict with colleagues in the struggle for an independent Ukraine in the 1930s and 1940s.

At the same time, nationalists are not represented in the Ukrainian Parliament. In the last election, not a single nationalist political party was able to win the five per cent. of the vote required to be so represented. A force that cannot enter Parliament is not a real political force.

In contrast, Ukrainian patriotism is more inclusive. The main prerequisite is to love one's country and here there is no enthusiasm for the creation of exclusive criteria. Crimean Tatar activists – mercilessly targeted by the Russian security services – mostly do not speak Ukrainian. They usually speak Russian and their native Crimean Tatar but nobody questions their Ukrainian patriotism.

I too am a Ukrainian patriot. Ukraine, as an independent state, matured before my eyes. I lived for 30 years in Soviet Ukraine and have been living in independent Ukraine for 31. Since independence, Ukrainian literature and culture have revived and a very different, European generation of new Ukrainians has grown up for whom everything Soviet is exotic. This generation has made the Ukrainian language and Ukrainian-language literature fashionable. In 2012, both the Russian- and Ukrainian-language versions of my novel *Jimmy Hendrix Live in Lviv* were released simultaneously in Ukraine. It was then that I realised, for the first time, that in Ukraine a book in

Ukrainian will sell better than the same work in Russian. Since then, my books in Ukrainian translation have always outsold the Russian language editions. Young Ukrainians read Russian less and less. The Russian language is losing its position in Ukraine. Frankly, this does not upset me.

In February, I decided to stop publishing my works of fiction in their original language – Russian. Let the books come out in Ukraine in Ukrainian, in France in French, and in Britain and America in English. Russian readers do not need my books. Publication of my books was first stopped in Russia in 2005, after the Orange Revolution in which I took part. The second time this happened was in 2008, following a short "thaw" during which time many of my novels were republished. Since 2014, Russian bookshops have been forbidden to import my books from Ukraine. I am used to the idea that, as an author, I do not exist in Russia. I do not have readers there and I do not regret that.

Lately, on Ukrainian Facebook, the Russian language is increasingly referred to as the "language of the enemy". The Kremlin has done everything possible – and much seemingly impossible – to make Russian-speaking Ukrainians switch to Ukrainian. Having said that, you rarely hear conflicts over language on the street, where people use both Russian and Ukrainian and the languages peaceably coexist.

The language question and arguments around it were the prerogatives of the political arena, in which, before the start of the war in 2014, the defenders of the Ukrainian language fought with the defenders of the Russian language – or rather, with the defenders of Russian influence in Ukraine. The current military aggression has removed the defenders of the Russian language from the political arena. Many of them turned out to be traitors, collaborators and even Russian spies, holding Russian passports.

In this situation, some Ukrainian intellectuals consider all Russian-speaking Ukrainians partly responsible for this war. It is true that Putin has made Russian speakers the apparent cause of the war by maintaining that his "special military operation" was required to protect them. His persistent repetition of this idea has led some Ukrainian nationalists to declare that if there had been no Russian speakers in Ukraine, then there would have been no war!

Some nationalists, such as Iryna Farion, seem to struggle to achieve an objective view of Ukrainian society. They do not see that Ukraine is a multicultural state with more than two dozen national minorities. Fortunately, few activists ignore the reality of Ukrainian society in this way and those who do, do not have much influence on state polity. However, they do use every opportunity to project their divisive opinions, encouraging the creation of a schism in Ukrainian society between national idealists and realists.

25.10.2022

Autumn in Ukraine – Apples and Jellyfish

It is strange that the horrors of war have not cancelled the pretend horrors of Halloween, a cultural import that took root in Ukraine in the late 1990s and that has since become popular among young people. In Kyiv, Halloween decor is as hot a commodity in October as Christmas tree decorations are in December. Even now, when the Ukrainian media is full of the visual horrors of war, bloody plastic heads, giant cobwebs and other Halloween accessories have appeared on the shelves of some shops.

Among these seasonal items, a new product has appeared – "Putin's coffin". Now on sale in Kyiv at the Zhitniy Market in Podil, it is a life-size wooden coffin, with Putin's name on the lid and a label that reads "souvenir coffin". Vendors say they are very popular with restaurant owners who are counting on customers wanting to celebrate the "horror holiday" with a good meal. I only hope that the Halloween festivities will not be cancelled by real Russian horrors, the missiles and Iranian drones which, at the very least, can cause power cuts and plunge cities into darkness. Such things may not be conducive to celebrations, even ghostly ones.

Arranging outings and festivities during a war is controversial but necessary. Excursions can reduce stress. Kyivites who rarely if ever went to museums before the war now make a point of checking which museums will be open at the weekend. The Khanenko Museum, containing Kyiv's largest collection of European painting, had to close after all the windows of this historical building were blown out by a missile explosion. The Museum of the History of Medicine is still open. And, of course, there is the Museum of Live Jellyfish on Independence Square. It is underground and could well serve as a bomb shelter. This is a private museum and the owner is clearly someone with a passion for this form of aquatic life. On display is the largest, if not the only, collection of rare, live jellyfish in Ukraine.

Although it has been open for some time, I refused to visit the museum for what now seems an absurd reason – its location! The large underground space in the very centre of the city was previously a public toilet. When the toilet was closed down, I was outraged. And when a private museum of jellyfish was opened in its place, I took it to be some kind of joke. Since then, two large public toilets have appeared in the nearby underground shopping mall and my indignation has lost its puff.

When the Museum of Live Jellyfish announced that entrance was free for Ukrainian military personnel, any negative feelings I might have retained evaporated. My son Theo recently spent almost two hours there, in the semi-darkness, looking at the slow, dreamlike movements of the creatures in large, backlit aquariums built into the walls. I imagine military folk would like this museum. For a short while, they can immerse themselves in a world far away from war.

Like mushrooms and yellowing leaves, I associate jellyfish with autumn. It is certainly autumn now in Ukraine. The leaves, yellow and red, are already falling from the trees and covering the gardens and the roads of cities and villages.

This autumn, many unpicked apples hang in the orchards and gardens around the burned-out houses in Donbas and southern Ukraine. Even in the more peaceful areas of the country, the owners seem not to harvest all the apples on their trees. Yet it is a bumper year, as if the trees were trying to compensate for the swathes of farmland rendered unproductive by the war. In my village too, apples are still hanging on the trees. A number of the branches have snapped under the weight of the crop. We have a lot of walnuts too this year. My son sent me photographs of himself posing under a tree with buckets full of walnuts.

The garden has become overgrown during our absence. There is much work to be done. My wife Elizabeth bottles apple puree every day. We also have an electric fruit dryer to make apple slices for the special Ukrainian drink, *uzvar* (a compote made from dried fruit and berries), which assumes importance at Christmas time.

Last week the village children started to again go to the local school for lessons. They had been studying online for two weeks. The last Iranian drone flew over the roof of our little house almost ten days ago. Since then, life in the village has fallen back into its quiet routine. All four of the village's shops are well stocked and fresh bread is delivered every day.

Recently, funeral music could be heard in the neighbouring communities of Kostivtsi, Stavishche, and Morozivka. Ukrainian soldiers, killed while defending their country, were brought home to be buried. Twenty-five men from our village are fighting in the war with Russia. They are all well. Fellow villagers often talk about them and immediately cross themselves while doing so, praying that they will all stay safe and come back alive. I know some of the soldiers from our village, but I do not know where they are fighting. You should not ask relatives about this as it is a state secret – even parents are not supposed to know.

Once more, children's voices can be heard in the village. Some young families from Kyiv have moved to the countryside to stay with their relatives, as they did during the pandemic. The capital has air raid warnings almost every day and life in the village seems safer. Children can study online and, unlike in Kyiv, there are virtually no power cuts. Few parents are thinking of returning to the city in the near future.

One indication that life in the village is returning to normal, and indeed, throughout the region, is that the crime rate is nearing its pre-war level. There is an increase in carjacking, theft, and robbery. Recently, there was even a police raid in our village, and arrests were made, with a number of young men from the area taken into custody accused of duping those wishing to travel abroad. The masterminds of the scheme could receive a prison sentence of several years.

The young men had pretended to be organising work abroad for Ukrainians and demanded up-front payment for arranging the paperwork. Once the payment was made, they disappeared.

The most surprising thing is that the organiser of this criminal scheme was the son of a friend, the owner of one of the village grocery shops. I remember him as a boy helping his parents: he seemed to spend much of his free time behind the counter. Several of the suspects were released on bail for the period of the investigation, but the main organisers, including the son of our friend, are sitting in a pre-trial detention centre.

If that had happened in Russia, those arrested would probably have been offered the opportunity to fight in Ukraine instead of sitting in prison. That is not an option for Ukrainian malefactors right now, although there have been discussions about offering prisoners the opportunity to volunteer for the Ukrainian army.

There is opportunity for cases of online criminal activity to increase in wartime. During war, online services take on new significance. People who are afraid to go out in case of an air raid can order whatever they need and have it delivered. There are always people ready to risk the street to earn money delivering stuff.

It is impossible to overestimate the anxiety and stress that haunts the residents of Kyiv. The carefree youth populating the cafés and bars in the city centre are far from typical. Take our friend Svetlana, who recently returned to Kyiv from Bulgaria, where she had spent six months. She is now considering packing her bags and taking a bus back to Ahtopol. By late September, she had quite recovered her peace of mind and was delighted to be in her own home, but the recent missile and drone strikes have thrown her back upon the unbearable nightmares she experienced during February this year.

Recently the war killed one of my Kyiv acquaintances, the rector of the Grinchenko Pedagogical University, Viktor Ognevyuk. He was 63. His death was not caused by an Iranian drone or a Russian missile. He shot himself with a pistol. He left a note explaining that he could not live like this anymore. I would like to believe that Ukrainians are not afraid of death and are not afraid of the Russian aggression, but this is not always the case.

Recently my old friend and neighbour, the musician Liosha Aleksandrov, was walking along Yaroslaviva Val, one of Kyiv's loveliest streets, when the air raid siren sounded, yet again. Before his eyes, people hurried out of the cafés and the doors were locked. Only the local beauty salon continued to work and, through the window, Liosha watched the lone salon employee continuing to give her client a manicure. One would like to think that beauty is more important than life!

Despite the missile and drone threats and the power cuts, there is a "business as usual" feel about Kyiv. McDonald's restaurants are reopening and long queues form outside, as if people see it as their patriotic duty to defend and support this sign of normality.

It has also become popular to buy bracelets made from steel produced at the once huge Azovstal steel plant now destroyed by the Russian army. The money raised from the sale of these bracelets goes to the Ukrainian army. Everything goes to the army now – and the army feels this support.

All Ukrainians, even those who live as refugees abroad, have become part of the Ukrainian army. Despite the stress and upheaval caused by the war, they think more about Ukraine than about themselves and constantly follow the news from the front. Every Ukrainian has their own vision of the front line and sense of how far away that front line is. Each advance of the Ukrainian army towards Russia brings happiness and hope of a speedy end to the war.

Only the television pundits try regularly to temper this hope.

They do not want people to believe in a quick and easy victory. After all, if this does not materialise, the disappointment and further stress could drive people to despair. Even three hours in Kyiv's Museum of Live Jellyfish may not then be sufficient to give them back their peace of mind.

07.11.2022

Candles in the War

This November, residents of many large Ukrainian cities have been able to enjoy the beauty of the night sky for the first time in almost a year. The stars have never hung so low over Kyiv, Kharkiv, Lviv, and Odesa. Their brilliance was always hidden by the brightly lit streets and houses. Not anymore. After the shock of the first blackouts, Ukrainians are becoming accustomed to frequent periods without electricity and water. Whenever possible, people fill their bathtubs and keep stocks of drinking water in five-litre plastic bottles. It is harder to store electricity. You can charge power banks and batteries, but you cannot connect your refrigerator to them, or a freezer.

Kyiv, as other cities, is adjusting itself to this new regime. There is a schedule of power cuts for each district. On a typical day, there will be no power from three o'clock in the morning until six, then from midday until four o'clock, and finally from eight o'clock until midnight. However, power cuts can happen more often, start earlier and last longer. No electricity means no Wi-Fi. So, Kyiv's army of I.T. specialists, including those who work remotely for foreign companies, must toil until the early hours of the morning and catnap during the day in order to get anything done.

Conscientious Ukrainians have stopped using their washing machines, dishwashers and kettles because they consume too much energy. Washing is done by hand, mostly in cold water. It is very tempting to use the machine, of course, but neighbours might feel the vibrations or hear the hum. You cannot predict how they will react to such an insane waste of kilowatts.

After the difficult, early years of Ukraine's independence, the electricity supply in cities became more reliable. Urban Ukrainians, however, tend to associate rural life with the lack of most things, including light. This is not an accurate picture although if, in our house in the village, you switch on the electric kettle in the evening, all the bulbs in the house grow dim. At least, they did. These days, nobody uses electric kettles. As in the towns, village people are doing their bit to save electricity.

Not surprisingly, the demand for candles has risen exponentially and they are now in short supply. The number of generators imported into Ukraine has also risen tenfold, although they are very expensive.

I used to make light of my wife's habit of giving beautiful decorative candles to friends and acquaintances as presents. I was equally bemused when candles were given to us. They seemed to end up gathering dust. But now their time has come – the time of donated candles. Suddenly such a gift makes perfect sense. A candle is a future light and it might be the only source of light during darkness. What is more, a candle is an opportunity to understand how people lived before the advent of electricity. It was a very different world. Without electricity and all our electricity-guzzling apparatuses we might be left in the dark but we are also able to return to philosophical reflection and eternal values. A burning candle slows down movement. You never walk past one too quickly because the gust of air might extinguish it.

The popularity of the candle as a commodity also raises the value of matches. They too now find a place of honour in the kitchen, or on the table near the candlestick, where they are easy to find in the dark.

The Ukrainian writer and artist Anatoliy Dnistrovy has discovered the process of painting by candlelight and is delighted. "It is very cool to draw by candlelight! The old masters knew something!" he told me. I asked Anatoliy whether he had switched to pen and paper when writing texts. "Of course!" he replied. He told me that he was writing two books at once without a computer: a diary about life during the war and a more philosophical, non-fiction text, also about the war.

Other writers and poets are gradually moving to pen and paper and finding special pleasure and self-affirmation in the physical process of writing. Previously they wrote by electric light on computers, now they use pen and paper by candle-light. It is proof that Russia will not force them to change their aspirations.

We are down to our last candles in our house. My wife has said that the local shops have run out.

"Go to the church and buy some!" I advised her on the phone and immediately realised what a silly piece of advice that was.

"You know the church is closed!" she said.

Yes, our church is open only on major holidays. We do not have a permanent priest and that means that you can only buy candles there a couple of times a year.

The most powerful candle-making industry in Ukraine has always belonged to the church. Throughout the country, hundreds of thousands of candles are burned every day in front of icons as part of religious ritual. Although very thin, beeswax candles burn slowly. I would not be surprised to find them burning in the houses and apartments of many Ukrainians today. Five years ago, in the novel *Grey Bees*, I described life without electricity but with church candles. The novel foretold the new Ukrainian reality. Eight years ago, it was already the reality for many people living in Donbas's grey zone.

At that time, Russian propagandists threatened Kyiv: "You too will live like Donbas! You will be flattened by bombs! We will destroy everything, wherever you are!" Donbas at that time was bombed by Russian "volunteer artillerymen". Now they are carrying out that threat and worse – bombing and shelling the entire country.

On the first evenings without electricity Kyivites were fascinated by what they saw. Social media was full of beautiful photographs of Kyiv without street lamps or lit windows. It is like a living being that had just lain down to sleep. Like other Ukrainian cities, Kyiv at night is now no longer visible from space. The dark hours protect the peaceful dreams of the city from its enemies.

Meanwhile, all over Ukraine, people are learning how to make candles. Not the usual kind that beekeepers might make from wax, but so-called "trench candles". Ukrainians no longer throw away empty tin cans. Instead, they use them to produce these crude but effective candles, which are then sent by the crate load to Ukrainian soldiers at the front. All you need to make a trench candle is some cardboard, a tin can, natural wax or artificial paraffin and oil – even palm oil will do. You cut a strip of cardboard and roll it up into a bundle to fit the size of the tin can, one piece of thick cardboard becomes a wick. You melt the wax or artificial paraffin on the stove, adding oil to it if you have some. The melted mixture is poured into the tin can, over the bundle of cardboard. Once the wax has solidified the candle is ready. It will burn for up to six hours and you can even brew coffee or heat food on it. As a source of heat, as well as light, a trench candle is important, especially as winter approaches and the soldiers' shelters are both damp and cold.

Trench candles have another name – "Finnish candles". It is said that they were first used by Finnish soldiers during the Soviet–Finnish war of 1939. It seems to me that the coming winter will be in many ways reminiscent of that confrontation when the Soviet Union attacked Finland. In that war, the U.S.S.R. lost 126,000 soldiers and officers, and about 250,000 were wounded. The war lasted 105 days. Having failed to capture Finland's capital Helsinki, the U.S.S.R. withdrew its army but retained part of Finland's territory – Karelia.

The war in Ukraine has already lasted more than 260 days. According to the Ministry of Defence of Ukraine, more than 76,000 Russian soldiers have already been killed. Russia claims that the true number is one tenth of that.

In 1939, fewer than four million people lived in Finland. Finland lost 26,000 soldiers during the war. They defended their independence, although for many years Finland remained under threat from its southern neighbour. I think that Russian politicians should have re-read the history of the Soviet–Finnish war before deciding to attack Ukraine.

In Russia, meanwhile, in their desperation to gain the upper hand against Ukraine, they are looking to the climate and "General Moroz" (General Winter Frost), which is seen traditionally by Russians as an effective ally in all wars. While in Ukraine, military ranks have never been bestowed on weather types, such as frost or rain, even in joke. In Russia, such concepts as "General Frost" and "General Winter" are taken extremely seriously. Russian Wikipedia even has a long article called "General Frost" which explains how winter has always helped the Russian army "to defeat its western European enemies". For example, the winter of 1708 helped to weaken the Swedish army of Charles XII before the Battle of Poltava.

Ukrainian civilians are acutely aware of the effect of winter conditions on soldiers at the front. In the south of Odesa region, near the town of Reni, is the village of Kotlovina, the capital of the Ukrainian Gagauz people, a Turkic-speaking national minority. Most of the women and even some of the men gather every evening to knit warm woollen socks for Ukrainian soldiers. The Gagauz are engaged traditionally in sheep breeding, so their wool stocks are plentiful. Kyivites have also looked out all the old knitted socks presented to them by grandmothers and great-grandmothers.

The central heating has finally come on in our Kyiv apartment building, but nobody expects the radiators to be more than tepid, so those warm socks will at last come in handy.

Curfew is still in effect in Kyiv. Bars, cafés, and restaurants close at around ten o'clock so that customers can be safely at home by eleven. The bars, often located in basements and even in former concrete bomb shelters, are still crowded. During power outages, they light candles and stop accepting bank cards. You can pay for your next single malt or bourbon in cash alone. The atmosphere becomes warmer and more romantic.

The other day Kyiv's mayor, Vitali Klitschko, inadvertently warned the capital's residents that they might have to evacuate the entire population, some three million people, if all the infrastructure is destroyed by Russian missiles. The people of Kyiv reacted quite aggressively. They have got used to having no heating in the bars and cafés, and the more customers who come the warmer it will be – evacuation is not an option!

The optimism of Kyiv's population seems at odds with common sense, but if positive thinking wins out and there is no evacuation this winter it will be remembered for generations to come as a dramatic period in the life of a country huddled around handmade candles, which remain bright and warm through the night, like the Ukrainian spirit.

15.11.2022

How Much is a Train Ticket to Crimea?

For elderly residents of high-rise buildings, hard times have come. Their biggest fear is getting stuck in an elevator for the duration of a power cut. They would like to sit on a bench near the house or in the park, but instead they sit in their apartments all day long. Younger people are boldly playing a new form of Russian roulette with the lifts. Kyivites are also applying their "We can do this!" spirit to deal with the challenge. On the floor in the elevators of some high-rise buildings you can find cardboard boxes with a supply of everything you might need in case of a power cut – water, biscuits, wet wipes, blood pressure pills, a mat, a flashlight. Some elevators also have a chair.

Last week, our friend Tanya finally arrived in Kyiv, bringing with her from Germany the ashes of her husband, Valentin, who died in September. There is a family grave at Kyiv's Baikove cemetery. Among the guests at the interment ceremony were several former colleagues from the hospital where Valentin worked until well into his eighties. Our elder son represented our family. During the wake, he recalled that Valentin had told him all about the difficulties of buying a car in Soviet times and how inexpensive petrol was in those days. Tanya is going back to Mainz, in Germany, where Valentin spent the last five months of his life, dreaming of returning home. Tanya has tried to

97

sell the garage and the car, but you cannot get a good price for anything right now.

Winter is approaching and at night the temperature is already dropping to zero or lower. In the morning, there is fog outside the window. It disappears only after a couple of hours, allowing the sun to heat the air to 10°C.

Our village neighbours, Nina and Tolik, are already thinking about Christmas but have not decided when to celebrate – with Europe on December 25, or with Russia on January 7. Our village has only one church and it is attached to the Moscow Patriarchate, which will curse those who celebrate Christmas separately from Moscow.

The Moscow Patriarchate must feel that its days in our country are numbered. In the Pechersk Lavra, the church's main monastery in Ukraine, the faithful have been praying for Russia and singing hymns glorifying "Holy Rus" during their services. Someone video-recorded this pro-Russian activity and Father Zacharias, who was officiating at the service, was suspended temporarily from church duties. Then several interesting stories surfaced about him. He has been compared to Rasputin and, as it turns out, he was the spiritual mentor of many Ukrainian politicians and statesmen during Yanukovych's presidency. He even performs miracles, such as predicting the dollar exchange rate.

Ukraine's Security Services recently paid visits to senior hierarchs of the Ukrainian Orthodox Church of the Moscow Patriarchate. Some of their homes were searched. Several priests were detained by the police for passing on to Russian curates information about the Ukrainian army and the mood of the population in different regions of Ukraine.

In Bukovina, in and around the ancient city of Chernivtsi, strange anti-Moscow "signs" have been observed. Cracks and dips have appeared in the ground surrounding the churches of the Moscow Patriarchate. It began at the Neporotovsky Monastery. According to local jour-nalists, potholes and cracks have also appeared near both St Nicholas Cathedral on Ruska Street and the Holy Vvedensky Convent on Bukovinska Street.

I was beginning to wonder whether we were, indeed, witnessing paranormal anti-Moscow activity, when the former adviser to the Chernivtsi governor, writer and public figure Volodymyr Kilinich quickly brought me back to earth. "There is a perfectly boring explanation," he told me. "Yes, there are cracks and potholes there, but nothing too huge and the reason is not divine but related to the poor condition of underground water pipes."

Still, the local people have perked up. The Chernivtsi newspaper *Chas* wrote gleefully: "This is a bad sign for Moscow priests! They should flee from Ukraine immediately, or risk falling into hell!"

———

Ahead of winter, the Ukrainian army accelerated its counter-offensive and liberated Kherson. The city met Ukrainian soldiers with joy and tears. There is no electricity, no heating, and no water. There is gas, which means you can cook food. Before fleeing to the other side of the Dnipro River, the Russian military blew up a television centre, a television mast and many other infrastructure facilities. What they did not have time to blow up, they mined. A couple of days later, the Minister of Culture announced that Ukrainian television was already available in Kherson. How you access it without electricity or a television mast is not clear. There is no telephone connection or Internet either but there is happiness and relief.

Ukraine's Department of Railways has promised to have

trains running between Kherson and Kyiv in the very near future. Train tickets to Kherson are already on sale on the national railway's website. On this site, you can also buy tickets for Donetsk, Luhansk, Mariupol and Simferopol – all in Russian-occupied territory. More than a thousand would-be passengers have already bought tickets to Simferopol, the capital of Crimea. No-one knows when the first train will leave Kyiv, but the Ukrainian railways need money to repair the badly damaged stations and rails and to restore the Antonovsky rail bridge across the Dnipro River. This bridge is vital for rail transportation to Crimea.

While optimists are buying tickets to Crimea, Ukrainian troops have closed Kherson for entry and exit and imposed a curfew from five o'clock in the afternoon. The de-mining of the city is under way, as well as the search for collaborators and Russian soldiers who did not have time to escape to the other side of the Dnipro River with the rest of the Russian forces. Some Russian soldiers have already been detained. They were in civilian clothes and trying to impersonate Kherson residents.

Two collaborators were also detained, but most people who chose to collaborate with the occupiers fled the city with the Russian troops. Some of them, they say, wept as they left. They could not understand how the Ukrainian army could return to Kherson if there were huge billboards on every street with the inscription "Russia is here forever!" Russia, as it turned out, was there temporarily, but that eight months must have seemed like an eternity to Kherson.

Before retreating, the Russian occupiers dug up the bones of Empress Catherine II's lover, Prince Potemkin. His remains have probably been taken to Moscow. Perhaps the Russian Orthodox Church is planning to promote the playboy reveller-prince to sainthood.

Potemkin's bones were not the only thing the Russian occupiers took from Kherson. They removed two monuments: one to the Russian Tsarist Marshal Suvorov and the other to Admiral Ushakov. More importantly, they stole the entire contents of Kherson city museum and the museum of Kherson region. Approximately fifteen thousand works of art were transported to the other side of the Dnipro, along with the archives from the pension fund and the police.

The occupiers also raided Kherson's mini-zoo, so beloved by the city's younger inhabitants, and kidnapped a donkey, two peacocks, and a raccoon. The raccoon did not want to leave and resisted fiercely. Oleg Zubkov, the owner of a private zoo in Yalta, Crimea, was brought in to deal with the troublesome creature. Zubkov grabbed the raccoon roughly by the tail and stuffed him into a box, unashamedly sharing a video of the skirmish online.

The raccoon is now famous. Even Russians have started to joke about how he was captured, suggesting that the war can now be brought to an end since the whole point of it was obviously the abduction of Ukraine's most militant raccoon.

While Kherson was being liberated, another animal-related story came to an end. It did not get as much media attention as the tale of the raccoon. The dog named Crimea has died. He survived the missile attack on Dnipro city that killed his owners: the little girl, Vassilisa, her brother, Ivan, their mother and grandmother. Crimea was shell-shocked and temporarily blinded. He could not react to anything around him, only tears flowed from his eyes. He was taken to a veterinary clinic for treatment. There, his heart stopped.

Every day there are more and more homeless pets in Ukraine but the number of volunteers willing to help with this problem has also grown and they are constantly finding new ways to help the animals.

Recently, an unusual "getting to know you" event was arranged in one of Kyiv's vegan cafés, Sereda, in Podil. The Sirius Animal Shelter brought a dozen puppies to the café where it had been announced that from midday until four o'clock you could come and choose a pet. "Defeating the darkness is easier with a faithful four-legged friend!" was the project's slogan. It is true that even getting stuck in the elevator is less scary if you have your dog with you. But they had better add more water and some dog biscuits to the emergency supplies.

22.11.2022

Waiting for Godot

What do Adam and Eve, Newton, and Steve Jobs have in common? My first thought was, if you adhere to the biblical story, Newton and Steve Jobs are both descendants of Adam and Eve. But there is a better answer: the apple has been very important to all of them.

In Transcarpathia, this idea is central to a sculpture created by Roman Murnik that was recently installed in the historic Shenborn Park, not far from Uzhhorod. Apple trees have been planted around the sculpture and the authorities hope that this "apple square" will become a popular tourist attraction.

Transcarpathia, a region bordering Hungary, Poland, Romania and Slovakia, is still relatively peaceful. Russian missiles do not explode here thanks to Hungarian Prime Minister Orbán's increasingly steadfast friendship with Vladimir Putin. Hungary is blocking European financial assistance to Ukraine. It is also in favour of lifting the economic sanctions imposed on

Russia by the E.U. Furthermore, Hungary recently announced its desire to develop economic relations with Iran.

At the beginning of the war, millions of refugees passed through Transcarpathia. More than 50,000 internally displaced persons from all over Ukraine are still in the regional capital of Uzhhorod. At first, these long-term displaced people kept a low profile but now they are making their presence felt in the region. Young newcomers to Transcarpathia have entered colleges and universities and are active in the many volunteer projects that have sprung up. At the same time, the Theatre Company of Re-settlers, known as U.Zh.i.K., has staged Shakespeare's "King Lear" in Uzhhorod and their production of Samuel Beckett's "Waiting for Godot" has just been premiered there.

The role of Vladimir in Beckett's absurdist play is taken by Oleksiy Dashkovsky, who used to teach English at a school in Irpin, one of the towns near Kyiv which was partially destroyed during Russia's disastrous assault on the capital. Estragon is played by Sophia Almaz, a refugee from Kryviy Rig. The amateur troupe has adapted the play, but the central themes of uncertainty and expectation are unchanged.

The U.Zh.i.K. theatre group looks set to grow and the Uzhhorod Philharmonic has provided them with use of its stage. In short, the theatrical life of Transcarpathia has been enriched since the start of the war. The Theatre of Re-settlers is preparing for its first tour of western Ukraine and dreaming of a tour of Europe.

In Chernihiv, near the border with Belarus, theatre life has practically stopped. The region is shelled constantly by Russian artillery and rockets. The bridges between Kyiv and Chernihiv, which were destroyed earlier in the war, have not been restored because of the danger that they will once more become the target for Russian missiles. Electricity is a rare guest in the homes of the region's residents, but the saddest things of all are the lack of street lighting, the non-functioning traffic lights and the darkness in general, which at this time of year falls at four o'clock in the afternoon.

The number of car accidents involving pedestrians has risen dramatically. People are afraid to cross the street, even at marked crossings. The local administration is trying to find a way to maintain lighting at intersections and pedestrian crossings, even when there is no power elsewhere. As a start, free reflective vests and armbands are being handed out,

In Kyiv, too, traffic lights stop working during blackouts, causing numerous accidents. There are fewer cars on the roads, partly because of ice and snow but also because electric car owners have found themselves unable to charge their vehicles. The boots of many electric cars now contain small generators and cans of petrol. Filling stations are well stocked, but prices have more than doubled since February.

In contrast, the trains still run – and usually depart on time. A few days ago, the first train to newly liberated Kherson rolled into the regional capital's station to cheers and applause. On board the train, which was decorated with patriotic graffiti, there were three types of passengers: journalists, relatives and friends of Kherson residents who wanted to be sure that their loved ones were alive and well, and other Ukrainians who had no particular business in the city but who wanted to share in this victory over the Russian army. Most of the passengers, including the journalists, did not remain in the city but returned to Kyiv later that day because there are no functioning hotels in Kherson.

I hope that the U.Zh.i.K. theatre troupe will soon be able to take a play to Kherson, although not "Waiting for Godot". Waiting is too raw a subject. The people of Kherson struggled under Russian occupation for eight months. They suffered terrible disappointment when the early spring announcement of a military campaign to liberate their city turned out to be disinformation designed to trick the Russians. Fortunately, Russia fell for it, allowing the Ukrainian army to liberate Kharkiv region relatively quickly, while Kherson was left waiting for freedom. Some 80,000 people still live in the city, in extremely difficult conditions. The government has offered to evacuate residents to the neighbouring Mykolaiv region or to western Ukraine for the winter, but getting messages though to Kherson's population is difficult due to the lack of Internet and mobile communications.

Work on de-mining schools and kindergartens is coming to an end. These buildings will not serve their usual purpose this winter but will be turned into "spaces for the invincible". The plan is to create a dozen community hubs, located throughout Kherson, equipped with generators where you can charge your telephone and computer and connect to Elon Musk's Starlink. Doctors and social workers will be on duty to give help and advice. Last but not least, you will be able to get a hot tea and have a snack. I would like to add books and other cultural activities to these spaces; however, when everyone is concerned with basic survival, culture may have to wait.

On the positive side, a supermarket and two banks have opened branches in the city and one or two cafés have started up. The authorities promise to resume partial electricity supply within two to three weeks if the Russians do not make further strikes on infrastructure facilities. That is a big "if".

Five hundred police officers have arrived back in Kherson. Three hundred more are working in the region. Martial law is still in force and the production and sale of alcoholic beverages is prohibited. There is practically no crime in the city – only

105

the debris and victims of Russian war crimes. Several buildings were found to have been used by the Russian military as torture chambers in Kherson. Thousands of townspeople, including teenagers who too openly showed their negative attitude towards Russia and the Russian military, experienced these fearful places. Now the occupation is over, but every resident who survived it can tell you stories that would fill volumes of horror novels.

Kherson's teenagers have now taken to the streets to show their support for the Ukrainian army. They are covering the walls of apartment blocks with murals of the Commander-in-Chief of the Ukrainian military forces, General Zaluzhny. His image has also been painted on the pedestal of the monument to Admiral Ushakov. This monument itself departed with the Russian army. I imagine that the city would now approve of replacing it with one of General Zaluzhny.

Kherson is awaiting good mobile communications, electricity, water, and heating. When these services are restored, it will be possible to plan for a fully fledged cultural life. That will be the icing on the cake.

29.11.2022

Chess Matches and War Games in Ukraine

The more often the Ukrainian authorities tell their citizens that there will be no offensive from the direction of Belarus, the more apprehensively Ukrainians look towards their northern neighbour. The border between Ukraine and Belarus is about 1,100 kilometres long and it passes through four regions of Ukraine.

Volyn region, in the north-west of Ukraine, borders both Belarus and Poland. Soldiers and police officers are now going around the villages there, visiting each household to give instructions about what to do in the case of an evacuation. So far it is calm there, but these visits frighten the population.

On the border of Zhytomyr region and Belarus, strange events have occurred. Night-time military patrols discovered footprints in the snow originating from several different pairs of boots. Later, six people from Pakistan and Bangladesh were detained.

Before the start of the war, Belarus had "terrorised" the European Union, using refugees from Southern Asia to do so. The refugees were offered visa-free entry into Belarus, so the migrants flew to Minsk in their hundreds and thousands and headed immediately for the border with Poland. Belarusian border guards helped the migrants approach the demarcation line and then stood forming a wall to prevent them from returning to Belarus. Every night the refugees crowded at the Polish border. These events seem almost like ancient history now, but the appearance of these new refugees, this time on the Ukrainian side of the border, has raised many questions. Why were they trying to reach a country at war? And how did they get past the Russian military units stationed along the border of the Belarusian side?

The answer to these questions is as simple as it is macabre. According to the detained migrants, people in military uniform had driven them to the border with Ukraine and given them directions. They set off on foot through the snow-covered forest, regularly sending G.P.S. data back to the military in Belarus, as they had been instructed. This is how the Belarusian and Russian military check whether the forests on the Ukrainian side of the border are mined, which sections of the Ukrainian border are less closely guarded and where there are still reliable footpaths into Ukrainian territory.

On top of such worrying stories, there was the unexpected death of the Belarusian Minister of Foreign Affairs, Vladimir Makey, who, although he served Lukashenko, was reputed to have pro-European sympathies. He died just before a scheduled meeting with Sergei Lavrov, the Russian Foreign Minister. Lavrov immediately cancelled his visit to Minsk. The purpose of all official Russian visits to Belarus is to convince Lukashenko to send troops to fight against Ukraine and to open the "northern front" so that the Ukrainian army is forced to reduce its counter-attacks in the south and east.

While Ukraine is monitoring military activity inside Belarus and awaiting Russia's next attack on the country's energy infrastructure, a blitz chess championship has been held in Zhytomyr, 140 kilometres west of Kyiv and a regular target of missile attacks. The competition had four categories: men, women, boys and girls. The tournament was organised by the regional chess federation and took place at the Zhytomyr Ivan Franko University. It was dedicated to the birthday of the chess federation's previous president, Artem Sachuk, who is now fighting at the front.

The games were played according to the Swiss system: games of nine rounds in which players have three minutes for each move, plus two seconds of additional time for each move. Forty-four amateur chess players took part in the tournament. The youngest was four years old and the oldest was 72. During the championship, money was collected for the Ukrainian army and all the funds raised were sent to Artem Sachuk's unit.

Slow chess is impossible in today's Ukraine where everything has to be done quickly or very quickly. If in peacetime we appreciate each hour of tranquillity, during the war we appreciate every minute.

While the Zhytomyr Ivan Franko University was hosting the chess tournament, the city's School No. 7 was busy with the regional girls' basketball championship. The competition lasted two days and ended with victory for the team from the Dynamovets Children's Sports School.

In the city of Cherkasy, 300 kilometres to the south-west of Zhytomyr, the national Greco-Roman wrestling championship was taking place. The well-known Afro-Ukrainian Member of Parliament from Zelensky's Servant of the People party, Zhan Beleniuk, became the national champion in the under 87-kilogram category. Beleniuk's father was a Rwandan pilot who died during the 1990–94 Rwandan civil war. Beleniuk grew up in Kyiv and, in 2020, he brought back Ukraine's only gold medal from the Tokyo Olympics. The Servant of the People party invited him to become a Member of Parliament (through the "party list" system) because of his determined character and popularity among sports fans.

As Ukraine's first black Member of Parliament, Beleniuk is also a member of Ukraine's National Olympic Committee, which has just held new elections. The results of the ballot have shocked the country. Almost all of the newly elected members of the N.O.C. turned out to be former representatives of pro-Russian parties, or oligarchs, or officials close to oligarchs. In protest, Beleniuk resigned from the N.O.C. and called on all other patriotic members of the committee to do the same.

The well-known international footballer, Andriy Shevchenko, heeded that call. He had just been elected to the position of vice-president. Shevchenko issued this statement: "At this most difficult time in the history of my country, I am proud to stand by Ukraine and help in any way I can for our victory. I consider it an honour to serve on the National Olympic Committee and I understand the importance of its development. At the same time, I cannot be part of such a line-up. We are paying an infinitely high price for our freedom with the lives of the best of Ukrainians. We must be worthy of them."

Among the new members of the National Olympic Committee is one of Ukraine's most prominent pro-Russian politicians, Nestor Shufrych. He also remains a member of the Ukrainian Parliament and Head of the Committee on Freedom of Speech.

While outrage over the composition of the National Olympic Committee continues, thousands of well-known Ukrainian athletes are fighting and often dying at the front. Three months ago, near Donetsk, Zhan Beleniuk's friend and colleague Igor Pastukh became one of the hundred athletes to be killed in action so far. They are known as "Sports Angels" and a website has been launched in their memory.

Although statistics indicate that Ukrainian young people are not in general believers, there is a common understanding that the number of angels in the sky over Ukraine is growing. The concept of the "Heavenly Hundred" first appeared in 2014, after the execution of protesters on and near the Maidan during Ukraine's Revolution of Dignity. To those angel throngs, we can add the hundreds of Ukrainian children killed by Russian missiles and mortar fire, as well as the tens of thousands of adults, including soldiers.

Ukrainians' willingness to support local sporting events is a form of resistance; however, interest in this year's World Cup in Qatar is at a record low. Only the news about a fan running onto the pitch in a T-shirt with a Batman logo and the inscription "Save Ukraine" attracted attention. Ukrainians are focused on their own battles and on staying strong.

As the Christmas and New Year season approaches there are new tensions around how to celebrate. In Kyiv, after lengthy disputes, the city's mayor, the multiple title holder and world boxing champion, Vitali Klitschko, has decided to allow the erection of the country's main Christmas tree in Sophia Square as usual. In answer to protests from representatives of the presidential administration and other activists, who said that putting up festive decorations in Ukrainian cities during a war was neither ethical nor moral, the mayor's office insisted that the war should not deprive Ukrainian children of their holiday. The Russian aggressors should not be allowed to rob children of seasonal good cheer as it has robbed them of electricity, heating and running water. I agree with Vitali Klitschko: war does not cancel Christmas or the New Year. The war only increases the significance of these holidays for Ukrainians. Every festive or sporting event that goes ahead contributes to people's morale and the future of the country.

I hope that very soon they will hold classical chess competitions in Ukraine. Those chess games will require prolonged periods of silence, uninterrupted electric lighting and conditions in which players need think only about their next move and victory.

12.12.2022

Sounds of War

On frosty mornings Kyiv continues to wake up apparently peaceful and happy. The snow crunches under our feet. We can look forward to a Christmas tree appearing in Sophia Square as usual. True, we will have to go without the festive market – and the wooden huts selling Christmas decorations, mulled wine and hot food – which usually encircles the huge tree and stretches along the streets of Kyiv's ancient "top town". Nobody wants crowds to gather. We never know where and when the next missile will land.

Warmer weather recently replaced freezing temperatures, leaving Kyiv wrapped in a thick fog. As well as warning of poor visibility, Kyiv's meteorological office informed the public that they should not panic if they hear explosions coming from the north-west of the capital, from the direction of Bucha and Irpin. Bomb disposal services would be blowing up unexploded mines and shells in the area. All day I listened out for them but no sounds of explosions reached my ears.

I am home at last. After nine months of telling people about Kyiv, I can finally walk the streets, sit down with friends and see the tired but determined glow in their eyes. I have become a listener. Everyone has their own story of the moment when the war came home to them. I have heard many such stories already, of course, but it is different hearing these things when you are standing in a battered front room or driving through the ruins of a village. When they have told you about how they survived, they always ask, "What do you think, when is it going to end?" as if my time away has made me clairvoyant. I usually respond, "Most likely in the new year, in 2023." But I am not sure why I say that.

Our friends Yuri and Olga live a three-minute walk away, down the hill from the Golden Gate. Olga has mobility issues and does not go out much, especially in icy or slushy conditions. Their apartment building has a lift, but nobody uses it, even when there is electricity, as they never know when the supply is going to be cut off. Their building seems to have more frequent and longer power cuts than neighbouring buildings. Olga spends most of the day sitting in the dark, sadly contemplating the apartment block opposite where the windows are almost always bright.

Kyiv's dark streets have a magical quality about them. The darkness is silvery blue. As you walk, circles of light come towards you that turn into people wearing head torches or carrying mobile telephones.

In the area around the Golden Gate, the bars stay open with or without electricity, at least until curfew-time approaches. The bars are often located in cellars, and you have to enter them with care. Once inside, candles and battery-powered lamps make for a cosy atmosphere. The bar staff are pleased to see you – businesses must survive. There are candles on the tables; beyond them, shadows and quiet voices. Where there is electric light, the volume of voices increases. In candlelight, people even laugh more quietly. There is a sense of hibernation; one of the customers has just fallen asleep.

Our friend Olga is having trouble staying positive and not just because of the power cuts. Her husband, Yuri, who works backstage for the National Opera and Ballet Theatre, will be in Paris with the ballet troupe over Christmas and New Year. Olga will be left to greet 2023 on her own, quite possibly in the dark.

The trip to Paris is good news for the theatre company. Their Christmas season in France and Japan will allow the performers to work in normal conditions for a while. Despite air raids, the company has been putting on fantastic shows for appreciative Kyiv audiences, who are seated only in the stalls and lower boxes so that they can be evacuated to the cellar if the sirens sound. Even with two troupes on tour, the theatre is still offering Kyivites "The Snow Queen" ballet over the holiday period. This ballet is performed to music by an array of composers, but none of them are Russian.

It is also a good thing that the Kyiv opera and ballet companies have the opportunity to show off their talents to international audiences. After all, it is usually the St Petersburg ballet and opera companies, the Mariinsky and Mikhailovsky companies, that tour Europe and Japan. This year, no-one in Europe dares to invite them and Russian theatres can tour only inside Russia.

On November 29, the Mikhailovsky Theatre hosted a gala concert with Russian opera and ballet stars in aid of the families of Russian citizens mobilised for the war against Ukraine. I wonder if that theatre is also involved in another initiative designed to support Russian soldiers and officers sitting in dugouts on Ukrainian territory. The Russian military command has asked citizens to donate harmonicas, button accordions, guitars and balalaikas. In St Petersburg, the collection points for donated musical instruments are the Museum of Military Medicine, the Military History Museum and the Central Naval Museum. I would like to know how these musical instruments will be delivered to the front line and how they will be distributed.

Intercepted telephone conversations between Russian soldiers and their relatives indicate that the frontline forces lack both food and warm clothing and there is no mention of any kind of entertainment. Playing musical instruments may warm them up, of course, especially playing the accordion. Perhaps Ukrainian soldiers will soon hear Russian folk songs and melodies from Soviet films drifting across no-man's-land from the enemy trenches. In the end, these musical instruments might become trophies for the Ukrainian army, or they could remain in the blood-drenched trenches, leaving a new "cultural layer" for future archaeologists to ponder over.

The sounds of war are many and miscellaneous. Generally, they have nothing to do with music. The sound that Ukrainians hear most frequently is that of the air raid siren. Three weeks ago, when I was driving towards Kyiv, another sound scared me. A strange noise appeared as soon as we entered Kyiv region.

Something like the roar of a jet engine but, most alarmingly, it seemed to be coming from under the car, from the wheels.

"Is it the bearings?" my younger son suggested.

Apprehensive, I slowed down, but the sound did not go away. It accompanied us all the way to Kyiv. The next morning, I took the car to the service station.

I told the mechanic about the noise. He smiled oddly. "It's resonance," he said. "All the road surfaces around here have been damaged by tanks and heavy tracked vehicles. The sound appeared when you entered Kyiv region, right?" he asked knowingly. I said it had. Just in case, the mechanic checked the wheels. They were in good shape. Now that I know that the problem is the roads, I have stopped paying attention to the aggressive rumble beneath my car. I have got used to it. More precisely, I have come to terms with another sound imposed on me by this war.

Recently, as we packed the car to return to Kyiv from the village, my wife put a yoga mat in the boot. I was surprised. "It will make the corridor more comfortable during air raids!" she explained. The corridors of apartments all over Ukraine have become living rooms, bedrooms, offices, and sometimes even tiny kitchens, equipped with small tables and folding chairs for breakfast or dinner. Some people have moved their sofas into the hallway. Others have installed a T.V. set. The main thing is to stay away from the windows, which a rocket explosion could shatter, spraying the room with glass.

In the Kyiv metro, there are adverts for apartments in newly built blocks. The posters show floor plans and I noticed that all the new apartments have rooms set around a spacious, window-less area – a clever design for wartime. Unfortunately, these new apartment buildings are almost always powered by electricity alone; a power cut means no heating, water or cooking facilities.

The Russian aggression has given electricity a very bad name. People in older buildings with gas stoves and ovens consider themselves very fortunate. They can cook and make hot drinks. What is more, bricks placed strategically on the gas hob can heat a room quite effectively.

In our village power cuts are rare, but my wife and I have bought a kettle for the gas hob, a small contribution towards saving electricity. I was also pleased to note our new kettle's gentle hum – much nicer than the rocket-like noise of the electric one.

23.12.2022

All We Want for Christmas…

A couple of days ago, my dentist Victoria and I spent an hour and a half in her surgery waiting for the electricity to come back on. According to the schedule, the power cut should have ended at four o'clock but we were still waiting at five. We talked by candlelight and when the candle burned out, we continued in the dark, comparing our trips around Ukraine and Europe and never mentioning the war.

At some point, Victoria recounted how a regular client had recently come running into the surgery with a terrible toothache. Just as he sat down, the electricity went out. The patient screamed in agony and asked Victoria to pull out the tooth without electricity. "We don't need any!" he yelled. "I'll hold a torch and shine it into my mouth." Seeing how desperate the man was, Victoria eventually agreed to try. He opened his mouth and held up his mobile phone to his face. The light was very weak and Victoria realised that it would be dangerous to pull out a tooth under such conditions. She refused to do it and her patient rushed off in search of a dentist's surgery with power.

By the end of this story, the electricity had still not come on. We decided not to wait any longer and agreed that I would come back the next morning, if there was electricity, of course. Before saying goodbye, Victoria told me another story, about how she recently went to the hairdresser's. Usually, you have your hair washed first, then cut while wet, then dried with a hairdryer. This time Victoria's hairdresser washed her hair and immediately grabbed the hairdryer. Victoria assumed that he had simply forgotten to cut her hair but he explained that he was drying it while the power was on. "You don't need electricity to cut hair," he explained.

Dentists and hairdressers are busy in the run-up to the festive season. Despite the war, people want to look good and feel good. Many Ukrainians also seem keen to celebrate the New Year in the usual way, out in the street. In most of Ukraine, the curfew forces civilians to remain indoors from eleven o'clock at night to five in the morning. City authorities throughout the country have been petitioned by residents to lift the curfew for one night on New Year's Eve. While surveys suggest that Ukrainians are going to spend very little money during the holidays, the stocks of red caviar and Champagne in Kyiv shops give the impression that supermarket managers are expecting to do good business.

Kherson's residents are taking a stand against Father Frost ("Dyed Moroz"), a character similar to Father Christmas who was, until recently, eagerly awaited by Soviet and post-Soviet Ukrainian children. "Father Frost" has been identified as a Russian deviation, and this year, Saint Nicholas will be the one congratulating children on the holiday. A "Saint Nicholas Residence" has been opened in Kherson's theatre where children can visit Saint Nick and receive presents donated by the Rotary Club.

In Kharkiv, an entire garden of decorated Christmas trees has been created underground, at the Pivdenny Vokzal metro station. Everything is brightly lit and families go down to take photographs. Sometimes Saint Nicholas appears among the trees, with his long white beard and red coat and hat. In the city of Mykolaiv, which is shelled every day by the Russians, the main Christmas tree of the city has been made from camouflage nets used in summer.

All the frontline regions, including Kherson, will be visited by "Saint Nick's Railway Residence", a specially decorated train with stocks of presents for children in these war-damaged areas.

Good health is what Ukrainians most often wish each other at New Year celebrations. In today's Ukraine staying healthy is more important than ever because hospitals are busy treating wounded soldiers. For civilians, getting quality medical care is much more difficult than before the war. This partially explains the "keep healthy" social advertising campaign that has appeared on city billboards. A veteran of the current war is featured in the posters urging Ukrainians to quit smoking.

The Ukrainian police too are involved in the fight against tobacco. Not far from Kyiv, they found an illegal cigarette factory on the premises of an industrial unit that had officially been closed down long before the war. The raid means there will now be fewer illegal cigarettes on sale. This will affect supply to Hungary and Slovakia because illegal manufacturers in Ukraine and Belarus tend to work for the wider Eastern European market.

Logistics chains connecting Ukraine's illegal cigarette producers to smugglers and points of sale in neighbouring countries were developed long ago. From time to time, the police succeed in blocking a contraband channel, but that channel is quickly replaced by another.

Before the war, batches of illegal cigarettes most often crossed the border in private cars and trucks. Powerful quadcopters are now the smugglers' vehicle of choice. At night, along the Ukrainian–Hungarian frontier, Ukrainian border guards use thermal imagers to monitor the darkness. They are not only interested in detaining the smugglers. It is just as important for them to intercept and capture the quadcopter drones before they enter Hungarian territory. When they succeed in doing this, the border guards have double joy – as well as thwarting a smuggling operation, they have won a prize for the Ukrainian army. All confiscated quadcopters are sent to the front where they are in particular demand for reconnaissance work and for dropping mines on enemy positions. The Ukrainian military also uses them for the swift delivery of emergency medical supplies and anything else that is needed at combat positions up and down the front line.

In the city of Bakhmut, in Donetsk region, where the fighting is most severe, a special "Saint Nick" unexpectedly turned up with gifts for the military – President Zelensky. His unannounced appearance on the front line coincided with Putin's lacklustre visit to Belarus. It is another slap in the face for the Russian army and for Putin, who seems to have set his heart on recapturing Bakhmut, as does Yevgeniy Prigozhin, the head of the Wagner Group. Ukrainians can expect further shelling of civilian infrastructure and more disruption to water, heating and electricity supplies, the only area in which the Russian army has had any success.

If the Russian army equates the theft of museum collections from occupied territories with some kind of success, they are not being very thorough even in these operations. After the liberation of Kherson, an icon of St Nicholas, unnoticed or forgotten by the invaders, was found in the city museum. Ukrainian security services also discovered an entire collection of ancient icons that the Russians had stolen from the residence of the Lithuanian Consul General in Kherson. All 120 antiques were returned to the consul, who immediately donated them to the Kherson Museum of Fine Art. For now, these works, together with the icon of St Nicholas, will decorate the walls of the museum in the place of the works stolen by the Russian occupation forces.

While "Saint Nick's Railway Residence" delivers gifts to children in cities near the front line, the Ukrainian Railway company has launched another passenger route. It is called "The Ski Express" and runs between Kyiv and the ski resort of Slavske. By Ukrainian standards, it is a very fast train, covering the 680 kilometres in six hours. Before the war, the journey took much longer. Skiing is expensive, but I hope there will be special deals available at the resorts this year, at least for war veterans and combatants.

I have two more visits to the dentist to fit in before the New Year. So, my personal wish list for the festive season has only one item on it – electricity in the dentist's surgery, for myself, and for other patients dreaming of entering 2023 with healthy, pain-free teeth.

Christmas Day in Kyiv

Snow has already covered the earth and, when the sun reigns in the sky, its rays add bright gilding to the snow cover. All my previous winters, all my previous Christmas celebrations, were peaceful. Snow emphasised the calm. The snow and the cold preserve life until spring, until the first warm weather. It seems to demand that everyone rest, avoiding unnecessary movement and noise. The snow affects the sounds of nature. It somehow keeps the sounds above the ground and prevents them from disturbing the hibernating moles and other inhabitants of Ukraine's rich black soil.

Our family agreed to donate money to Ukrainian causes this year instead of buying presents. Late on Christmas Eve, however, I noticed my wife placing the children's red stockings around the stove – bulging with gifts as usual. "It's just practical stuff!" she explained. In the morning, more presents appeared from the children. "It's all made in Ukraine!" they declared.

Christmas 2022 is not only special because it is tumultuous and war-scarred. This year, Ukrainians can choose to celebrate Christmas according to the Gregorian calendar, that is, with all of Europe, or according to the Julian calendar, as they did before, with Russia and the Orthodox Church of the Moscow Patriarchate. Last year, my village celebrated Christmas on January 6 and 7, together with Russia and, in the village church of St Alexander Nevsky, with a priest called Alexander, a rather portly man with a habitually dissatisfied expression. It seems his wife had left him, taking the children with her. He remained alone, complaining often that his parish brought him little income. He earned extra money as a taxi driver and used-car salesman.

Alexander has gone now and the church is closed. Zina has the keys. It was Zina who paid for the construction of the church after the death of her husband. They moved to our village from Siberia about fifteen years ago. They bought one of the cottages built for those being resettled from the Chernobyl zone. They enlarged it and added outbuildings.

Zina is a businesswoman and makes money in Moldova selling nutritional supplements that are supposed to be good for your health. They are made from powdered corals. Where she gets these corals and who grinds them into powder nobody knows. The instructions on the packaging say that the powder can be added to soup, porridge or tea.

Zina was always busy with her business, but her husband had nothing to do. He walked around the village with his dogs. Sometimes he drank. One sad day he died of heart disease. Zina buried him and started building a brick church, overlooking the river in the centre of the village. Village church services had previously been held in a simple wooden hut.

Building the new church was a slow process punctuated by numerous scandals. Builders came and went. Sometimes construction stopped for several months. Nonetheless, the day came when Zina was able to invite hierarchs from the Kyiv-Pechersk Lavra of the Moscow Patriarchate to consecrate the church. It was dedicated to St Alexander Nevsky.

The church has been served by a succession of priests, all relatively young and all dissatisfied with their parish. The villagers go to church only twice a year, at Christmas and Easter. The rest of the time the church is empty. And now it is empty and locked up. The little chapel constructed near the sacred spring just beyond the village, which was also paid for by Zina, is also locked up. The spring, though, remains accessible and residents regularly come for its clean, ice-cold water.

01.01.2023

New Year in the Corridor

Even during a war, the approach of New Year makes you feel more relaxed. On December 31, our old friend Stanislav came to visit us in Kyiv. Owing to Covid and the war, we had not seen each other for a couple of years.

Just as he arrived, we heard the moan of the air raid siren but still we sat down at the dining table and began exchanging news over lunch. For eight months now his wife and two daughters have been living in Britain. He wants them to stay there until the end of the war but he suffers from loneliness. He was just showing us photographs of his wife enjoying the snow in London when an explosion sounded somewhere nearby. We got up quickly and moved to the corridor. Stanislav began to search the Internet for information about the air strikes. Then he called his mother, who lives on the other side of the Dnipro River, and told her that he would pop in shortly to see her. We heard her scared voice saying, "Don't come today. It's dangerous!" But Stanislav said he would come anyway. When he had gone, my family began to prepare food for our New Year dinner.

I was planning to cook turkey legs and suddenly realised that there was no rosemary in the house. I set out for the super-market. The streets were already dark. As I passed the French embassy, the three Ukrainian soldiers standing guard with Kalashnikov assault rifles looked me up and down. I greeted them and they relaxed and returned to their conversation. The supermarket had no rosemary or any other fresh herbs, so I bought olives with anchovies and some baking foil.

By ten o'clock the dinner was ready. My brother Mikhail and his wife Larisa arrived with salads. Our daughter Gabriela had to reach her apartment before the eleven o'clock curfew. She and her boyfriend stayed as long as they could and then ran home. Just before midnight, I poured Prosecco into glasses and we managed to clink glasses and toast the Ukrainian armed forces before the air raid siren rose into the quiet of the night. Almost immediately, explosions rumbled right above our house – our city's air defences had started working. We took our chairs into the corridor. A chess table that I work at during air raids was already there.

"Strange," Larisa said, "Explosions usually start a while after the siren."

"The military probably did not want to spoil the New Year moment for us," my brother Mikhail suggested. "Otherwise, we would have been sitting in the corridor since last year!"

Maybe they wanted Ukrainians to watch President Zelensky's televised New Year's speech without interruption, I thought. Corridors are rarely equipped with T.V. sets and, as I could see on Telegram, the air raid warning covered the entire country.

That night, all of the 32 drones directed at Kyiv were destroyed before they hit their targets, but debris caused damage to some houses and cars.

Now and then, our younger son Anton went out onto the balcony to look at the exploding sky. He reported to the rest of us sheltering in the corridor that, on other balconies, our neighbours were standing with glasses in their hands and shouting in chorus "F . . .# Putin!" after every explosion. Sometime after three in the morning, we gave up waiting for the all-clear and went to bed. Kyiv seemed quiet enough by then.

Now I recall this night with some sadness; it was probably the strangest New Year's celebration of my life, a sombre marking of the passing of time. The curfew, despite petitions and requests to the city authorities, was not cancelled. There could be no fireworks or visits to friends. The police patrolled the streets to ensure compliance. As it turned out, they were not too strict with those who were caught outside after curfew, as long as they had some I.D. on them.

In the corridor during the air raid, we thought about all those Ukrainians who had been killed by Russia and who could not greet the New Year. We also remembered families unable to celebrate for reasons connected with the war. The December 31 lunchtime drone and missile attack left dozens of apartments in high-rise buildings without windows and doors. It also destroyed a private house on the left bank of the Dnipro, making its residents homeless. I like to think that the people who suffered were still able to join relatives and friends to greet the New Year. In any case, today they will be facing the stark reality of their damaged or destroyed homes.

Despite the ban on fireworks, some Kyivites were determined to add brightness and noise to the sky. In addition to the fire trucks and ambulances rushing to where drone debris had fallen, police patrols were reacting swiftly to any sightings of fireworks. At least one violator was detained. He turned out to be drunk but this is unlikely to save him from punishment. He could get up to five years in prison.

At five in the morning, the air raid warning was cancelled. We sat down to our first breakfast of the New Year at ten o'clock. In past years, this meal was enlivened with Champagne, but today I did not feel like eating or drinking. We went out for a walk. The sun was shining and, to our surprise, many cafés were already open.

We had lunch with our friend Irina. Her daughter, Alyena was full of news about the outdoor gatherings that had gone on through the night near their apartment building. In the space between the high-rise apartment blocks, out of sight of the police, neighbours had set up tables and shared food and Champagne.

All over the city, on December 31 and January 1, charity kitchens were open for anyone who needed sustenance. Charitable organisations, both Ukrainian and international ones, recruited internally displaced people from the east and south of Ukraine to help with the food handouts. Those so displaced, so often at the receiving end of charity, were happy to be helping others.

During 2022, patronage and charity became the norm for most Ukrainians. The concept of charitable giving is even used in local marketing campaigns. It is sometimes hard to tell where charity ends and commerce begins. There are notices in bars announcing that half the money paid for a particular cocktail will be donated to the army. Customers are particularly happy to order these cocktails. My wife and I went to a bar specially to drink some. I have forgotten the taste, but I remember that everyone in the room seemed to be enjoying the cocktail.

Unfortunately, there are also losers in this situation. Before the war, parents of sick children would collect money on the Internet for costly medical treatment. There are fewer appeals like this now. Parents are simply ashamed to ask for money when there is a war going on.

There is still a shortage of doctors and medical staff in Ukrainian hospitals. Planned operations are almost always cancelled. Only emergency treatment is available. Maternity hospitals and children's hospitals work best. In these hospitals, you can expect almost the same quality of treatment as before the war, at least in the unoccupied parts of Ukraine. In the occupied territories, most hospitals now treat only wounded Russian soldiers. And they do not have enough beds for the injured.

The Russians are turning schools, sanatoriums and even

maternity homes into military hospitals. In the city of Pervo-maisk in Luhansk region, the maternity hospital was taken over by the Wagner private army. Patients and staff were evicted and 150 wounded fighters were moved in.

———

At the maternity hospital in Uzhhorod on the border with Slovakia the first child to be born in 2023 was a girl – the daughter of a 24-year-old internally displaced person from Nikopol in Dnipropetrovsk region. She arrived in Uzhhorod on December 29 and went into labour on the evening of December 31. The baby girl, whom her mother wants to name Ayramiya, was born at five minutes after midnight on January 1, 2023. The second child born in this maternity hospital was also a girl and the daughter of another displaced person, this time one from Kharkiv. In total, on the first day of the new year, four children were born in Uzhhorod: three girls and one boy.

This year, the city with the highest number of births on New Year's Day was Kyiv. Thirty-one children were born here, including triplet boys: Matviy, Bohdan and Vladislav. All of them, like all Ukrainian children born after February 2014, can be called "war-time children". Soviet "war-time children" qualified for subsidies on fuel. I am not sure whether these new Ukrainian citizens will be offered any special benefits, but they will know much more about war than my generation. Ukrainian children can already tell the difference between the sound of a blast made by air defence systems and the noise of the explosion of a missile hitting its target.

Most children can also recognise the sound of an Iranian Shahid drone's engine. These drones are nicknamed "mopeds" because of the engine-like quality of their sound. Young people try to record these sounds on their smartphones and exchange the audio files for "educational" purposes. This means trying to stay near the balcony during air raids – an extremely dangerous exploit.

For the celebration of Orthodox Christmas on January 6 and 7, Putin has proposed a 36-hour ceasefire. He might have expected Kyiv to agree, but Kyiv has rejected the offer, sure that the Russian forces would only use the time to reinforce their now weakening positions along the front lines. For Ukraine, a few hours of peace would make no difference after the months of bombardment the country has suffered.

Since the beginning of the war air raid alarms have sounded hundreds of times in Kyiv. The frequency of danger has blunted people to the fear of death. With three million people living in the city and new children being born, perhaps there is a false sense of security. At certain moments it seems that the war has stopped, the threat evaporating as if it had all been a bad dream. Only the sound of the next air raid siren brings the people of Kyiv back to reality.

———

What awaits us in this new year? Most likely, the continuation of the shelling, the continuation of the war. Russia is discussing further mobilisation. It was probably in support of new conscription that Vladimir Solovyov, one of Russia's principal television propagandists, has been insisting that, "The value of life is exaggerated, and one should not be afraid of death, because it is inevitable." This message was clearly directed at those who may soon be sent to war in Ukraine. Today, after Ukrainian artillery destroyed a Russian army base in Makiivka, near Donetsk, killing large numbers of mobilised Russian soldiers and officers, Solovyov's message is especially relevant.

The people of Russia are only now beginning to believe in

the extent of their army's losses. The announcement from the Russian General Staff that "only" 63 people died in the college building, where about 700 soldiers and officers were garrisoned, provoked loud criticism, even from pro-Putin propagandist bloggers. In reality, between 350 and 450 Russian soldiers and officers died in Makiivka. They died because the military had stored shells and rockets in the same building. The detonation of the warehouse means that nothing now remains of the very large building of the technical college.

Meanwhile, the owner of the Wagner private army, Prigozhin, has complained to the Russian Ministry of the Interior, and even to the Russian Ministry of Health, about the employees of the Luhansk mortuary, where the corpses of hundreds of Russian soldiers, including soldiers from his private army, have been lying for weeks. He has accused mortuary staff of sabotage because they take weeks to release the bodies of soldiers so that they may be sent to their relatives in Russia for burial. The bottleneck seems to be the pathologists, who do not issue death certificates. The pathologists may have been instructed to space out the return of bodies so as to avoid panic and defeatism among ordinary Russians who, in general, remain very supportive of Putin's war.

The Luhansk regional mortuary is littered with black bags containing the remains of Russian soldiers. The staff must be exhausted. The beginning of a new year is not only about reviewing the old one but also about looking to the future. It is difficult for me to imagine the hopes and plans of mortuary employees in the occupied territories. I do not envy their having to count corpses day in, day out.

America's Choice

There is a proverb in Ukraine, "However you greet the New Year, that is how you will spend it!" It used to mean that you should celebrate cheerfully and with optimism. This year's celebration was not cheerful, neither are our expectations of the near future a cause for optimism. Nonetheless, the beginning of any new year does provoke thoughts about the changes it could or should bring.

Our plans were finalised towards the end of December. My wife and I decided to go to America for a few months, taking up the offer of a short-term teaching post at Stanford University. On January 1, we finished packing our bags and by the evening we were already at the station. Much to our surprise, our journey to the other side of America went according to plan. We took an overnight train to Mukacheva, in Transcarpathia, where we changed to a small and very slow Slovak diesel train which took us across the border and into Košice. This town has an airport which is designed for only a few flights a day, but one of them is always to London. From London, we made for San Francisco.

We were met there by Stanford University professor Yulia, who had previously lived in Kyiv. She and a colleague had worked hard to prepare accommodation for our arrival. They dedicated yet more time to helping us settle into a residential complex within easy reach of the university campus. We did not expect such generous and selfless help, but I understand that, apart from them being very nice people, they were guided by the desire to help us as "people from the war zone", as residents of Ukraine.

Despite the great distance from Ukraine, the desire to help the victims of the Russian invasion is felt in villages and towns throughout America. In early December, a poll by the Ronald Reagan Institute showed that 57 per cent. of American citizens believe that the country should continue to send military and financial help to the people of Ukraine in their fight against Russia. Some 76 per cent. of Americans consider Ukraine an ally, a significant increase on 2021 when only 49 per cent. of respondents felt that way.

Of course, hundreds of thousands of Ukrainians live in the United States. The first Ukrainian emigrants arrived in the 1850s, but Ukrainians who came to the United States after 1991, after independence, are the backbone of the active Ukrainian diaspora. They are the catalysts for volunteer projects and the organisers of demonstrations and events that rally people, raise money, and collect all kinds of goods to support the war effort and to relieve suffering in Ukraine.

How Ukrainian Americans perceived Russian aggression can be seen in the example of a former Kyivite called Boris, who moved to the northern part of San Francisco some years ago and made a successful career for himself as a programmer. At the end of February 2022, when Russia unleashed its invasion on the whole of Ukraine, he lost his centre of gravity. His psychological state deteriorated. He lost twenty kilograms in weight and had trouble sleeping. But then Boris pulled himself together and decided how he could be useful in the new situation. He regained his stability immediately.

He told his friends, Margaret and Joe, a Ukrainian-American couple, that he was going to raise money to buy drones for the Ukrainian army. Very soon, he had collected $2,000 and bought his first drone. One hundred dollars of that money was brought to him by 75-year-old Lyudmila, who had moved to America from St Petersburg. With the first news of the Russian invasion, she sided with Ukraine and straightaway made herself a Ukrainian flag to wave at demonstrations.

An active group of Americans and Ukrainians gathered around Boris, who within two more weeks had raised another $8,000. Then a question arose, how could they deliver the drones to Ukraine? Shipping the equipment in containers or by mail seemed expensive and unreliable. In the end, they found a Ukrainian who was planning a trip to Warsaw and was willing to act as a courier. Ukrainian volunteers met him in Poland and, a month later, Boris was sent a photograph from the front line which showed a Ukrainian soldier holding one of the drones. The logistics have now been tried and tested. Almost everything sent by volunteers from California to Ukraine is sent through Warsaw.

Some people simply collect money for Ukraine and then use this money to buy necessary medicines and medical supplies in Poland. The medical supplies are then distributed to both military and civilian hospitals in Ukraine.

American individualism is reflected in how they arrange support for dozens of humanitarian projects. Margaret recently attended a "bring and buy" picnic organised by Ukrainians in the Bay area. Having purchased several pies from different participants, Margaret realised that each seller was raising money for a different project. One woman was going to buy sleeping bags for the Ukrainian military, another towels and linen for an orphanage evacuated from the now-occupied territory. Each person had heard about a need and was responding to it.

Margaret's husband Joe, a retired energy engineer, helps with fundraising events and also tries to spread information about the war in Ukraine among Americans who, in his view, are ill-informed or not sufficiently interested in what is happening outside America. The other day, over a coffee in Palo Alto, he complained that he had been blocked on all the pro-Russian English-language Telegram channels. He had sought out these channels to argue with pro-Russian commentators. Eventually he realised that he was arguing with Russian propagandists and bots who target English-speaking audiences and work for the Kremlin. Now the phone number he uses to connect to Telegram channels is known in Russia and he is simply not given access to the platforms. He told me he was no longer upset about this, although the way he spoke indicated that he took this affront to his freedom of speech very hard.

Americans love to argue about politics even, or perhaps especially, with people they meet at random. Joe uses this national trait skilfully to enter into conversations with anyone who will stop to chat. He tells them what he thinks about the Russian invasion of Ukraine and asks them what they think. I see him as a kind of missionary.

Recently, Boris learned that a Ukrainian military unit needed three scopes for sniper rifles. It turned out to be easy to buy scopes in America. The problem was the licence you need to export them. Boris and his team found a Ukrainian aid fund in California that already had a licence to ship such items to Ukraine. Whenever necessary, the two teams now work together.

Among the Ukrainian volunteers, there are people with different political views and attitudes. Occasionally tensions arise. Nina is a Russian citizen who moved to California from Moscow fifteen years ago. She works hard to help Ukrainian refugees in the Bay area and asked the Ukrainian community to accept her into their closed Facebook group so that she could be even more useful to refugees and the Ukrainian army. Upon learning that Nina was from Russia, the Ukrainian activist group flatly refused to cooperate with her. This did not stop

Nina. She continues to support Ukrainian refugees, helping them to complete official forms, driving them to interviews with social services and generally helping them to adapt to American life. At the same time, she houses and looks after the son of Moscow friends who fled Russia when mobilisation was announced.

Sometimes American-Ukrainian volunteer groups on Facebook are more tolerant than the ones that rejected Nina's offer of help. In some groups, you are allowed to post in Russian, while in other groups this is forbidden.

Americans who support Ukraine are often unaware of these tensions and when Americans learn that the popular view in Ukraine is that there are "no good Russians", they regretfully chalk it up to the trauma of war. In California, it is customary not to judge people by the colour of their skin, their religion, or their passport.

Russian media often states that the majority of Americans are against extensive military aid to Ukraine. So far, I have not come across a single American who was anything but in favour of supporting Ukraine.

The war is featured constantly in radio and television programmes that often have their own fund-raising projects for humanitarian needs. For many Americans, the war in Ukraine has almost become "their" war. Perhaps such emotional involvement is made easier because, unlike in Iraq or Afghanistan, there are no American forces on the ground. And perhaps California is not typical of the whole country, as it seems that many people in this state are willing to spend time and money supporting Ukraine.

Blogger to the President

In the late 1980s, the Soviet Union was slowly approaching its collapse, but no-one imagined that, within a couple of years, it would cease altogether to exist. Grandad Danylo, our elderly neighbour in our village near Kyiv, was the only person on the street who subscribed to a newspaper.

All the major newspapers expressed the official view of things, but the Soviet papers, like *Pravda* or *Izvestiya*, were trusted more than provincial or city papers. Every morning, a postman cycled up to the gate of Danylo's house and left a newspaper between the slats in his fence. Danylo immediately pulled it out and read it from cover to cover before beginning his "anti-Soviet" activities. He walked along the street stopping to talk with everyone he met, calling over the fence to neighbours if he saw a potential interlocutor in a courtyard. First, of course, he greeted them and then he told them, in detail, what the Soviet press was lying about that day.

There was already plenty of cynicism in Ukraine about Moscow and the direction it was taking the country. By no means everyone trusted the official press. Nevertheless, Danylo's authoritative and clear exposure of the lies that were being presented as news never failed to surprise me. He was perhaps an early equivalent to a blogger.

On January 12 this year, Ukrainians were asked to answer the question, "Whom would you call the politician of 2022?" The first two places in the ranking, based on this poll, were occupied by President Zelensky and General Zaluzhny, Commander-in-Chief of the Ukrainian armed forces. Nobody is surprised to find these names at the top of the list. However, the Ukrainians gave third place in the ranking to Olexiy Arestovich, a non-staff adviser to the head of the Office of the President, the "presidential blogger".

Despite his obvious popularity with the Ukrainian public, on January 17, Arestovich resigned from his advisory position. His dismissal was demanded by Ukrainian intellectuals and activists because he had stated in one of his video broadcasts that the Russian missile which blew up an apartment block in Dnipro had been shot down by Ukrainian air defence and that it was debris that fell on the building, killing about 50 of its residents and injuring more than 80. The Armed Forces of Ukraine refuted Arestovich's claim. Soon a video showing the flight and explosion of the rocket became available. Arestovich had got it wrong. He apologised but his suggestion that Ukrainian air defence had caused the deaths was already being used by Russian propaganda as proof that Russia only shoots at Ukrainian military facilities and not at civilian targets.

"I am just tired," Arestovich said in his defence as he resigned. But he has not disappeared from the informational space. He remains a popular blogger with 1,700,000 subscribers. His popularity and his undoubted talent as a communicator prompted Andriy Yermak, head of the presidential office, to appoint Arestovich in December 2020 as his non-staff adviser on strategic communications in the field of national security and defence. Yermak said that Arestovich was tasked with "providing comprehensive answers to counteract the spread of disinformation and accusations in the Ukrainian media space".

Until Zelensky's presidency, television was considered the most reliable tool for protecting one's position of power and maintaining high ratings in Ukrainian popularity polls. Previous presidents had their own pool of journalists who served the government's informational goals. For a journalist, getting into one of these pools could lead to a successful career. Zelensky became president largely thanks to the popularity of his T.V. comedy shows and television movies on Ukraine's 1+1 Channel. Once in power, the President tried to estrange himself from the oligarch who owned the channel, Ihor Kolomoisky. However, this left Zelensky and his party with no media clout, few if any friendly journalists and scant defence against criticism of his party and administration.

One strategy to increase Zelensky's media presence involved "Press Marathons" – televised, round-table press conferences during which several groups of journalists took turns to ask questions of the President. Each group had a set amount of time to ask questions before the next group took over. The first marathon was held in October 2019 and revealed the ambitiousness of the concept, but the marathons did little to endear Zelensky to the press corps. Another strategy was required.

The idea of gathering a group of pro-government bloggers was first mentioned by Mykhailo Podolyak, deputy head of the Office of the President, in July 2020. He announced that a pool of "positive bloggers" would be created. He said, "I think they will speak publicly about positive trends in domestic politics, and not just hate! In our country, unfortunately, 90 per cent. of the informational space is taken up by hate. It is believed that the negative sells well and that you can do well out of it. This is a big problem, which is more than twenty years old."

Bloggers very often look more like boorish hooligans than T.V. presenters, but many are professional journalists who became disenchanted with their role as servants of one or other party. They set out to work for themselves and for their own audiences, mostly the youth and the middle class. Volodymyr Zelensky relied on the same audience during his election campaign.

Although there was never officially any attempt to create a "pool of positive bloggers", some journalists do seem to have been recruited informally by the Office of the President actively to promote the new government's messages and to defend the new government from criticism and attacks. One of the well-known Ukrainian bloggers whom Mykhailo Podolyak wanted to attract to the government's "pool of positive bloggers" was Serhiy Ivanov, a man with a bright biography, from the now-occupied Luhansk. He had worked there for ten years as a prosecutor and criminal investigator. After 2014 he was forced to move to Kyiv, where, having created his own YouTube channel called I.S.L.N.D. T.V., with more than 460,000 subscribers, he has made a successful career as a blogger. Apparently, Serhiy Ivanov turned down the offer to join the presidential pool. A year later, he agreed to work as a talk show host on the Ukrainian Parliament's R.A.D.A. channel.

The well-known journalist, Serhiy Leshchenko, another non-staff adviser to the head of the President's administration, became a "counter-blogger" – entering into fierce battles with anyone who published negative content about Volodymyr Zelensky. Beneath almost every critical article about President Zelensky or the government, you will find extended and passionate commentaries by Leshchenko, who tirelessly counter-attacks the enemies of the President and of the Servant of the People party. True, since February 2022, there has been very little criticism voiced on any platforms of the President or the government.

Aleksey Arestovich was the government's brightest fighter on the media front. His biography is rich and varied. He was fond of esotericism, studied theology, graduated from a military institute in Odesa, and then served in military intelligence, retiring with the rank of major. Arestovich has also acted in films and television commercials and run courses in public speaking, acting and negotiation techniques.

He joined the radical nationalist organisation the Brotherhood and in 2004–5, together with the organisation's leader, political scientist and playwright Dmytro Korchinsky, he opposed the supporters of the Orange Revolution. He even travelled to Moscow several times to talk at conferences organised by Alexander Dugin, the ideologist for the Eurasian Platform, who is said to have had a great influence on Vladimir Putin. There, Arestovich also called on Russian nationalists to fight against American influences and the "colour revolutions" in the post-Soviet space. In 2008, however, Arestovich's political views changed course. Predicting Russia's future annexation of Crimea, he began to develop a strategy for the defence of Crimea from Russia. In 2019, he said that Russia would attack Ukraine sometime between 2020 and 2022. His predictions came true, further increasing his credibility among Ukrainians.

The significance of Arestovich's media role in the first months of the war can hardly be overestimated. Starting from the end of February 2022, he inspired Ukrainians with optimism and faith in victory through videos that he produced several times a day. His assurances that the war would end in two or three weeks helped hundreds of thousands of Ukrainians to control their fear and stave off depression. It is not for nothing that he is still called "Ukraine's chief psychotherapist".

Sometimes this does feel like a televised war. All the main T.V. channels joined forces immediately after February 24, 2022 to produce a television marathon of news reporting. However, the stream of official news can hardly compete with the inventive, colourful, and sometimes shocking collage of blogger shows and independent news channels available on various platforms including YouTube. Ukraine's "blogosphere" has been following the main European trends for years. Blogs on motherhood, cooking, travel, show business, fishing and fashion are very popular even today. However, since the beginning of the all-out invasion the sphere has been expanded by military bloggers. Many Ukrainians are turning to them and to the less formal blogger news channels to get information about what is happening.

Taras Bilka, with 73,000 followers on Instagram, is a professional journalist who turned to blogging before the war because he began to doubt the integrity of the profession in Ukraine. He is now serving in the army, but he still finds time to report on the emotional state of Ukrainians, both soldiers and civilians. Bilka, whose motto is "Don't be afraid!", speaks earnestly and with authority to a camera mounted on a car dashboard.

More controversially, a combat drone operator with the call sign "Madiar" (248,000 viewers on Telegram) records videos on the front line showing conversations with prisoners of war and the corpses of Russian soldiers after battles and military operations.

From February 23, 2022, the start of Russia's new offensive, I was a huge consumer of blogger material. I found that this took up a great deal of my time. When I could no longer ignore my doubts about the authenticity of some of the information, I stopped watching the blogs and switched to reading reports from professional journalists on the Internet. After a break of about three months, I returned to a number of bloggers about whom I felt more confident. I cannot assume that everything they say is objective or true but, like Danylo in the village 30 years ago, they do a great job of exposing the Kremlin's lies.

Hello Darkness

Ukraine has entered 2023 as if going into a dark room without light and no light switch. There are windows but it is dark behind them too. People are waiting for the dawn, or the restoration of the power supply. While there is neither one nor the other, darkness provokes a deep sense of fatigue.

The Lviv University teacher and well-known Ukrainian poet Halyna Kruk has noticed an unsettling pattern in her life. During a blackout, the power banks and batteries that feed her flashlights and lamps always seem to run out of power about half an hour before the electricity comes back on. Once they fail, she finds herself in a darkness that seems even more profound than that before the lights went out, a darkness with which it was still possible to cope, unlike this new darkness. These half-hour periods of impenetrable darkness, when you feel helpless, are the most difficult both psychologically and physically. Time stretches to infinity; space shrinks and it becomes terribly cramped. You feel at once acute hunger and the desire to sleep. Your muscles lose strength and physical movements require energy that is no longer there. Halyna Kruk experiences this state every day and now dreads these half-hours without light.

In complete darkness, without additional sources of energy, a person becomes defenceless. You might have a candle, but it gives only just enough light to reveal your fear in the mirror, your inner condition written on your face, welling up in your eyes. Electricity allows communication with relatives and friends and the surrounding world in general. It is impossible to communicate with a candle, except to send the signal from the window: "I am alive!"

Many of my acquaintances have spoken about this sense of helplessness as the periods of darkness drag on and become more frequent. Some seek advice about how to cope. They exchange information about new, more potent power banks and rechargeable batteries, about L.E.D. lamps with brighter bulbs that work from portable chargers for a longer time, that might allow you to read books for several more hours. There is also advice on taking vitamin D. Apparently, the lack of this vitamin exacerbates depression, a key danger for people who regularly find themselves in complete darkness.

Absolute darkness, when nothing and no-one is visible, makes you think more about yourself. You pay more attention to physical problems and are more likely to find your inner voice both anxious and nagging.

When light conquers darkness and the electricity is turned on, there is temporary calm and thoughts switch from yourself to the world around you. Halyna Kruk thinks about another parcel of medicines that she recently sent to the Ukrainian military in Bakhmut. Has it already been delivered? Have any of the soldiers found the medicines useful? Usually, packages for the Ukrainian army reach the addressees at the speed of courier mail and so feedback from the front comes quickly.

Supporting the war effort has become a form of therapy, if not a cure, for many Ukrainians. Halyna Kruk wants to write poetry about life and love, but she stops herself. She is not sure that during a war you can write about anything other than war; but if you write only about war, then the war is, as it were, magnified.

Halyna Kruk's friend, Irina, who also lives in Lviv, is ironical about the darkness forced upon the city's apartments. She is sure that the city can expect a population explosion during the coming year. She says the lack of electricity and the Internet

142

might also bring children and teenagers back to live communication, which she feels is no bad thing. Many parents dream of their children learning to live without the Internet but communication in the dark is not very pleasant. What is more, children and candlelight are not a safe combination.

Children are also affected by the darkness and power cuts. The son of our Kyiv friends, thirteen-year-old Artem, does not grieve when the electricity goes out during the day. He studies remotely through online lessons, so no Internet means no classes. But if there is a power cut in the evening, Artem gets bored and his mood deteriorates.

Artem and his parents live on the nineteenth floor and they have to walk up the stairs to their apartment several times a day. Using the lift, even when there is electricity, is too risky as you could be stuck for several hours. Artem and his parents might have improved their fitness, but they also go to bed earlier owing to fatigue and the lack of electricity.

Artem falls asleep much later than his parents. During the day, when there is electricity, he downloads movies and music videos onto his smartphone and then, in the dark, he watches the downloads until the battery on his smartphone runs out, or until he falls asleep.

Nature itself will soon come to the aid of those Ukrainians suffering from depression associated with the darkness and lack of electricity. The days are becoming longer and the nights shorter. If there is good news from the front added to this mix, then it will be easier for Ukrainians to gain a more optimistic mood. For now, they are holding on, sometimes with the last of their strength and willpower – holding on to their belief that Ukraine will win and restore everything that Russia has destroyed, including the electricity supply.

05.02.2023

Our Railway Fortress

At the end of last month, the European rail industry gave their "Rail Champion" award to Ukrainian Railways (U.Z.), recognising "the railway's remarkable resilience and continuation of transport services in times of war and unimaginable hardship".

On February 24, 2022, Russia deprived Ukraine of civil aviation for the foreseeable future. Regular flights to airports all over the world and chartered planes to holiday destinations disappeared from the sky. In their place came Russian missiles, directed at every region of Ukraine and bringing destruction and terror. When the first explosions sounded at five o'clock in the morning, hundreds of thousands of Ukrainians rushed to their cars and headed for the western borders, creating hundred-kilometre traffic jams. Even larger numbers of people did not have cars and so made for the railway stations. There were tens of thousands of traumatised people at every terminus. They had left almost everything behind them. Now their only thought was to get on a train going west.

Having a ticket made no difference to your chances of boarding a train. Railway personnel could not control the waves of people storming the carriages. At some point, it was decided that only women with children and elderly people would be allowed onto trains, and that they did not need tickets.

Those who made it onto trains in the early days of the war will never forget the journey. Twelve people packed into sleeping compartments designed for four, sitting in silence, listening to the knocking of the iron wheels, fearing new explosions from Russian missiles. The trains would stop in the middle of fields and forests, in front of bridges, standing for hours while the train drivers waited for instructions as to when to go further.

Since the start of the war, more than four million Ukrainians have been evacuated from their home towns by train. Many of them subsequently left for elsewhere in Europe, and most have not returned.

We left Kyiv by car and went to Uzhhorod on the border with Slovakia. Friends there helped us with accommodation. Almost immediately our son, Anton, announced that he was going back to Kyiv. We could not stop him. "I am nineteen and I decide what to do!" he said. He bought himself a ticket for the four o'clock train that day. We went to see him off. The train was already standing at the platform. The conductors at the door of each carriage looked haggard. They had arrived from Kyiv on the same train only an hour earlier. The journey had been slow and difficult. There would be no bed linen for Anton. There had been no time to organise it. The train's prompt departure was the priority.

Boxes and packages were being loaded into one of the carriages, but we saw no other passengers. We said goodbye to Anton and watched him take a seat alone in a four-berth compartment. He waved to us through the window and I noticed that the glass had been completely covered with two-inch wide strips of Sellotape. We had done the same for our windows in Kyiv, to prevent shards of glass from flying across the room if a missile landed nearby but we had not done the job anything near as thoroughly. One carriage must have required a great deal of Sellotape and, I imagined, created a lot of work for the exhausted conductors, who were just now pulling up the steps and shutting the carriage doors.

Suddenly there was a shout and a car screeched to a halt almost on the platform. Two men leaped out and, shouting instructions to the conductor of the nearest carriage, pushed several dozen cardboard boxes onto the train.

"It's medicines," I heard one of the men say. "They'll be picked up in Kyiv. What time are you likely to arrive?"

The conducted gave a tired shrug: "Who knows?" When the last carriage of the train, wagging like a dog's tail, disappeared around the bend, we stood alone on the platform. The station was now empty. The first few hours of that train journey through the Carpathian Mountains are beautiful. My wife wondered whether Anton would notice.

There followed an anxious wait. I kept checking the news feed. We watched as missiles struck cities all over the country. Russia has been actively targeting the Ukrainian railways. Missiles fall on electrical substations, bridges, stations and track. The next morning, Anton called to say that his train had arrived on time. The railway station was tightly controlled by soldiers who checked the documents and bags of everyone going in or out. As one of the few people arriving in Kyiv, he got through in no time at all.

The war changed everything, including your reasons for travelling. Rail passengers could now be divided into two categories: those evacuating a city and those returning. In most cases, their "return" was temporary, when family members went home to check the apartment was secure and to pick up things they found they required where now they were living. My wife returned to Kyiv in May, taking a suitcase of winter things home and bringing back summer clothes. She took the same train as our son, number 81. This time, it was full of passengers.

Ukrainians have great faith, not only in their army but also in their railways, as well as in those who are responsible for the system's safety. Rail traffic in Ukraine has not stopped for a single day during this war. I have the impression that it would be impossible to bring it to a complete halt. Trains can no longer reach areas occupied by the Russian forces but within days of the liberation of Kherson a passenger train arrived there.

You can blow up the rails, but teams of workers proceed at once to repair the damage. You can blow up railway stations and kill passengers waiting for your train, as happened in Kramatorsk on April 8, 2022, when 61 people died and more than 120 were injured. Yet even this tragedy did not disrupt the railway connection between Kyiv and Kramatorsk, or deter people from using the trains.

The Ukrainian railway was constructed when the territory was part of the Russian empire. The Russians built their tracks some 89 millimetres wider than the Stevenson gauge used elsewhere in much of Europe. Some historians suggest they did this to make invasion from the west more difficult. Needless to say, Soviet authorities saw no reason to change the gauge. The result is that Ukraine's railway system is almost entirely cut off from the rest of Europe, the Mukacheve–Košice line from Ukraine to Slovakia being one notable exception.

On March 15, 2022, only three weeks after the invasion, the first international delegation arrived in Kyiv, but because of the difference in gauge, they had to make the journey from the border on a *Ukrazaliznitsya* (U.Z.) train. The Prime Ministers of Poland, Slovenia and the Czech Republic were the first V.I.P. passengers to arrive. Their arrival in the capital at a time when Russian troops were still occupying the suburbs of Bucha, Borodyanka and Irpin inspired Ukrainians and strengthened their faith in victory.

Since then, hundreds of foreign politicians and diplomats have become U.Z. passengers. More than 300 foreign delegations have taken the train from the Polish border to Kyiv for meetings with the Ukrainian government and then on further towards the combat zones and cities which are constantly shelled by the Russian army – to Kharkiv, Kramatorsk, Mykolaiv and Kherson.

It would be hard to find a European politician or high-ranking diplomat who does not now know what a Ukrainian train's sleeping car looks like, or who would not recognise the U.Z. conductors' uniform. They are all enthusiastic about this service that continues to operate as if there were no war in Ukraine. Boris Johnson was keen to shake hands with the railway personnel of the trains he took, including the engine driver. The Finnish President said he had never enjoyed such a good night's sleep as he had on the train to Kyiv.

Without the Ukrainian Railways, the visits of high-ranking foreigners would have been much riskier and perhaps impossible. If all those top-level meetings had taken place in border towns, or outside Ukraine, the foreign guests would have been deprived of crucial insights into the situation on the ground and the Ukrainian people would have been deprived of essential morale-boosting moments in their extremely stressful lives.

Ukrainian Railways continues to play a vital part in Ukraine's struggle against the Russian assault. Perhaps most crucially, it enables the supply of frontline areas and war-damaged cities with essential goods and equipment for both civilian and military purposes.

How did Ukrainian Railways become this unshakeable bastion? During the Soviet era the railways were centrally controlled and, in essence, part of the military machine. In 1991, when Ukraine became independent, U.Z. became a state within a state. A state-owned joint stock company, it is the world's sixth largest passenger rail company and, at least until the start of the war, the seventh largest rail freight company. And yes, it is a monopoly.

The passenger network is relatively simple, with several trains a day between Kyiv and regional capitals and some other large cities. Then there are a number of local networks of electric trains serving the areas around each regional centre. Until 2012 almost all trains ran at night. All journeys lasted from teatime to breakfast. It did not seem to matter what the distance was. Then, in 2012, daytime "express" trains were introduced on many routes. They proved popular with people travelling on business. Leaving Kyiv at six in the morning, for the first time you could be in Kharkiv by midday, a journey of almost 500 kilometres.

Not all is perfect in the railways. As in every area of Ukrainian public life, top management has been accused of corruption. For years, passengers have complained about poor service – tatty or damp linen in the sleeping cars and the lack of air conditioning or heating. During the 1990s and early 2000s, it was often impossible for ordinary folk to buy tickets. The tickets were being bought up by insiders and resold at inflated prices. In 2013, this scheme was stopped by the introduction of tickets that include the name of the passenger. Now you must show photo I.D. to get on a train.

Despite corruption, the U.Z. infrastructure has gradually improved, funded by the money made on the freight side of the industry. Responsibility for the railway system was considered one of the toughest government-appointed jobs. Perhaps the country's most famous railway minister was George Kyrpa (1946–2004). In the early 2000s, he was first the General Director of U.Z. and then the Minister of Transport and Communications. Under his leadership, dozens of railway stations were renovated and numerous railway bridge construction projects launched. He shot himself, or was murdered, at the end of 2004, during the Orange Revolution.

There had been rumours that Kyrpa had been preparing to stand in the 2004 presidential election, which Yanukovych won using falsified results. In the days of Kyrpa, U.Z. had 400,000 employees and most of them would have voted for their "railway president", although they never got a chance to. The circumstances of his death remain a mystery.

Since Kyrpa's time, U.Z. top managers tend to remain in the job for short periods. It is as if someone in the President's office is afraid that the Ukrainian railway industry will once more nominate its own presidential candidate. Oleksandr Kamyshin recently left his post as U.Z.'s Director General after less than a year in the post. He has now been tasked with developing cooperation between U.Z. and European railway companies. Who will replace him at U.Z. has not been announced, although this choice is unlikely to affect the train schedule – and that is what Ukrainians care most about. Presently, up to 99 per cent. of Ukrainian passenger trains depart on time and 96 per cent. arrive on time. I spent many hours in the autumn of 2022 on the German Bundesbahn (D.B.). Of the twenty-plus trains I took, only one reached its destination on schedule.

Wartime conditions impose discipline on all technological and logistical processes. They suggest that the price of any mistake, any moment of unjustified relaxation, could be too high. The Ukrainian railway works like a Swiss clock because it works in extreme conditions. Since February 2022, more than 360 U.Z. workers have been killed while on duty and 800 others have been injured. Yet railway personnel continue to volunteer for work on trains sent to evacuate civilians from frontline areas or to deliver equipment to the army.

On March 4, 2022, a Russian missile exploded over the main children's hospital in Kyiv. The windows and doors of the central building of the hospital shattered. The young patients were in a bomb shelter at the time. Their evacuation by train began a few hours later. Information about the train and the route it would take was known only to a very few, although we know that the operation to evacuate the children was successful.

U.Z. has even seen some improvements in its services since the invasion began. Before the war, U.Z. ordered one hundred sleeping cars adapted for wheelchair users and the last fifteen of the cars recently went into service. Routes that have had to be abandoned owing to hostilities have been revived wherever possible, including that of the Slobozhansky Express, which runs from Kharkiv via Sumy to Konotop. This route runs parallel to the border with Russia and the front line.

Now U.Z. managers are also working to revive passenger routes shut down for economic reasons. The question is, where will the money come from in the future? Although ticket prices seem high to Ukrainians, by European standards they are very low. Anton's Uzhhorod–Kyiv ticket cost about twenty dollars. Income from passenger travel is not keeping the railways going. In the past it was freight that paid for the system and its maintenance. Much of that freight originated from the heavy industries located in territories which are now either under Russian occupation or have been devastated by Russia's military assault.

09.02.2023

Approaching the Tenth Anniversary of this War

On February 20, 2024, the Russian–Ukrainian war will be ten years old. We cannot forget that it began with the annexation of Crimea and then spilled over into Donbas. Of course, no-one is thinking about the tenth anniversary of the war, not yet, as it is still a whole year away. But the first anniversary of Russia's full-scale assault on Ukraine is nearly upon us. You can touch it, you can hear it and feel its hot breath on your skin.

It seems this anniversary will be heard and seen around the world. Russia is preparing for a new all-out attack, for another blanket missile strike on Ukraine. The criminal aggressor wants to seize as much territory as possible before Ukraine gets the tanks promised by Western Allies – and the planes not yet promised by them.

We are again standing on the edge of a precipice. At the bottom is the hot lava in which our happy, pre-war life was incinerated and into which high-rise homes, churches and universities are still falling – a gaping furnace that has already destroyed hundreds of thousands of lives. To be a Ukrainian today is to suffer this terrible illness, with which we have been infected intentionally. We may feel we are healthy, but there are no entirely healthy people in war or close to war. Like a disease, war takes control of your behaviour, your thoughts and even your feelings. War starts to think for you. It makes decisions for you.

I too suffer from this illness and I have not sought treatment. I am used to it. I am not a soldier or a doctor, but I am a citizen of Ukraine. I love my country and my former life. When confronted with the fact of war, I had to choose a front for myself. I needed to feel that I was doing something useful. So, every day, starting from February last year, I write and think about the war. I surround myself with the war and allow its horrible mass to pass through me. Closer to midnight, I fall asleep, only to wake up to check the news from the front line, from cities and villages all over Ukraine: news from my friends and acquaintances, including those who are now fighting at the front and who could be killed at any moment by Russian bullets and mortar fire.

What is the worst thing in today's Ukrainian life? You might think that it is the rocket attacks on residential buildings in peaceful Ukrainian cities. Yes, that is frightening. I have experienced it and my family experiences it every day, but I am not sure that this is the worst thing. The worst thing is that the death of a person has become something commonplace. War is a production line of death.

When, at the beginning of the war, a Russian missile ripped through the apartment of my friend, killing her instantly, I could not believe the fact of her death. She was a young journalist with plans and dreams. Since then, several other of my friends have died and several acquaintances have passed away owing to stress, or because they did not get to see a doctor in time. I know what they were thinking: "How can I worry a doctor right now? How can I think about my own health when my country is in danger?" And the reality is that there are too few doctors. Many are now refugees in Europe. In big cities and towns, further away from the front, they were partly replaced by internally displaced doctors, those from the territories in the south and east of the country which have been occupied by Russian forces. But there are still too few. Some doctors from western Ukraine also left home to go to the east to treat wounded Ukrainian soldiers. Never before have so many Ukrainians had to uproot themselves and make haste in all directions, either to support the war effort or in search of a safer place for their families.

Despite this, despite the struggle to maintain any semblance of normal life, despite the anguish of losses and the anxiety about a future that is impossible to imagine, Ukrainians are trying to prove to the world that they are O.K., to prove to the world that they can survive and that they will win this war. I am sure that we will win. We have already won once, when we prevented Russia from capturing our capital, Kyiv. We won again when we liberated almost all of Kharkiv region from the Russian invaders and prevented them from taking the city. We won once more when we freed Kherson. How many more victories do we need to end this war once and for all?

This is a rhetorical question. This war will not end on its own. Will one more victory, or many more victories, suddenly bring this horror to an end? It can only be stopped by Russia leaving the occupied territories and bringing to an end its aggression against Ukraine. Will this happen? Yes, but I do not know when. For this to happen, the Russian generals and the leaders of the Kremlin need to understand the utter senselessness of continuing hostilities.

If this does not happen before the summer or autumn, then we can expect a Ukrainian victory by the tenth anniversary of the start of the Russian–Ukrainian war, by February 20, 2024. This also would be quite logical: the war began with the annexation of Crimea and should end with its return to free Ukraine. Justice must be done.

20.02.2023

The Munich Security Conference

Flying all the way from San Francisco to Munich for one day seemed like a crazy idea. But I did it because I was invited to the Munich Security Conference. The "cultural block" of the conference was organised primarily for the general public, and Claudia Roth, Germany's Minister of Culture, and I were to speak in a dialogue on the topic "The role of cultural figures in wartime". The packed hall of the Munich House of Literature indicated that the subject was of interest to ordinary people.

Before my event, however, there was lunch, and meals at the conference, I was told, could be more interesting than some of the reports. I was lucky. I found myself sitting next to the famous retired American general Ben Hodges. Some politicians and representatives of civil society made short speeches between courses. There was only one topic – help for Ukraine.

Ben Hodges spread his optimism all around the circular table at which seven of us were seated. "Ukraine will win," he repeated several times. "I can read military maps! I see that Ukraine will win!" For some ten minutes he explained to me how and when Ukraine would win, stamping out any doubt I might have had about his prediction.

The next morning at Munich airport, the border control officer leafed through my passport for a long time, his eyebrows raised. He finally put my passport down and stared into my eyes. "Where is the stamp for entry into the Schengen zone? When and where did you enter?"

"Yesterday. Here." I replied. "I flew from San Francisco on a Lufthansa flight." "Then where is the stamp?" he asked again.

I took the passport and looked for the stamp myself, but I could not find it. "Your colleague must have forgotten to stamp it," I ventured.

An expression of shocked disbelief came over his face, but I managed to find my boarding pass from the day before still in my jacket pocket. The officer studied it and, nodding, handed back my passport without stamping it. I had not officially entered Germany, so I must leave the country unofficially as well. It would be as if I had never been there.

I pocketed my passport and headed out with Ben Hodges' words still ringing in my head: "Everything will be O.K.! Ukraine will win! I can read maps!"

Between Light and War

Despite continuing attacks on the energy infrastructure, the last two weeks have been brighter for many Ukrainians, not only because of the outpouring of support at high-level meetings, including President Biden's visit to Kyiv, but also because there is more light in Ukrainian streets and more electricity in Ukrainian homes. Trams and trolleybuses are running again in Odesa and Kyiv following a five-month break. In Uzhhorod and Lviv, street lighting has reappeared.

Some Ukrainians are cautious or cynical about these apparently positive developments: why is the electricity supply suddenly better when infrastructure is still being destroyed by Russian missiles and Iranian drones? Have Ukrainians learned to conserve electricity so effectively that it now supplies all our needs? Or did the frequency and length of the blackouts reflect more the need to conserve energy rather than the inability to supply it? Or is the government trying to calm the nation's nerves on the anniversary of the invasion, demonstrating that the situation is not only under control but that things are improving?

Or could it be that Ukrainian engineers have learned to repair damaged lines and substations very quickly? It was reported that some blackouts were carried out prior to when attacks were expected because it is easier to repair systems that have been switched off before an air raid. It would be possible to create a television series about the courage of the electrician repair teams, or perhaps I should say battalions, because they work like military units – unarmed but facing regular military threats. They are shelled constantly by the Russian army and often have to work in areas that have been mined by the enemy. As with the railways, this army of specialists also suffers losses. On January 20, it was announced that 127 electricians had been killed and many more wounded.

When Ukrainians are asked how life has changed over the last year, they rarely have a swift answer. What usually comes to mind are the faces of dead or missing acquaintances, friends and relatives. It seems to me that every Ukrainian knows someone who has been killed by Russia. Everyone has heard the funeral music for those who died in the war or because of the war. In many villages and towns near the front line there are simply no people left. It is hard to imagine anyone returning to these places as there is nothing for survivors to go back to. The villages and towns have been reduced to ruins by Russian artillery, they remain only as memories and as names on the map.

Statistics show that during the last twelve months the population of Ukraine has read less, eaten less and drunk much less wine. Behind the numbers is the simple truth that there are now many fewer Ukrainians in Ukraine. Compared to a year ago, there are many more of them in Poland, the Czech Republic, Germany and America.

"What do we need to do to get you back?" I might ask the eight million Ukrainians who have ended up abroad.

I can imagine their answers: rebuild the housing, give us security guarantees, index our pensions, so that we can survive. Answers like these would come from only a portion of the refugees. Others would remain silent because they do not believe that they will return, or because they have already decided to stay abroad. The most enterprising refugees, often younger adults, have already found jobs or started their own businesses. When travelling in Europe and America I have noticed a number of young Ukrainian couples, sometimes with children. I cannot help wondering how conscription-age men managed to leave Ukraine.

Some Ukrainians were of course already abroad when the war started. I met a few in the south of France: for example, a young couple from Chernihiv and their seven-year-old daughter who were on holiday in Egypt on February 24 last year. Their return flight to Kyiv was cancelled. They called their relatives in Chernihiv and could not decide what to do. The hotel expected them to leave as per their holiday dates but then allowed them to stay when no new Ukrainian tourists appeared to replace them. After several days of thought, they flew to Europe. The husband, Igor, is a cook, his wife is an accountant. Neither speaks good English. After a short stop in Spain, they ended up in a refugee centre in Marseille. During our short conversation, Igor did not mention how he got a job there as an assistant cook in a hotel. That is what he was doing when I met him last summer.

The hotel bartender asked me where I was from. When I told him, he was overjoyed. "I have a colleague from Ukraine," he cried. "Hang on. I will call him!" Igor had fallen on his feet. The owner of the hotel had not only given him a job but also taken in his family, providing accommodation for them in the hotel. They were happy with their situation and were not thinking about the future. Dressed in his chef's white jacket and apron, his curly hair showing beneath his chef's hat, Igor was the spitting image of a Frenchman.

How other young men ended up abroad, one can only guess. Many left in the very first days of the war, before martial law was introduced. Some would say they were the lucky ones. No-one knows how many men have left Ukraine illegally. A week ago, in a single day, border guards in Transcarpathia stopped seven men who were trying to cross undetected. Since

February 2022, hundreds of Ukrainian men have been detained while trying to leave the country. Some attempts to leave must have succeeded. The illegal enterprise of providing "border guides" has become a profitable albeit risky business for residents in those regions. The guides charge between 1,000€ and 8,000€. Those who pay perhaps see this as the price for being saved from possible death at the front. On Ukrainian social media, there is a great deal of discussion about these young male refugees. For the most part, their situation is regarded with a degree of sympathy. The strongest accusation against them is that they lack patriotism.

While some men continue to storm the country's western borders, others volunteer to join the army and yet others, who may not be so keen to fight in the war, are mobilised. Following an information campaign designed to make it clear that a man of conscription age can, by law, be presented with a summons to the military draft board anywhere and at any time, the Ministry of Defence has sent "draft assault brigades" out onto the streets. Summonses to the draft board are being handed out in cafés, shops, fitness clubs and even in the sanatoriums hidden in the Carpathian Mountains.

Odesa has recently seen several mobilisation incidents that have raised an outcry, where men have been detained physically on the street so that summonses to the draft board could be put into their hands. In Ternopil, in western Ukraine, there is outrage over the tragic case of 33-year-old Bohdan Pokitko. He had never served in the army, so had no military experience. However, he was mobilised and sent straight to the front line in Donbas without training. He died five days later. His indignant relatives and friends demanded that Ternopil's Regional Governor should explain how this could have happened: "Is Ukraine now recruiting its citizens into the army as they do in

Russia – to be used as cannon fodder?" they wanted to know. The Ternopil military registration and enlistment office is investigating this case.

The Ministry of Defence does not report data on Ukrainian losses. They are certainly significant. Continuous battles in Donbas, in and around the towns of Vuhledar, Soledar, and Bakhmut, take hundreds of Russian lives every day. European military analysts suggest that Ukrainian losses are comparable, although Ukrainian spokespeople insist that Russia is losing many more soldiers than Ukraine. The recent acceleration of the mobilisation campaign in Ukraine indicates that more soldiers are needed.

Not surprisingly, Russian special services are stepping up their efforts to sabotage mobilisation in Ukraine, sending tens of thousands of messages to Ukrainian numbers through the Telegram messenger app. The recipients are urged to save their lives and refuse to be mobilised. Ukrainian intelligence agencies have identified more than 40 fake Telegram accounts from which these anti-mobilisation messages are sent. Interestingly, many of these same accounts were previously used inside Russia to spread propaganda in support of Russia's war in Ukraine.

In Russia, public figures are demanding more strikes on Ukraine's energy infrastructure, even on nuclear power plants. Apparently, they have also noticed the return of street lighting, trams and trolleybuses in Ukrainian cities.

24.02.2023

One year on

It is difficult for me to remember life in pre-war Ukraine. It is not that I have forgotten, not entirely. It is just that it now seems like a fairy tale, like something I heard about as a child when I believed in magic.

My family and I used to love our road trips around Ukraine, including to Donbas and Crimea. I wanted my children to know Ukraine in all its variety: how the Donbas differs from Zakarpattya, northern Ukraine from Bukovina. Many of the towns and villages we fell in love with during our travels have since been reduced to rubble or have been occupied, seized by Russia's tyrannical regime.

At the very beginning of their new offensive, the Russian army occupied Novooleksiivka, a small and cosy town just north of Crimea. The town had been a haven for many Crimean Tatars who had fled Crimea, their historical homeland, when the Russians annexed it in 2014. When Novooleksiivka was occupied, many of them fled once more. Others remained under occupation and some of them have now been arrested or kidnapped.

I want to say that the last twelve months are the most tragic in Ukraine's history, but can one really compare tragedies? In 1932–3, several million Ukrainians died owing to the famine orchestrated by Stalin and the Communist Party, the Holodomor. Only openly discussed since independence, that tragedy is still a raw wound in Ukraine. In 1943, the entire Crimean Tatar population was deported from their homeland. Many died on the journey into exile. They all lost their homes. In 1989 they were allowed to resettle in Crimea. Now they must lose their

161

homes again or live under a regime that does not give Crimean Tatar culture a significant place in the peninsula's life and fabricates criminal cases against activists and those who try to defend them.

Can a past tragedy strengthen you against a current one? In Mariupol, entire apartment blocks, with the residents still inside, were pummelled by Russian artillery until they were structurally unstable and then pulled down by the aggressors, the dead residents still inside.

Tens of thousands of Ukrainian soldiers and civilians have been killed. New mass graves of civilians are discovered regularly. The Ukrainian prosecutor's office has already recorded more than 70,000 war crimes committed by the Russian army and the Wagner mercenaries. Who will investigate these crimes and when, if every day continues to bring new atrocities?

This war is being broadcast live to the whole world. We are watching the past in a battle to the death with the future – bigotry pitched against Ukrainian culture and identity. A battlefield where representatives of Ukraine's cultural and business elite must fight against professional criminals released from prisons. The Russian convicts were promised freedom if they survive six months on the battlefield. Some of them have already returned home as "heroes". Some of those killed are buried as heroes in Russia's "Alleys of Glory", next to the graves of scientists, politicians and artists.

Among the soldiers of the Ukrainian army, you find I.T. specialists, musicians, businessmen, poets and farmers. They are fighting and dying for Ukraine every hour, every minute of the day. They do not ask for rewards or privileges, all they want is victory in this brutal war that has been imposed on them and on us all by the Russian invader.

An anniversary is often considered a reason to take stock.

I do not want to sum up the results and the consequences of this outrage. The war is not yet finished. Any war ends with a counting of the dead and wounded, the number of destroyed houses, schools and universities, churches and museums. This terrible inventory will be drawn up, but later, when the war is over. For now, I can say only that Ukrainians are not giving up. They believe in their victory. They are already restoring houses around Kyiv destroyed in March last year. They are thinking about the future after the war, after the liberation of all Ukrainian territories occupied by Russia.

On January 1, when I was walking past the playground in Shevchenko Park, where one of the Russian missiles exploded last October, I heard children playing in the sandbox using the "F" word about Putin. Kids will always pick up such phrases from grown-ups. I do not blame the parents, the whole country thinks and speaks the same way. The phrase is now commonplace, but it makes me think of that lost innocence, the fairy-tale life we lived before February 24, 2022.

25.02.2023

The Pen and Poetry

The sound of a Ukrainian word reaches the Atlantic coast of America before it can be turned into a printed word in Ukraine. Now everything is sound: explosions, shots, cries of despair – and spoken words. Words that say what is happening to us and our country. Words that tell the outside world about us. Words that help us to share and deal with our pain.

Books, newspapers and magazines require weeks, months, and even years to produce. It is difficult to find the time for such to be born in a country at war. And where could they be born, when so many of the print shops and publishing houses were bombed in the early spring of last year? What is more, readers, publishers and writers have become soldiers at the front, or volunteers who make haste to and from the front with help of every kind.

If journalists tell the news to the people of their country, writers and poets tell the whole world and future generations. Somebody still needs to write.

On my way to the Munich conference, I met Amelia Glaser and Yulia Ilchuk at San Francisco airport. They are excellent translators and were flying to Japan for a conference. They let me see an advance copy of a volume of English translations of poems by the Ukrainian poet and Lviv University professor Halyna Kruk. Amelia and Yulia were thrilled to be taking this book with them. The collection of poetry is called *A Crash Course in Molotov Cocktails*. Halyna Kruk's poems have yet to be published in their original Ukrainian. They will be read first in English by Japanese academics, then they will appear in American bookshops.

Do we need poems about the war in Ukraine? We do. We need them in Ukraine perhaps more than elsewhere. They have the power to rescue, heal and sustain. Poetry has also become a powerful engine for fundraising in support of the army. We saw this with the cult Ukrainian poet and prose writer Serhiy Zhadan. His poems are like gunshots – they launch, ignite, then freeze for a moment, long enough for several images from the poem to become embedded in the reader's memory. During a war, people are very sensitive to precisely chosen words, intonation and images.

I am sure that after this war even more poetry will be read in Ukraine. At the front, where time is so precious, many soldiers have discovered their first taste of poetry. Poets only use important words. A single phrase can take you home or back to the past – to the peaceful past.

P.E.N. Ukraine members are fearlessly travelling close to the front line to visit soldiers and civilians. They talk to everyone. They share their creative energy but they also gather information about the crimes against Ukrainian culture committed by the Russian invader. They also help to restore cultural and social life in recently liberated towns and villages. They write too, of course, chronicling every day of this war.

P.E.N. Ukraine also keeps a close eye on Ukrainian political prisoners held by Russia, including Crimean Tatar activists and citizen journalists. The war has not made us forget about the unjust trials that target anyone in Crimea who refuses to accept the Russian annexation of the peninsula.

Poets are not alone in being able to convey the drama of today's Ukraine, the pain of a war that has destroyed the lives of millions of Ukrainians. This pain is transmitted to the world through many channels: prose, journalism, music, documentary and feature films.

Ukrainian writers try to share our experiences and the truth about the war by all available means. Are we succeeding? Sometimes yes, sometimes not. But Ukrainian writers and poets cannot but talk about Ukraine, about the war, about our losses and hopes. Who else can tell the world about how Oleksandr Kislyuk, a professor and translator of classical antique literature, was shot dead in front of his house in Bucha in early March? Who knows better than the Ukrainian writer Victoria Amelina about the tragic fate of her colleague, the children's author Volodymyr Vakulenko, whose body could not be found for several months and then, for another two months after it was found, could not be identified? He was buried finally a full eight months after his death. His thirteen books remain his legacy in Ukrainian literature – an unlucky number.

Two bullets from a Makarov pistol were taken from Volodymyr's body. Russian soldiers do not have pistols, only machine guns. Officers have pistols. Volodymyr was executed. He was killed because he loved Ukraine and the Ukrainian language, culture and history. They killed him because they saw strength in him. They killed him because he did not kneel before them, did not beg to be left alive and did not switch to Russian in conversation with them. This is how Russia kills, how it has always killed Ukrainian culture. In 1937–8, they shot a generation of Ukrainian writers, poets, playwrights, and scientists in the Karelian camp of Sandarmokh and on Solovki Island in the White Sea.

Dozens of Ukrainian poets, writers, translators, publishers and journalists have perished in this war. More of them, like Artem Chekh, Markiyan Kamysh and Artem Chapay are still fighting, not with a pen and notepad but with a machine gun. They shoot and then write. They shoot and then give Skype interviews. They are the powerful voices of a country at war. Without them, the world would know less and empathise less strongly with our daily drama.

The world has learned a lot about Ukraine during this war. All over Europe there are new books about the history of Ukraine and the history of Russian–Ukrainian relations – about the 300 years of Russia's unceasing quest to assimilate Ukrainians and destroy Ukrainian culture. The time when nothing was known about Ukraine is over. People want to know more, but it is difficult for Ukrainians to talk about anything except war. Perhaps, if I were a poet, it would be easier.

I sometimes close my eyes and listen to the past. I hear and see the pre-war Ukraine, the places that always surprised and fascinated me. I see the town of Sharhorod – an ancient Jewish town in the south of Vinnytsia region, close to Moldova where there is one of the oldest synagogues in Ukraine. It stands white-washed and renovated, waiting for people to visit it. I remember Kamenets-Podolsky with its deep canyon, along the bottom of which flows the Smotrych River. I remember Bakhmut, a place of dark mines, sparkling wine and wartime atrocities old and new, and Solidar, a salt mine turned into an enormous concert hall where I once heard the Donetsk Symphony Orchestra play Vivaldi. Was that really me?

27.02.2023

Recycling Everything

Even if you know something about church holidays you may not be familiar with St Tryphon, the patron saint of wine-makers. This saint is particularly loved in Besarabia, the largely ethnic-Bulgarian part of Ukraine's Odesa region, where the February feast of St Tryphon is a much-awaited event. The festival usually heralds the start of the tourist season in Besarabia. It is the moment when the vineyard owners begin the solemn work of pruning the vines. Processions of festival participants enter the villages to visit wineries, taste the new wine, sing songs and choose the best vineyard of the year, "The King of the Vineyards". When the merrymakers can drink no more, they sprinkle wine on the vineyards to ensure that the next harvest will be even better.

This year the festival of St Tryphon began on February 14 as usual but without any tourists. Villagers pruned their vines and celebrated quietly by themselves, recalling, not without sadness, past holidays attended by tens of thousands of visitors from all over the country and abroad. Given the tragedy of war, this tradition could have been abandoned altogether. A number of local men have died at the front and in the village cemeteries their grave mounds are still fresh. However, the authorities chose to maintain the festival which has underpinned their communities for hundreds of years. To give up the tradition would be a form of capitulation and no-one is prepared to capitulate, or even to think about doing so.

The wine in this region is very good. Unfortunately, the scarcity of tourists last summer meant a big fall in sales and a loss of income for the wineries. However, 2021 was a good year. The vintage can be sold at higher prices in the years to come. Apart from that, the less interesting wine can be recycled into very interesting grappa.

The feast of St Tryphon is also the beginning of spring. The Besarabian steppe is beginning to warm up. Villagers are clearing their gardens and farmyards of winter debris, trying to free up space within and outside their homes. Local Roma support this process, driving around the villages in horse-drawn carts and calling through loudspeakers so that people know to bring out any scrap metal, unwanted pots and pans and old car batteries.

It will take much more than a few horse-drawn carts to deal with the scrap metal cluttering swathes of Ukraine's farmland further east, for we are talking about hundreds of thousands of tons of military hardware scattered throughout areas that have seen hostilities. As of February 20, the Ukrainian army has destroyed 3,310 Russian tanks and more than 6,500 heavy armoured vehicles. Efforts are made to salvage and renovate whatever can be used by the Ukrainian army but many of these vehicles are beyond repair.

Each tank weighs at least 45 tons. By law, all military scrap belongs to Oboronprom, the state defence industry. Oboronprom cannot deal with the volume of scrap metal currently available for processing. In neighbouring Poland and the Czech Republic, prices for scrap metal are three times higher than in Ukraine. However, according to another law, scrap metal is a strategic resource and cannot be exported even though Ukraine lacks scrap metal processing plants. Two-thirds have either been destroyed or are located in occupied territory.

While large-scale military scrap remains abandoned on the ground, smaller-scale waste, such as cartridge cases, is being recycled in projects that are more artistic than industrial. Dozens of artists, professional and amateur, are painting on the spent cartridge cases. The resulting works of art are sold through online auctions. The proceeds are given to the army, or used for humanitarian needs. Most of this cartridge-case art is sold in Ukraine, but the best works are sent to charity auctions in Europe. True, the export aspect of this project raises a good many questions among customs officers.

One such project was set up by Victoria Matvienkiv, an art and design student at Ivano-Frankivsk University. Her father is fighting in Zaporizhzhia region. Victoria asked him to bring her some cartridge cases so that she and her friends could paint them and raise money for the army. Her university has agreed to host the auction of the finished works on its website. Prices for the artworks start at eight euros, but many fetch ten times more.

"We cannot but support our students and our Ukraine," says Ivanna Babetska, vice-rector of the university.

As well as cartridge cases, Kharkiv artists are exhibiting

painted helmets in Ternopil, in western Ukraine. This project was initiated to help the family of Nazar Myalikguliev, a soldier who was killed at the front. His widow and three children could no longer afford the rent for their apartment. The plan is to buy them a new home.

Artistic recycling of military items is not limited to metal goods. Enterprising Ukrainians are also making use of the many wooden shell crates made available by the war. The Odesa region winemaker, Oleksandr Shushpanov, who courageously opened a wine-tasting cellar in Odesa in late October 2022, uses these crates to package gift sets of his products. Oleksandr also orders grenade-launcher tubes from the front. Once cleaned up, a tube can hold a bottle of wine and two glasses. Oleksandr gives the money from the sale of these unusually packaged gift sets to his wife Olena, who runs a volunteer project producing light battlefield stretchers. Oleksandr and Olena's son, Volodymyr, is currently serving in the Ukrainian army.

In Kyiv, there is another ongoing recycling project, that of turning Russian-language books into pulp to raise money for humanitarian projects. This campaign is not spearheaded by the state but by Ukrainian-language writers and cultural figures who believe that the preponderance of Russian-language books in libraries, both public and domestic, is an aspect of Russian aggression. Putin has very often justified his "special operation" as a way to protect those who use the Russian language. Putin's words may allow you to believe that if nobody in Ukraine used Russian, there would be no aggression. Since so many of the Ukrainian civilians killed by Putin's army are Russian speakers, we have to conclude that he does not care what language his victims use.

Even museums are being recycled. In 1990, the Pushkin Museum was opened in Kyiv, based on a large collection of artefacts donated by Yakov Berdichevsky. On March 3, 2022, the museum was renamed and redefined, in my view appropriately, as the Museum of Early Nineteenth Century Life in Kyiv.

Another museum, that some would like to see "recycled" in this way, is the one dedicated to Mikhail Bulgakov. The museum is in the very building in which he lived after the Bolshevik revolution during the dark days of the civil war. It has been suggested that the premises should be given over to a museum in honour of the choirmaster and composer Oleksandr Koshyts, who was little known in his homeland until recently. In 1919, on behalf of the government of the Ukrainian People's Republic, which had then just declared independence from the Russian Empire, Koshyts left Ukraine on a tour of Europe, together with the chamber choir he had created. The aim was to acquaint the European public with Ukrainian song culture. His story is worthy of a three-hour Hollywood biopic and I hope some other building can be found for a museum in his honour.

It is not yet clear how the Bulgakov Museum story will end but in Mariinsky Park, in the centre of Kyiv, the story of a monument to the Soviet General Nikolay Vatutin recently ended with the monument's demolition. In 1943, Vatutin commanded the Soviet forces which liberated Kyiv from the German fascists. A figure associated with Soviet and Kremlin power, the removal of his monument and his grave, which lay in front of it, has long been demanded by Ukrainian activists. Their wish has been granted. The monument is gone and Vatutin's remains have been moved to a Kyiv cemetery.

Heartened by this news, a village near Kharkiv which bears the name Vatutino, after the Soviet general, has appealed to the Ukrainian Parliament requesting that the name of the village be changed. Residents have already held a referendum to select a new name for their village. It only remains for Parliament to vote and confirm their choice. The name chosen is Zaluzhnoe, in translation, "beyond the meadow". The surname Zaluzhny means the same thing and this also happens to be the surname of the Commander-in-Chief of the Ukrainian army. The village leadership claims that the connection with General Zaluzhny's name is purely coincidental. I wonder what Parliament will think about this. There might well be an onslaught of similar requests if the change is granted.

For now, the residents of Vatutino can focus on Masliana, the week-long religious holiday that precedes Lent. Unlike St Tryphon's festival, Masliana is traditionally celebrated throughout Ukraine, with singing and much eating of pancakes, and this year is no exception.

15.03.2023

The Tale of the Shevchenko Prize

Since Soviet times, there has been one unchanging tradition in Ukrainian cultural life. The period leading up to March 9 is one of high tension because on that day, the birthday of Ukraine's national poet, Taras Shevchenko, the winners of the National Prize that is named after him are announced. According to the rules, the selection committee puts forward a list of laureates, which is confirmed in a decree signed, until 1991, by the secretary of the Communist Party of Ukraine and since 1992, by the President of Ukraine.

For sixty years, without interruption, March 9 was when the winners of the national awards for achievements in the arts and literature were announced. This year, on the morning of March 9, there was the usual tense, expectant air as the country's cultural elite waited. No presidential decree was forthcoming. Instead, the chairman of the Shevchenko prize selection committee, Yuriy Makarov, posted that the wartime environment justified changes to the rules of the prize. In his announcement, Makarov admitted that other members of the committee had not agreed with him.

The Shevchenko Prize Committee met to make its final decisions in February. They agreed on a list of laureates in various categories. Since then, the list has been with the President's office, awaiting a signature. On March 9, when it became obvious that the President was not going to sign the committee's decision into law, the committee took the unprecedented step of publishing their list of laureates without the presidential decree.

The winners are, in my view, worthy representatives of Ukrainian culture and literature. Among them are: Irina Tsilik, the author of the documentary film "The Earth is as Blue as an Orange", for which she has already received many international awards; Katerina Kalitko, a well-known poet and translator of Balkan literature; the musical ensemble Chorea Kozatska (the Cossack Choir) which maintains Ukraine's ancient vocal and instrumental traditions under the leadership of the legendary musician and music historian Taras Kompanichenko; and Vitaliy Portnikov, one of the country's brightest essayists and journalists.

Instead of confirming the committee's decision, on March 9 President Zelensky called together cultural figures for a meeting during which he spoke at length about the need to create new "content" that would correspond to Ukraine's wartime situation and which would constitute an important contribution to the victory over Putin's army.

It has been a long time since Ukraine saw such indignation among artists, film directors, writers and members of the world of theatre. Social networks boiled over in fury. A dozen conspiracy theories were put forward, based mostly on the assumption that the President's administration intended to push forward their own candidates for the award. Another version, more plausible in my view, was that the journalist Vitaliy Portnikov was held to be unacceptable as a laureate. Portnikov often criticises Zelensky's administration, while he is much less critical of the previous President, Petro Poroshenko.

At the meeting with the President, Yuriy Makarov suggested, apparently spontaneously, that the announcement of all the laureates could be postponed until May 22, the day when Shevchenko's remains were buried at Kaniv in Cherkasy region. He commented that before that date, some new nominations could be considered which were relevant to Ukraine's wartime situation.

One of the selection committee members, the artist, Vlada Ralko, resigned on March 9. There are numerous explanations or rumours as to why she did. Certainly, she had already served three years, the usual term for committee members, but it is also true that no prize was awarded for fine art this year. Then another committee member resigned and on the third day of the scandal, with no resolution in sight, Yuri Makarov himself resigned.

The problem remains that, according to the rules of the award, the laureates must be announced in a presidential decree and no decree has been signed. So, there is no point congratulating the winners. The now decapitated Shevchenko Prize Committee itself is silent. Nor is there confirmation of some kind of ceremony with the announcement of the laureates, the ones already selected plus some "new content" on May 22.

What surprises me most of all is that there is now more heated discussion about the Shevchenko Prize on social networks than news from Bakhmut and other hot spots of the war. I imagine that many commentators appreciate the incongruity of the situation. We should all be focused on supporting our armed forces. However, Ukrainian intellectuals also have a responsibility to defend traditions that strengthen the country's cultural life.

It is very hard to understand how it has been possible to drive the sturdy tradition of the Shevchenko Prize into this dead end, creating a scandal on the very day that we should have been marking the poet's birthday.

17.03.2023

Permission to Travel

Against the backdrop of news from the front lines, especially from Bakhmut and Vuhledar, we may fail to notice reports about the possible cancellation of fundraising concerts in Europe by Ukrainian performers, including those by the popular band Kazka and the jazz-punk group Hypnotunez. We might be about to see a sharp reduction in the number of events involving male representatives of Ukrainian culture, as it becomes more difficult for them to leave Ukraine.

All Ukrainian men between the ages of eighteen and 61 are liable for military service and men planning to take part in cultural projects abroad must obtain permission from the Ministry of Culture to leave Ukraine. An exit permit carries with it the obligation to return within the period specified in the document.

Since the start of Russia's all-out invasion, the business of getting permission to leave has added new layers of stress to the organisation of foreign tours. The application has to be made well in advance and permits are often issued only one day before the planned trip. Nonetheless, a good many Ukrainian cultural events have taken place in Europe and America during the last year.

Two recent cases of "betrayal" have made the process much more complicated. These incidents involved the stand-up comedian Andriy Shchegel and the film director Taras Golubkov. It has emerged that Shchegel had been granted permission to leave Ukraine even though he had already received three summonses to the military registration office. Shchegel is now in Turkey, where he plans to wait for the end of the war before returning home. "I have based my actions on the fact that it is the choice of the guys to die," Shchegel said in an interview with Ukrainian journalist Roman Skrypin. "I sincerely sympathise with everyone who is now forced to defend Ukraine out of love for it. I sincerely sympathise with Ukraine, which is experiencing the worst tragedy in its history."

Shchegel went into hiding in Turkey instead of performing in stand-up comedy shows at venues outside Ukraine, as was indicated in his permit to leave the country. Golubkov's crime is even more heinous. He gained permission to travel abroad to make a film about the war in Ukraine but, instead, he went to Moscow and there worked on a music video with the Russian singer Klava Koka, who openly supports the Russian aggression. No Ukrainian journalist has managed to interview Golubkov. He no longer responds to emails or calls and has closed his Facebook and Instagram accounts.

Two "betrayals" from the cultural sphere may not seem like a large number, but show business is high profile. Perhaps this is why the Cabinet of Ministers has felt obliged to introduce new rules for all military-age men wishing to obtain permission to travel abroad. They must now first receive a document from the military registration office confirming their status. The issue of trust and confidence, not only regarding cultural figures but men in general, is a two-edged sword. The increasing focus on keeping men in Ukraine may affect negatively the population's confidence in the state and this, in turn, could affect the strength of their loyalty to Ukraine.

Since 2014, Ukrainian cultural figures have been very active in supporting both the army and the civilian population affected by the Russian invasion. Many of them have become volunteers in a broad array of projects including fundraising activities in support of the army and humanitarian needs. Until recently, Ukrainian groups and individuals from the cultural sphere who already had a reputation outside the country had no problems obtaining permission to go abroad. The poet and rock singer Serhiy Zhadan, the band Okean Elzy and their lead singer Stanislav Vakarchuk and the folk group DakhaBrakha are among those who have travelled abroad in recent months. It is not clear how these same people will react to the new travel permission rules, but concerns over the matter of trust are already being raised.

Commenting on the cases of Shchegel and Golubkov, Zhadan said, "The example of these two scoundrels should not undermine the efforts of thousands of representatives of Ukrainian culture who have been working for our victory for more than a year, who have invested so much in our common struggle . . . Let's be frank, without volunteer assistance to the armed forces of Ukraine, our army would be in great difficulty. The activities of Ukrainian cultural figures result in millions of dollars being raised around the world. Essential things are bought with this money."

The Long Path to Self-identification

While Ukraine is struggling against the invasion, it may seem strange to spend time remembering the collapse of the U.S.S.R. in 1991. Yet I find it useful to reflect on those events. New, unexpected insights appear which sometimes provoke a shift in my attitudes, allowing me to reassess the past from the point of view of today's tragedy.

In 1991, the U.S.S.R. was physically disintegrating, crumbling like an old, abandoned building. Now Putin's dream of restoring the U.S.S.R. is also crumbling and nostalgia for the Soviet past is dying.

I met the collapse of the Soviet Union in 1991 with optimism. For that country, which fell apart painfully, bit by bit over a long period, bringing new difficulties for its inhabitants each day, there was no choice but for it to disappear. It had to make way for the formation of a new state on its territory. I was then 30 years old. I saw myself as already quite mature. Yet I was still a young man, one who had managed to get a higher education, complete my army service and who was working in a state publishing house as an editor.

I have always believed that the most important thing in life is to have a choice. This is the essence of freedom. Choice gives the opportunity to better understand yourself, the purpose of life and your own role in it. In Soviet society I could not choose a role that would suit both me and the Soviet system.

In my student years, I was an anti-Soviet Soviet person, as were many of my peers. I disliked many things about the U.S.S.R. I often argued with my communist father about the wrongness of the Soviet regime. And yet, I did not believe that the regime could be changed, that it could be made "correct". My father did not like to argue, although he always defended the Soviet system in his calm, lazy manner. His positive attitude towards it resulted from his belief that the Soviet system had allowed him to realise his dreams. Since childhood, he had wanted to become a military pilot and he became one. He rose to the rank of captain, spending several years in the Soviet occupying forces in defeated Germany. He returned to the U.S.S.R. and, had it not been for the Caribbean crisis and Nikita Khrushchev's unilateral disarmament policy, he would have risen to the rank of colonel. Following that crisis, having faced the threat of a third world war, Khrushchev wanted to show the world that the U.S.S.R. was a peace-loving state. This meant that my father, along with tens of thousands of other military men, was sent into the reserve army, to live a peaceful life. I am still grateful to Khrushchev for this beautiful peacekeeping gesture. Without it, I would not be a Ukrainian today.

After leaving the army, my father began to look for work in civil aviation. He was fortunate. My grandmother, my father's mother, lived in Kyiv where one of the largest aircraft factories in the U.S.S.R., the Antonov factory, produced civilian passenger and cargo aircraft. It was for this plant that my father was invited to work as a test pilot and so our whole family moved to Ukraine – more precisely, to the Ukrainian Soviet Socialist Republic.

I was not yet two years old. Therefore, the Russian village of Budogoshch in Leningrad Region, my mother's home and where I was born, is preserved in my memory only through the stories told by my mother and maternal grandmother. In my memories of early childhood only Kyiv features – Kyiv and Yevpatoriya in Crimea, where our family spent the summer holiday every year.

I have no non-Ukrainian memories of childhood, although it

is difficult to call the memories I do have "Ukrainian" as they were Soviet, albeit connected geographically to Ukraine. The "Ukrainianness" of the country at that time was expressed only in Ukrainian folk song and dance, as if the Soviet republics differed from one another only in these narrow areas.

My parents considered themselves Russians all their lives, but in fact they were people of Soviet nationality. They were brought up in Soviet, not Russian, culture. They did not sing Russian folk songs. They liked the Soviet songs from popular Soviet films.

After 1917, Lenin dreamed of creating a special "Soviet man" – a person cut off from his ethnic roots, from the history of his specific small homeland. Of course, Lenin took the Russian person as the basis of the "Soviet person" – someone with a collective mentality, loyal to the authorities and who values stability more than freedom. And, of course, this Soviet person had to speak Russian. Without the Russian language, the control of one Soviet People was impossible. Therefore, the Soviet political system, which had initially abandoned the tsarist policy of Russification in the early 1920s, returned to this policy in the mid-1930s. The dramatic flourishing of distinctly Ukrainian culture in the 1920s ended in 1937–8 with the mass executions of all those who had been responsible for the Ukrainian cultural revival.

In Kyiv, in the 1970s, most schools taught all subjects in Russian. Ukrainian schools were looked down on as institutions for the children of janitors and cooks, for children with no ambition and whose future could never be bright.

At Russian school No. 203, only one of my friends was from a family in which Ukrainian was spoken at home. But at school, he spoke Russian, like everyone else. At that time, if someone spoke Ukrainian in Kyiv, it was assumed that they had come to

Kyiv on business from some outlying village, or that they were nationalists.

At school, we were taught Ukrainian twice a week. Some of my classmates were excused from these lessons. All you needed, in order to be exempt from Ukrainian lessons, was a letter from your parents stating that, in connection with a possible future move to another region of the U.S.S.R., their child did not need to learn Ukrainian. I went to these Ukrainian language and literature classes, but I do not remember enjoying them. Strangely, I cannot remember either the name or the face of our Ukrainian language teacher. I do not even remember if it was a man or a woman but I do remember my Russian teacher very well. Her name was Bella Mikhailovna Voitsekhovskaya. She taught us Russian literature with great enthusiasm, constantly reciting Pushkin, Lermontov and even the officially frowned-upon Anna Akhmatova.

Now, when I think about the Ukrainian language and literature teacher who has disappeared from my memory, I suspect that he or she did everything possible to remain unremarkable, as if there was some shame in teaching the subject, as if the subject were something second-rate and insignificant.

The Ukrainian language was not banned during those years. There were Ukrainian-speaking communists and university professors. When I was a student at the University of Foreign Languages, we had a professor who lectured in Ukrainian, the legendary translator from English, German and Italian, Ilko Korunets. At that time, books by Oscar Wilde, Fenimore Cooper and Gianni Rodari were published in Ukrainian in his translations. Strangely, of all the professors who taught me, he is the only one whose name I can still remember.

After university, I worked for half a year as an editor at the Dnipro publishing house. I edited translations in Ukrainian of foreign novels. Inside the publishing house, everyone spoke Ukrainian – that was the unwritten rule of the place. I remember walking down the street to work with my colleagues. As we approached the doors of the publishing house, we would be talking about something in Russian, but as we went inside we automatically continued the same conversation in Ukrainian.

Knowing the Ukrainian language did not automatically make me a Ukrainian. Even though I had lived in the capital of Soviet Ukraine since early childhood, "Russian" was written in the nationality column of my Soviet passport. When I received a passport from independent Ukraine, I discovered that there was no nationality column in it, only the name of my new homeland, "Ukraine", embossed in gold on its cover. Without crossing any borders, I found myself in a new country. I did not change much and my attitude towards freedom of choice did not change. I continued to write literary texts in Russian but I called myself and considered myself a Ukrainian writer. Some of my Ukrainian-speaking colleagues treated my self-identification with hostility. They stubbornly called me a Russian writer and insisted that if I wanted to call myself a Ukrainian author I should switch to writing in Ukrainian. In the period from the mid-1990s until the middle of the first decade of the twenty-first century, I participated in dozens, if not hundreds, of debates on this topic and I do not ever remember any of the participants shifting in their opinion. On the other hand, some Russian-speaking writers did start using Ukrainian as their language of creativity.

The current war has caused a new wave of language migration. The most famous Russian-speaking writer from Donbas, Volodymyr Rafeenko, turned his back on the Russian language last year. This war has made many ethnic Ukrainians start to use Ukrainian in everyday life. They no longer feel any need for Russian.

The concept of identity is usually associated with belonging, being at home in a particular community with a shared culture, history and language. Although I cling to my native language as a writer, I feel that I am part of the Ukrainian community and so I need to know the Ukrainian language and understand Ukrainian history and culture.

The issue of self-identification has become one of the main themes of public discussion. Soldiers from the front are asking friends to send them books on Ukrainian history. We have seen an explosion of interest in classical Ukrainian literature and modern Ukrainian poetry. Putin, with his statements to the effect that Ukrainians do not exist, provoked in us a desire to feel and act as Ukrainian as possible. The process of Ukrainisation is now unstoppable. Ukrainianness has become a powerful weapon in the defence of our country.

Ukrainian has long been the language I use for public communication, for radio and television interviews and meetings with readers. I also write articles for newspapers and non-fiction in Ukrainian, although I still write novels in my native language. Now, because most bookshops refuse to sell books in Russian, my books are immediately translated into Ukrainian for the domestic market. Morally, I am prepared for the fact that my books will not be published in the language in which I write them. Russian will become my "internal" language, just as Ukrainian was the internal language of my school friend who was forced to speak Russian at school, while with his parents at home he used Ukrainian.

If I am honest, I can see that my self-identification as a Ukrainian is more important to me than my native language. To be Ukrainian, especially now, means to be free. I am free. Using this freedom, I maintain the right to my native language even though the language itself has gained the status of "the language of the enemy".

Ukraine was and remains a multi-ethnic state with a dozen active national minorities, each with their own culture and literature, often written in their own language – Crimean Tatar, Hungarian, Russian, Gagauz among them. I see all these languages and cultures as part of my Ukrainianness. Tolerance in inter-ethnic relations is a Ukrainian tradition and the harmony that flows from such tolerance should again flourish in my country, once we have peace.

27.04.2023

"Do I have the right to be tired of this war?"

Speech for the Geneva Conference

No, I do not have the right to be tired of this war. I am not in the trenches. I am not driving a tank on the front line. I am just a slightly displaced civilian, one much less drastically affected than many millions of others. And yet, I regularly feel as though I am homeless. I am not, of course. My house in the village is safe. It was the neighbouring village that was partially destroyed by Russian shelling.

It was in Bucha, Borodyanka and dozens of other towns that thousands of civilians were killed, where women were raped and whole families with children burned in their cars as they tried to escape the Russian atrocities. I saw the burned-out minivans of families that did not make it to western Ukraine, that were unable to carry their passengers far enough away from the merciless aggressors.

We made it. We left Kyiv on the second day of the new invasion. With the sound of artillery fire ringing in our ears, we joined the traffic jam that stretched from Kyiv to the western border.

We have learned what it means to be displaced persons and what it means to be refugees. You cannot completely understand what it is until you have experienced it yourself – leaving your home, knowing that perhaps you would never return but nonetheless hoping that you will be able to, perhaps in just a few days. Hope is the stronger emotion.

Millions of Ukrainians were caught between hope and reality in February 2022. Fifteen months have passed since the day Ukraine was woken up by missile explosions and I have not returned home. I have visited, yes. I went to my home in the same way that I visit my parents' grave, like revisiting your past in your thoughts.

My colleague, Volodymyr Vakulenko, an author of children's books, decided not to leave his home near Kharkiv. He could not imagine becoming a displaced person or a refugee, travelling who-knows-where with his son, who has a learning disability. As soon as his village was occupied, he was taken for interrogation. He returned home, but several days later the Russian military came for him again. This time he did not return. His body was identified only in November. Two bullets from a Makarov pistol were extracted from his body. He was executed in the beginning of March and his body was put into a forest grave alongside those of hundreds of other Ukrainian civilians from in and around the town of Izyum.

When I think of him and his violent death, I cannot help but reflect on the entire history of Russian–Ukrainian relations, of the mass deportations of Ukrainian peasants to Siberia in the 1920s, the generation of Ukrainian writers and poets sent to the

Gulag and executed there in 1937–8, the deportation of Crimean Tatars from their homes on the Crimean Peninsula in 1943 and the ban on their return to their motherland, which was lifted only after the collapse of the Soviet Empire.

Now we are all dealing with a Russian Empire that kills those who want to stay free and independent. We are dealing with a Russian Empire that imprisons Crimean Tatar activists and journalists on fabricated charges, that bans other Crimean Tatars from returning home to their homeland, one that has once more been stolen from them.

Thinking about what Russia has done to Ukraine is painful and tiring. Writing about it is even more painful and tiring, but this is what writers and journalists can do. It is what we must do.

Volodymyr Vakulenko wrote a diary. Before he was taken away by Russian troops for the last time, he buried it under a tree in his garden. His elderly parents knew about this. Once his village was liberated, the diary was dug up. This is his last contribution to Ukrainian literature. It is, indeed, his testament.

I have no right to complain about being a displaced person or refugee. I did not need to hide my diary. I left my papers at home in Kyiv and Kyiv was defended by the Ukrainian Army. My diary travels with me. I make entries most days and I look back at the recent times because it is easier than trying to look ahead. My future and the future of Ukraine depend on the Ukrainian army and the receipt of military and humanitarian help from our allies and partners.

Ukraine is documenting crimes committed on Ukrainian soil by illegal occupiers. More than 80,000 war crimes have already been registered, but this is far from the final number. Ukrainian writers are also engaged in documenting war crimes. They are tracing the whereabouts of thousands of Ukrainian children who were kidnapped and taken to Russia and are trying to find out what happened to the thousands of civilians who went missing in Mariupol, Marinka, Druzhkivka, and the dozens of other towns and hundreds of villages that have been erased from the surface of the earth by Russian artillery and missiles.

Millions of Ukrainians are still displaced. Millions are still living as refugees in Europe and America, even in places as far away as Iceland and Japan. They are all victims of Putin's Russia. Like me, they have no vision of their future. We will not be able to envisage our future until the war is over and Ukraine is free.

In the first volume of *Diary of an Invasion* I wrote of what life is like for this displaced person.

Do I have a right to be tired of writing about the war and the lives of Ukrainians at this time? No, I will have no such right until after the war is over and until the last Russian soldier has left Ukrainian soil.

29.04.2023

The Building Blocks of Victory

The word victory has slowly become banal. It is included in all kinds of greetings, including birthday wishes, "Here's to your birthday, and to victory!" We are, indeed, longing for it and yet we do not quite understand how to achieve it. Many are not even sure what victory would look like.

The most common formula for victory comes from the Office of the President and it is clear and understandable: the return of all occupied and annexed territories to Ukrainian control. This will be the restoration of the Ukrainian state within internationally recognised borders and that means war until the last Russian soldier has left. To achieve this, there will have to be considerable successes on Russian territory, preferably facilitated by Russians themselves because the Ukrainian army will not go into Russia. Ukraine has never had aggressive imperialist intentions.

For Russia to stop wanting to fight, the political elite in the Kremlin must change. Its imperialist values must be replaced by democratic ones. Someday this will happen, although obviously not in the near future. Those who strive for power after Putin will use the same jingoistic slogans and follow in his path because the idea that democracy is no good for Russia, that the country needs authoritarian imperialism, is deeply rooted in the minds of Russian citizens.

Georgia has been living with the consequences of Russian aggression for fifteen years now and, surprisingly, the country's leadership has come to terms with the loss of territories and is trying to restore "normal" relations in air traffic and trade deals. Russian citizens calmly enter Georgia and do so without visas to escape from being mobilised in the war in Ukraine. Getting used to the consequences of an unjust war pushes aside thoughts of possible victory or revenge. This, it seems, is what has happened in Georgia.

In Ukraine only one other word can compete with the word victory in terms of how frequently it is used. That word is counter-offensive. For many Ukrainians, these two words have become almost synonymous. They are sure that the counter-offensive will lead to victory. Any sober-minded person, while realising that victory is impossible without a counter-offensive, understands that after the counter-offensive a new line of contact, a new front line, will be created. Only once that line is the border with Russia will it be possible to shift focus to ensuring that Ukraine's eastern neighbour does not break in again.

I want to believe that the Ukrainian army will reach the border with Russia, as it did during the liberation of Kharkiv region, but if this does not happen, Ukraine will have to prepare for a further counter-offensive. Again, we will need to accumulate ammunition and weapons – and do so under constant shelling.

The word victory in its new Ukrainian meaning is more specific than any of the Russian versions of the word. At first, Russia defined victory as the capture of the entire country, then the capture of all of Ukraine except its western territories, and then the capture of Kyiv. Now Russian "victory" means the capture of the ruins of Bakhmut, Marinka, and Avdiivka. Yet the Russian army is struggling, even with this victory. They are not ready to lose this war, although they have been losing it for a long time. This is precisely what explains the constantly changing stated goals of the "Special Military Operation".

Ukraine has already achieved many small victories that work towards a future big victory and not all of them are directly linked to the Russian aggression. Ukraine will need victory many times over and on many domestic fronts: on the front line against corruption and incompetence, on the reform front and even on the ideological front. Victory is needed because a significant part of the population remains in silent opposition to any change, seemingly indifferent to the future of their country.

For several months, in the town of Pervomaisk in Donbas they have discussed the renaming of their city. What should replace the Soviet-era name which honours May 1, Labour Day? Young activists proposed a dozen new names and even organ-ised online and offline voting, which determined that the name Dobrodar (Good Gifts) was the most popular. However, the local council decided not to consider the issue. The activists were given to understand that only about 700 out of the 30,000 residents took part in the vote, the rest appearing satisfied with the old name of the city. That is probably how it is.

The question now is whether the activists will give up, or continue to fight to get rid of the name associated with Soviet history. Knowing our national character, I assume that the struggle will continue and, in the end, will achieve victory for the new Ukraine. But will this happen before the big victory or after it? I do not know.

I do not doubt that these tiny battles inside Ukraine are being carefully watched by Russia and any defeats for pro-European forces will motivate Russian politicians to fight further. They say that they want to liberate Ukrainians, the ones who sit quietly on their sofas and wait for the war to end and for everything to go back to being as it was. It is they who are being addressed when the Russians promise to return all the renamed Ukrainian cities to their former Soviet names, to reinstate Lenin and Marx in street names. Inside Russia, they are even going to change the name of the city of Volgograd, reverting to the former Soviet name of Stalingrad. This demonstrates to Russians, Ukrainians, and the whole world the position to which the authorities wish to return the country and all the lands that Russia manages to seize.

It would be more just to rename Volgograd as Bakhmut, in memory of that destroyed city and the tens of thousands of dead Ukrainian civilians who died as a result of Russia's criminal attack on a neighbouring country. This could be considered a significant act of repentance.

After that, we could talk about a big, full-fledged victory – after Russia's victory over itself.

02.05.2023

A Displaced Person

It is sad when age or illness brings radical and unwanted changes to our life. Yet we might be able to accept these changes as a natural part of life. What we cannot accept are changes that are forced on us by violent acts of cruelty. When this happens, a person feels that they still have the same character, the same abilities; what has changed is that someone decided to destroy your house, your street, your city, and even your country. You are then forced to leave your home. You go on thinking that you will return in a couple of days, that the aggressor will be stopped and everything will soon be put in order. You do not take much with you because you are sure you will return soon. After a week or so, you begin to understand the term used to describe your new status – you are a "displaced person". It is not only the physical person who has become displaced. Your thoughts and actions, your vision of the past, the present and the future have all been tossed into the air. If you worked, your job is gone. If you were retired, your retirement is over. You now need to be active again to survive, to help others and to keep abreast of what is happening in a world turned upside down.

07.05.2023

War Films and War Reality

The other day, in reports from the front, my attention was drawn to the news that the Russian screenwriter Leonid Korin was killed during fighting in Bakhmut. At first, I assumed that

191

Korin had been in Bakhmut as part of some television film group, sent from Moscow to record the Russian army's "heroic struggle" against the "Ukrainian fascists". However, it soon became clear that the screenwriter had signed a contract with the Wagner private army a few months earlier and that he had been killed during a battle with the Ukrainian army. In other words, just like the infamous writer Zahar Prilepin, Korin had exchanged the pen for a Kalashnikov assault rifle and had gone to kill Ukrainians. As a result, he has met his own end.

Between 2012 and 2015, Korin was one of the scriptwriters for the ambitious Russian–Ukrainian film project "Battle for Sevastopol", a film about the most famous female sniper in the Soviet army, Lyudmila Pavlichenko. In 1942, Pavlichenko participated in the battle to defend Sevastopol during which, according to Soviet military historians, she shot and killed 309 German soldiers. While those historians were no more concerned with the truth than today's Russian propagandists, this number is not unrealistic. Pavlichenko was Ukrainian, born near Kyiv.

The film footage was used to make both a feature film and a television series. Its original language was Russian but Ukrainian and English versions were also made. The main roles in the film are played by Russian actors, with episodic roles played by Ukrainians. 70 per cent. of the film's budget came from Ukraine, including money from the Ukrainian state budget. Russia invested 30 per cent. The film was shot largely on location in Sevastopol, although some filming was carried out in Kyiv, Odesa and in a small town on the border with Moldova. The most interesting thing about this is that the filming ended only in July 2014, that is, after the annexation of Crimea and the start of the war in Donbas. The premieres of the film in Russia and Ukraine took place on the same day, on April 2, 2015. Yulia Peresild, who played the sniper Pavlichenko, travelled from Moscow to Kyiv to attend the premiere; this was during one of the bloodiest phases of the Russian–Ukrainian war.

True, in Ukraine, the film was renamed. It was released under the title, "The Unbreakable", so as not to irritate Ukrainians with mention of Sevastopol in the recently annexed Crimea. By the way, the television premiere of the film also took place simultaneously in Russia and Ukraine, on May 9, 2015, fifteen months after the annexation of Crimea.

Very little has been written about this film in Ukraine. Probably, the Ukrainian producer, and the apparent author of the idea for the film, Yegor Olesov, as well as other Ukrainian participants in the project, were by then not very comfortable about advertising their joint Russian–Ukrainian film project about World War II, while Russian attacks on Ukraine were taking place. Nonetheless, the project was completed and the distribution rights to the film were acquired by 20th Century Fox.

You can probably understand why, when I learned about the death of screenwriter Leonid Korin, I imagined that he had been killed by a sniper – perhaps even a Ukrainian female sniper. That would be poetic, although it did not happen like that. Korin died in Bakhmut from shrapnel wounds after a shell exploded nearby. Significantly, there is a scene like that in the film "Battle for Sevastopol", where the partner of the main character, a male sniper, covers the heroine with his own body when a shell explodes. He too dies from shrapnel wounds.

The Ukrainian producer of that joint Russian–Ukrainian film project, Yegor Olesov, is now preparing a feature film about atrocities perpetrated by the Russian invaders in Bucha. Meanwhile, Sergey Mokritsky, the Russian director of the film "Battle for Sevastopol" and his wife Natalia, who was the film's producer from the Russian side, are shooting an adventure film near annexed Sevastopol. The film is about a treasure hunt set around a British ship that sunk in the mid-nineteenth century during the Crimean War. The same Russian actors from "Battle for Sevastopol" are involved, but unless you include the regular drone attacks against military facilities in Sevastopol, there is no Ukrainian participation in this project.

The première of this adventure film is scheduled for 2023 but I am not sure it will take place in Sevastopol. Crimea is gradually being turned into a huge fortress. Several lines of trenches have been dug on the beaches and kilometres of concrete fortifications have been built close to the isthmus that unites the peninsula with mainland Ukraine. Crimea is not expecting tourists but a major war, that of the Ukrainian army's counter-offensive, which has been heralded many times by Ukrainian military leaders and politicians, including President Zelensky.

In all the occupied Ukrainian territories, the Russian army is waiting for the Ukrainian counter-offensive. In Kherson region, residents of occupied villages and towns close to the front line are being forced to evacuate their homes and Russian troops are moving into their apartments and houses. The same thing is happening in the occupied areas of Zaporizhzhia region, where the Russians are trying to force more than 18,000 residents to leave.

Ukrainians, who have been also looking forward to the Ukrainian counter-offensive since April, continue to wait. There is already a hint of annoyance and fatigue. Explanations that the wet weather is causing the delay do not convince all the country's citizens. Many begin to suspect that the West has not yet provided the Ukrainian army with the necessary stocks of weapons and ammunition to mount the counter-offensive.

In Russia, people are also living in a state of tension. Increasingly, they ask, "where is victory?" and more and more often, T.V. commentators or talk show guests make excuses – "Russia is fighting against N.A.T.O. and almost the entire world. Under such conditions, it is impossible to win quickly!"

Recently, fewer promises of an early victory have been heard from the lips of Russian politicians. Even in the daily television talk shows about the war, which are supposed to maintain a high degree of vigorous patriotism in Russian society, doubts about the possibility of victory over Ukraine are being voiced increasingly often. Viewers are losing interest even in once-popular propagandists like Olga Skabeeva or Vladimir Solovyov. On the other hand, there has been a sharp increase in interest in Russian mass media in the mostly non-Russian "foretellers of the future" and other such visionaries.

In recent months, Russian television has been popularising the Afghan mathematician and "Nostradamus of the twenty-first century", Sediq Afghan, who studied in the U.S.S.R. in the 1980s and who later lived in Moscow for some time. Sediq Afghan has already promised Russian television viewers that the American presidential election in 2024 will be the last before the collapse of the United States of America. He predicts the complete disintegration of the European Union in the period 2027–32. He has also assured Russian viewers of complete victory for Russia over Ukraine and the revival of the Soviet Union. By the way, in spring 1991, Sediq Afghan was deported from the Soviet Union for predicting that the U.S.S.R. would break up into 44 different states.

Not so long ago, Russian television found another visionary who inspires confidence. In the minds of less well-educated Russians, a real seer should be blind, like the famous Bulgarian soothsayer Vanga who, by the way, predicted in 1993 that the

Soviet Union would be reborn by 2025 and that Bulgaria would become part of the new U.S.S.R.

Nikolay Tarasenko, an elderly, severely visually impaired man from Donbas, began to predict the future in 2014. Before that, he is said to have had the power of healing through touch. His televised messages mirror those of Russian politicians but he uses simpler words; he speaks "in the language of the people".

"America is finished," he said on the popular Russian T.V. channel N.T.V., "not because I want that, but because America has outlived itself. The United States, as a state, will not exist at all. Geological, climatic and social cataclysms will begin. The people are now ready to break up into smaller states, into republics."

According to him, the American financial system will also be shaken. Other states will move away from settlement in American dollars and this will undermine the country's economy. "Soon dollars will fly like litter in the streets," he said in an interview on the N.T.V. channel. He also predicts catastrophic inflation in America, blaming the war "unleashed by the Americans in Ukraine" for all of this. He predicts victory for Russia by Easter 2024.

Against this background, Ukrainian television looks pale and boring in comparison. Not a single seer, visually impaired or sighted, has predicted the date of Ukraine's victory over Russia. Perhaps that is why in discussions and television shows on Ukrainian television they more often argue about something else – what could be considered a victory for Ukraine and what kind of victory it should be.

Everyone agrees that the liberation of all occupied and annexed territories of the Ukrainian state can be considered a victory for Ukraine. However, everyone also agrees that even after the possible liberation of the occupied territories, the Russian threat will remain. This means that the war should end not only with a military victory but also with a peace treaty with Russia and security guarantees for Ukraine from individual Western countries and the N.A.T.O. military bloc.

For me the final proof of Ukraine's victory would be a joint Ukrainian–Russian film production about the fate of one of the many Ukrainian female snipers in this war. It might be called "Battle for Bakhmut". Russia will volunteer to pay 70 per cent. of the budget and Ukraine can put in 30 per cent. Of course, the main roles would be played by Ukrainian actors, while Russian actors can play secondary roles, such as that of the Wagner Leader, Prigozhin, the film scriptwriter Korin, or the roles of ordinary Russian soldiers and mercenaries.

17.05.2023

Rain, Snow and Ashes

The Battle for Ukraine's Collective Memory
(Speech to the American Academy of Arts and Letters)

What do I remember about my early childhood, about the time when I could already hear and see the world around me but could not reflect on it or describe it in words? This was the time when my vocabulary was limited to sounds that I used almost exclusively to draw attention to myself.

I remember an old, two-storey, wooden house, with blackened walls. I remember a wooden staircase leading up to the second floor, the creaking of those steps under adult feet. At least, I think I remember that house and how it was so old that it sometimes wobbled quite perceptively, although not so much as to scare me. I was still wobbly myself. Was I confusing the building's instability with my own?

Beyond the windows of this house, it rained constantly. Water poured down the windowpanes, blurring the world outside. At first, I could not understand what rain was. I thought the windows were crying, that they were the eyes of a house in pain.

I spent the first 24 months of my life there and have returned only a couple of times afterwards, to visit my grandmother at the age of four or five. One of those visits took place in the winter and I arrived to see the roof of the wooden house covered in snow so that it looked like a white-haired old man. The snow was trying to hide everything dark and ugly, to give our eyes a rest and to make the world appear more beautiful, cleaner and more kind.

Of course, I remember later moments of my life much more clearly – or I think I do. All too often, when I reminisce out loud, my older brother or my wife will correct me, "It wasn't quite like that! It was different!" Yes, I cannot claim objectivity in my memories: they are both documentary and artistic, like a novel based on real events. My memory edits the story of my life. A country's collective memory can be a bit like that too. Significant events can be forgotten or misrepresented out of fear or ignorance, or even out of love. Equally, a new generation can "adopt" and feel they own the memories of previous generations.

It was both personal and collective memory that made my mother save every scrap of stale bread, the memory of the hardship she experienced as a child during World War II. I did not go through that, but I could not help adopting my mother's memory. I "remember" the cruelty of the local people in the village to which she and my grandmother were evacuated, who gave them only potato peelings, and I remain careful not to waste food myself.

Regular bombardments of Kyiv are to blame for my new habit of checking the thickness of the external and internal walls of any building I enter. I am following the "rule of two walls", which may at least save you from being injured by flying glass. I am sure my grandchildren will know this rule too, though they are yet to be born.

Our collective memory affects how we think and act, impacting what happens today and how history will be written about tomorrow. All Ukraine is involved in the creation of new "rooms" in our collective memory – and not only Ukrainians. You too are involved. Your attitude, your support and understanding, your practical and financial help are putting a positive stamp on Ukraine's collective memory. This is something that makes me proud to become part of the American Academy of Arts and Letters.

Right now, the world is acquiring collective knowledge of Russian aggression in Ukraine. The depth of that knowledge, the clarity and the nature of the memory it stamps on us, depend on the communities with which we are associated. I share a memory of this horror with three overlapping but distinct communities. The first is the largest. It is all the citizens of Ukraine, wherever they may be – a population that has agonised over the war since 2014 and, since February 2022, must agonise on the run, under shelling, or (hardest of all) under occupation.

The second group is that of war-displaced people. I became one of them on the second day of the new Russian invasion, when my wife and I left our apartment in Kyiv and drove to western Ukraine, in the opposite direction to the front line. Four months later I "upgraded" to the status of refugee in France.

My experience of joining that community turned out to be no less dramatic and no less fascinating than the previous two.

Last autumn, I managed to return to Kyiv and tried out life under air raids. When I left Kyiv again, it was not as a fugitive but as a person who had something to tell about the war, about the Russian aggression and about Ukraine.

I now realise that the Ukrainian collective memory has become one of the important energies in the struggle for our existence and the independence of our country. It is like a living organism being fed every day with new information and experiences, mostly with negative energy but with some sparks of light too.

The experience of war determines national interests and national taste in literature and art and, as if in a Freudian experiment, sets the themes of our dreams. It also pushes us into self-censorship of our words, thoughts and even our feelings. These side-effects of the war also affect our collective memory; doubtless, some aspects will be challenged in the future – in a peaceful future.

The current history of Ukraine is full of stories of fierce individualism and an unwillingness blindly to follow authority. And yet, these stories are the rallying cry that has welded the population into a living fortress in which we stand united against the enemy. I cannot help but ask myself what is this magic that changed a notoriously unruly population of individualists into a disciplined, fighting force? (I am talking about ordinary Ukrainian civilians here, not our military, of course!) How many Ukrainians grew up treasuring the history of Ukraine's struggle for independence? How many of us shared in Ukraine's collective memory? I did not, for one. The old house I told you about was in Russia. My parents were Soviet people. Their behaviour was shaped by the hardships of wartime life and the restricting pressure of the Soviet regime. Some 40 per cent. of Ukrainians come from a similar background.

Until recently, very few Ukrainians had any idea about the country's history, especially about Russia's negative impact on Ukrainian culture and language. For both the tsarist and the communist regimes, Ukraine's independent spirit was a major threat. Both those regimes did their best to undermine that spirit and to silence any mention of the policies they used to suppress it, or the tragedies that resulted from these policies. Not surprisingly, in 1991, independent Ukraine was born with collective amnesia.

Since then, a truer picture of Ukraine's history has emerged gradually. Individuals and groups studying this picture have used their newly acquired knowledge to analyse the conflicting forces at work in Ukrainian society. After two revolutions, and now this war, almost all Ukrainians have had an opportunity to compare the falsified "history" presented by Russia with other, more reliable, accounts.

It seems that we Ukrainians are clinging to this newly unearthed history, even those of us who are first-generation Ukrainians. We cling to it as if it were our own grandparents who were shot for speaking Ukrainian or starved to death for refusing to join a collective farm. This newly acquired understanding of Ukrainian history, the accuracy of which has been so demonically confirmed by Russia's current aggression, allows each Ukrainian to claim ownership of the fortress that is the country's collective memory.

In the most recent works by Ukrainian artists, you may be upset to find that ruins and desolation predominate. You may see burnt-out cars and murdered people; images of a previously happy life covered with ashes. Even our abstract artists have taken to painting figuratively, portraying the hard reality.

This year, spring flowers are not a subject for Ukrainian artists. In Ukraine, the end of May is usually a time of thunderstorms and heavy, green, pollen-filled rains. The thunderstorms will frighten many Ukrainians for a long time to come, but rain will always be welcome. It washes away the superficial traces of the atrocities we have witnessed, the blood and the ashes. These elements will blend into the soil, nourishing life and this, in turn, will nourish our future, indirectly feeding our love for our country.

I hope that next winter's snow will cover some of the ugly signs of destruction and decorate the new buildings, bridges, and parks that are already appearing, as Ukraine makes tentative steps toward its future.

Do I look forward to next winter's snow? Not really. I look forward to this terrible war becoming history, to the fixing in our collective memory of a moment when peace returned to Ukraine – a tender word alongside euphoria that will transfer into poetry and novels, movies and symphonies, fine art and architecture. The memory of that moment will remain as a monument to the value of human life, freedom and independence.

Alas, the ashes of this war will also remain in Ukraine's collective memory for generations to come.

22.05.2023

Icons and Other Messages

Even when I am abroad and visit someone, the first thing I pay attention to automatically is the thickness of the outer and inner walls. Without conscious thought, my brain independently checks the level of security of each location. I am planning for shelling by Russian missiles or Iranian drones. I am afraid this automatic habit will stay with me for a long time. This war has accustomed us to danger and the need to be ready for anything, including a nuclear explosion. However, being prepared does not guarantee survival.

When a person is constantly preparing for an external threat, he forgets about the internal threats, about his or her health. The number of Ukrainians dying from heart disease has increased dramatically and from other diseases too. The reason for this is both stress and the notion that medicine should now devote all its attention to the wounded soldiers, not civilians. Many people find it inappropriate to go to the doctor with their problems when the country's problems are a thousand times more serious. These people, who are dying from treatable but untreated illnesses, not from bullets and shells, are also victims of Russian aggression.

For three weeks Kyivites have been sleeping in their corridors or bathrooms. The most indefatigable have grab bags ready and go to spend the night sitting or lying in bomb shelters or deep in one of Kyiv's metro stations. When morning comes, cafés open and people go to work as if there was no war. How long can this go on and how does it affect the human psyche? For people who have remained in Ukraine, their anger and hatred towards Russia and all Russians must be accumulating.

Meanwhile, there are various signs that some Russians are still opposing the war, though not in public and usually only at night when everyone is asleep. For example, in Novosibirsk, on the night of May 15, somebody wrote the words "Thou shalt not murder" on the fence of an Orthodox church dedicated to the new holy martyrs of Russia. This is, of course, a direct quote from the Old Testament's ten commandments. However, in the Russian news, the inscription was called provocative, and a representative of Novosibirsk's metropolitan described what had happened as "an act of barbarism and lawlessness". The police and Russian special services are looking for the author of the inscription, but the results of this search have not yet been reported.

In mid-May, a church court in Moscow defrocked a priest by the name of John Koval who served in the church of St Andrew in the Moscow district of Lyublino. Koval was found guilty of making an unsanctioned change to the "Prayer for Holy Rus" which has been read during services in all orthodox churches in Russia since the country invaded Ukraine. He replaced the word "victory" with the word "peace". For this, the priest has been expelled from the church. Most likely, his problems will not end there.

May has been rich in news concerning Russia's spiritual life. At the beginning of the month, Putin sent two identical icons to the south and east of Ukraine, where Russians are fighting. Each icon is accompanied by a priest who must ensure that the icons visit all Russian military locations, including the frontline trenches and dugouts. Except for Muslim soldiers, each Russian combatant will touch the holy image with their lips, so that the icon can imbue them with confidence in Russia's victory.

Father Vyacheslav, who is accompanying one of the icons across the southern territory, believes that it will take him more than a month to visit all the Russian troop positions. Commenting on the reaction among the troops, he said, "To see this image, received from the hands of the President in their dugouts is, of course, an honour and joy."

According to the plan, both icons and their attendants should meet at some point on the front line. Surely, the priests will look for an undamaged church in which to hold a solemn service, during which no-one will dare to replace the word "victory" with the word "peace". However, as far as I am aware, no churches anywhere near the front line have survived the terrible devastation. Perhaps the priests and the Russian military will have to be content with a religious procession along the sad streets of some ruined settlement. They may decide that it is prudent to hold the service in a bunker. After all, the entire front line is the target of artillery fire day and night.

While the Russians look for a quiet spot to reflect on the mystical messages exuding from Putin's icons, some of the projectiles fired at them from Ukrainian cannons carry a rather different kind of message – words inscribed on their metal surfaces. While not strictly in accordance with military regulations, nobody in Ukraine would associate these short texts with "barbarism and lawlessness". On the contrary, the inscriptions on the shells and rockets from multiple-rocket launchers help Ukrainian gunners to expend some of their pent-up emotion. Most often, they write the names of their dead comrades, or the names of cities and villages destroyed by the Russian army: "For brother Kolya", "For Bakhmut", "For Irpin".

Russian gunners also write messages and threats on shells and these battlefield telegrams have been flying in both directions for some time. But recently on the Ukrainian side this activity has transformed into an international movement that can bring tangible help to the army. Several Internet sites now allow you to order your own inscription on a projectile that will fly toward Russian positions. The service is reasonably priced, from $40 to $250. In return, the "customer" receives a photograph showing the inscription they chose embossed on the projectile and sometimes even a video showing the very moment that the missile was launched at the enemy. Naturally, the money received for these inscriptions goes to help the army.

This method of killing several "birds" with one missile was

devised by a twenty-two-year-old student from Cherkasy, Anton Sokolenko. Having realised that many of his friends were serving in the army, including in the artillery forces, he created some Internet advertising that suggested the possibility of "congratulating" the occupiers with a choice message. He was surprised by the enthusiastic response his suggestion received. It turned out to be reasonably simple to negotiate with the Ukrainian soldiers about "the production end" of the project. Apparently, the junior commanders had nothing against it. The higher authorities were not informed about it initially, although they soon caught on. Officially, nobody gave permission for this type of fundraising but no-one forbade it either.

Sokolenko is now a registered volunteer and works with the N.G.O. Centre for Assistance to the Army, Veterans, and Their Families. With the money received from the shell telegrams, he has already bought two Starlink systems, a jeep, and a night vision device for the army.

The inscriptions on the shells are becoming increasingly diverse and some are quite memorable, such as "From Albania, with love" and "Happy Father's Day!"

09.06.2023

Seeking Shelter and a Summer Holiday

Since the destruction of the Kakhovka Dam, Kyiv has experienced fewer air raids. The lack of bomb shelters in urban areas nonetheless remains a big issue. Throughout May, the whole country suffered intensive missile attacks and on June 1, a young woman and a child were killed in Kyiv, near the entrance to a closed bomb shelter. Air raid shelters are now being checked all over Ukraine. The results of these checks are not encouraging. Although a huge budget was allocated for the setting up and repair of shelters, a large number have been found to be in an unfit state or closed, or both.

The two recent deaths in Kyiv have given rise to new attacks on the city's mayor, Vitali Klitschko, including from Zelensky's administration. These accusations have somewhat backfired because the responsibility for bomb shelters is shared equally by the civil administration and the city's military administration, whose officials are appointed directly by the presidential office.

Schools and other educational institutions are also now under scrutiny. According to the rules, their shelters should allow for the continuation of education during air raids. A year ago, Uzhhorod State University was able to hold entrance exams in their underground shelter. However, not all educational institutions have bothered about such facilities and prosecutors' offices are now using threats of legal action against the directors of schools and colleges in order to force them to clean up their basements and make education possible.

In Chernihiv, the regional court recently ordered the director of a school in Kozeletsky district to repair its shelter. The judge did not accept the director's excuse that no funding had been allocated for the work. Indeed, many tasks aimed at ensuring the safety of the civilian population are being carried out without any extra funding. To some extent, this stems from the Soviet tradition of requiring parents to pay for and carry out repairs to school premises during the holidays. The city administrations are finding other free sources of labour for such tasks. For more than a year, the "Army of Renewal" has been working in Chernihiv. This consists of people who are officially registered as unemployed and who agree to participate in work to repair shelters and other facilities in the city and the wider region. Some 3000 unemployed people are currently helping in this way.

Chernihiv region, located on the border with Belarus and Russia, is large and sparsely populated. There are few roads and many swamps and rivers. Some villages are difficult to reach. When the Russian army seized part of the region in March last year, it was unable to gain much of a foothold because of the nature of the terrain. In the end, they had to retreat.

In recent months, Russia has regularly attacked border villages and towns with rockets, drones and artillery but has made no new attempts to seize territory. That is probably why the Mezinsky nature reserve, which covers more than 300 square kilometres and is only an hour's drive from the Russian border, has opened its hotels and started inviting lovers of nature and ornithologists to come and enjoy the summer there. The reserve boasts two museums and, for archaeology enthusiasts, there are more than 50 sites of interest, including the remains of an ancient settlement from the Paleolithic era that is more than 20,000 years old. The war has required some adjustments to the rules for visiting the reserve. You can no longer go kayaking and boating on the rivers and lakes but you can ride jeeps along a specially prepared forest route. For S.U.V. owners, there are also opportunities to test your driving skills and the capabilities of your car.

The thousand-year-old city of Chernihiv is trying to live an ordinary life. Shops, cafés and theatres are all open for custom but tourists from other regions of Ukraine are in no hurry to visit. The all-Ukrainian competition for young pianists, which is held in Chernihiv every two years, was this year attended by participants from only two other regions of the country – the frontline regions of Kharkiv and Mykolaev. Anastasia Grushko, from Kharkiv College of Music, who won first prize in the competition, said that the biggest challenge had been the constant air raid warnings, which made preparation very difficult. Nonetheless, she has two reasons to feel lucky – there were no sirens during her performance and she fulfilled her dream of playing with a symphony orchestra.

The border with Russia in Chernihiv region can certainly be called a front line. Few people live there anymore. The villages have been mostly left in ruins. In contrast, the border with Belarus is quiet and calm, running as it does through impenetrable swamps and forests. Locals, of course, know all the secret paths and tracks, but for strangers this terrain is deadly. During World War II, thousands of German soldiers died in these swamps.

Now the checkpoints on the border with Belarus are closed, official trade with Russia's ally is prohibited, but smugglers continue quietly to ply their trade. Smuggling activity here is very different from what goes on along the western borders of Ukraine, where cigarettes are the principal illegal commodity. Judging by the latest news, the main product being smuggled from Belarus is insect repellent. Before the appearance of the Russian army, the main enemies of residents of Chernihiv region were mosquitoes.

Recently, local entrepreneurs tried to smuggle a batch of repellent by car from Belarus through Poland to Chernihiv region. Almost three and a half tons of fumigator plates were discovered by Ukrainian customs officials. The cargo was confiscated, but I hope that it will eventually end up in Chernihiv region, one of the most mosquito-blighted regions of Ukraine. Apart from anything else, the less Chernihiv region residents need to worry about mosquitoes, the faster they will be able to put their bomb shelters in order.

Since the start of summer, more buses have appeared on

Ukrainian roads leading to Moldova and Poland. The buses run between Ukrainian cities and airports in neighbouring countries. Ukrainians who can afford to and who are free to leave the country, are keen to go on holiday to Greece and Turkey, where the sea is warm and where there is no gunfire.

There are fewer Ukrainian holidaymakers abroad this year than in pre-Covid years, but they have become more demanding. Many Ukrainians planning to go to Turkey ask travel agencies to find them hotels where there are no Russians. Last summer, resorts in Turkey saw many conflicts and even fights between Ukrainians and Russians. Russians often wear T-shirts adorned with the letter Z or other symbols to show their support for the war in Ukraine and for President Putin. Ukrainians also wear T-shirts with their national symbols like the trident and often sport clothes in the colours of the Ukrainian flag, yellow and blue.

In Turkey, a list of hotels and hotel chains guaranteeing a "Russian-free holiday" has already appeared. They tend to be more expensive, five-star operations, and include the hotel chains Tui Blue, Tui Magic Life and T.T. Hotels. They have all announced that they no longer accept bookings from Russian tourists. The list of hotels without Russians is growing.

The number of Russian tourists going abroad has also decreased owing to the war and the worsening economic situation. Internal tourism is nonetheless being widely advertised, for example, for trips to Siberia and Lake Baikal. For Russians living in the Far East, China has entire resort towns ready to welcome their neighbours.

This summer the Black Sea coast of the Russian North Caucasus is unlikely to boast an influx of tourists. The only Russian-owned cruise ship in the Black Sea, the *Prince Vladimir*, has cancelled its cruise schedule for this summer, which traditionally featured visits to Sevastopol and Yalta. It will now only sail between the city of Sochi, where Putin's summer palace is located and the region of Abkhazia, seized from Georgia in 2008. Russian tourists who want to relax on the Black Sea coast will mostly go to Georgia, which is both safer and cheaper.

It seems the economic benefits from the influx of Russian tourists and "mobilisation refugees" are too enticing for Georgians to ignore.

In the occupied territories of Ukraine, in Mariupol, Novo-azovsk, and other Azov Sea coast towns, residents share the beaches with the Russian military, although they prefer to relax away from hotels and resort complexes where Russian soldiers and officers are now barracked – and which tend to be the target of Ukrainian rockets.

Life in the occupied territories has become strangely quiet, if not silent. After regular attacks on collaborators and the Russian military by Ukrainian partisans, teams of Russian intelligence officers have arrived in the regions to identify residents with pro-Ukrainian views. Initially they focused on using taxi drivers, ordering them to chat with their passengers so that the passengers revealed their political views. The taxi drivers were supposed to denounce those who appeared dissatisfied with the occupation. In the occupied territories, taxi journeys now take place in silence. A taxi in the occupied territories is not a good place to let down your guard.

Employees of the Russian special services also pay special attention to those residents of the occupied territories who do not want to take Russian citizenship. There are so many of them that Putin has signed a special decree allowing the deportation of Ukrainians from occupied territories if they refuse to take Russian citizenship.

Nonetheless, plenty of Ukrainians have taken up Russian

passports. For men, the main drawback is that they can be drafted into the Russian army and sent to the front. Over the past year, among enemy soldiers captured by the Ukrainian forces, an increasing number are residents of eastern or southern Ukraine. The Ukrainians captured in Russian military uniform rarely want to return to the occupied territories through the prisoner exchange scheme. That would mean a return to the front.

Ukrainian law recognises that these men were issued with Russian passports illegally and often under pressure. However, as citizens of Ukraine, if captured with weapons in their hands, they are traitors to their homeland and will either be charged with treason in Ukraine or exchanged for captured Ukrainian soldiers, a lose-lose situation for those involved. Perhaps Ukraine could use these unhappy people to create a special "army of renewal" for the repair and construction of new bomb shelters across the country. After all, the entire centre of Kyiv, destroyed during World War II, was rebuilt by captured German soldiers.

16.06.2023

Hotbeds of Civil Society

Since the Soviet era, the etiquette of alcohol consumption in Ukraine has dictated that before you take each sip of alcohol, a toast must be made. It might be a long speech or a short phrase but, traditionally, you cannot take a drink until someone has announced to what or to whom you are drinking. For fifteen months now, at home, in restaurants and bars, Ukrainians have been drinking "To victory!" As we watched the arrest in Moscow of an ex-F.S.B. man, the pro-Russian war nationalist

Girkin, a more recent phrase was the now oft-repeated toast, "Let's drink to them all destroying each other!"

During this war, while restaurants and cafés have maintained their role as centres of gastronomic culture, bars have tended to become platforms of civil society where like-minded people gather to share in and develop a sense of national unity. Regular clients feel like members of a family sharing mutual concern and a strong desire to help in Ukraine's future.

Recently, the well-known Kyiv bartender Bohdan "Bodya" Kuzminsky took leave of his friends. He was going to join the army. Bodya was seen off by all his colleagues and the regulars at Kyiv's legendary bar Barman Diktat, which is located under 44 Khreshchatyk Street. The entrance to the bar is through a narrow yard. Going into it is like entering a bomb shelter. Quite possibly that was one of the earlier functions of these spacious subterranean premises. The cellar was privatised and has since been resold several times, becoming what it is today, a very cosy and much-loved bar for Kyivites and brave expatriates who, despite the almost daily rocket and drone attacks on Kyiv, have not been driven out of the city.

There are several such underground bars in the centre of Kyiv. They are usually open by four o'clock in the afternoon. In the evening, they become very crowded, although no-one complains. The patrons have a dual motivation for choosing these underground "watering holes" – to relieve stress and to spend a few hours in the safety of their underground shelter. The bars are able to go on with their programmes of cultural events and entertainment uninterrupted by missile attacks.

At Barman Diktat, concerts are often preceded by meetings of the History Lovers' Club, featuring "Stories for Adults" – discussions about relevant historical topics. These discussions are sometimes led by the writer Oleg Kryshtopa, sometimes by the literary critic Nastia Evdokimova, and sometimes by the two of them together with specially invited guests, experts in one or another area of history or contemporary life. The discussions are recorded on video and posted on a YouTube channel under the same name, "Stories for Adults". Slowly, the channel is gaining popularity and the number of subscribers has already passed the quarter of a million mark.

The topic of one of these discussions was the personality of the writer Mykola Gogol. The main question asked was, "Can Gogol be considered a Ukrainian writer?" Over one or two glasses of whisky – after all, the hour-and-a-half discussion took place in a bar! – the participants concluded that he can indeed be considered Ukrainian. However, they added that the theme of Gogol's identity could be explored to eternity as he will always be seen as bestriding both Russian and Ukrainian culture. When staying in a German hotel he registered himself as Ukrainian, but he described himself as a Russian writer.

When that public discussion about Gogol took place, Bodya was still standing with his colleagues at the bar, making cocktails and pouring whisky and rum for customers. Now he is in a military unit, defending Ukraine.

Among the regular customers at the Barman Diktat, there are many veterans who have returned from the front, some owing to injury. The bar is a labyrinth of rooms and the veterans usually gather in one of its furthest corners. When they leave, they have to walk through the main bar area, which is always crowded and noisy, where the stage is set at one end. As the veterans pass, a perceptible hush falls over the room. Both fear and admiration show in the hidden glances of the other customers.

The bar's lively atmosphere might give the impression that everything in Kyiv is fine, but everyone present is aware of the plethora of problems that the war has brought to the city, both above and below ground. The business of checking access to bomb shelters has exposed another problem. Some of the officials responsible for keeping the shelters open have defended themselves by saying that they keep the shelters closed to keep the homeless out. With the outbreak of the war, the term "homeless" has taken on new meaning. Now in Kyiv and other major cities, volunteers and charities are feeding tens of thousands of people living on the streets, including a huge number of those who have been made homeless by the Russian bombardments. The number of homeless people in Kyiv has increased many times over.

Residents of the destroyed cities and villages of Donbas, Zaporizhzhia, and Kherson regions have also become *de facto* homeless. Today, a percentage of Kyiv's homeless are former residents of these regions. They have not been able to find a job or get temporary housing in Kyiv. Many have lost their documents and so are unable to access government assistance programmes.

Kyiv has long suffered from a shortage of shelters and organised social assistance for the homeless. One of the most active charitable organisations helping the homeless in Kyiv is the Catholic group San Egidio. They are now also helping internally displaced adults and children in Kyiv and other cities in Ukraine.

In the town of Vinniki near Lviv, another organisation has been helping the homeless since 2003. Oselya (Home) is a mutual aid centre and partner of Emmaus International, an organisation created after World War II by the French activist Abbé Pierre. During its twenty years of activity, Oselya has facilitated a return to normal life for several hundred formerly homeless people, many of whom suffered from alcoholism. The main rules for those accepted to live in the centre are the complete rejection of alcohol and a willingness to work in the commune. At Oselya, people learn new skills, including techniques for repairing old and antique furniture – skills that allow the residents to earn money, as well as to improve their own home environment.

At the beginning of the Russian invasion, the twelve former homeless people who were living at Oselya volunteered for the army. Their places were taken immediately by other homeless people who came from the east and south of Ukraine. Since the start of the war, under the leadership of Natalia Sanotska, Oselya has built another two-storey centre to serve refugees in Vynnyki, who can now also be called homeless. The centre has showers, washing machines and a free hairdressing salon. On the second floor, there is a cinema hall where films are shown free of charge in the evenings. Natalya Sanotska selects very carefully the films to be shown. They should be films that help relieve stress and support a certain level of optimism. Recently, Natalia had to make a difficult decision – to repurpose the furniture repair workshops into living space. It is big enough to house twenty or more people.

The distinction between displaced persons, refugees and those traditionally thought of as homeless is gradually becoming blurred. None have enough money to live on. All have problems with housing and it is very difficult for any to imagine their future. True, having a vision of the future is difficult for all Ukrainians now, whether they are living in their own apartments, or wandering around the world, or living as displaced people in Ukraine.

Now Ukrainians who have not had to leave their homes are automatically considered prosperous. They tend to be those who have also been able to keep their jobs, which means they have money to live on. Even so, they can still suffer from stress, just like those who are in much worse situations. There is an almost universal need to get away from reality for a while. For this, some go to the theatre, others have taken up yoga and yet others visit the bar. However, the war has firmly and permanently entered into every sphere of life and every art form. It is hard to get away from it. Ukraine's theatres have cancelled performances of classical Russian plays and replaced them with Ukrainian plays about war and refugees. In the bars veterans from the war are increasingly visible. Some of them wear camouflage out of habit.

Bodya's colleague, a bartender at a partner bar on the left bank of the Dnipro River, also called Barman Diktat, has already returned from the front but with one hand missing. He is currently unemployed and dreaming of returning to his former workplace. His colleagues are organising a fundraising campaign to buy him a high-quality prosthesis. The campaign will include more "Stories for Adults" events and concerts.

I hope that Bohdan "Bodya" will be back from the war safe and sound and will stand behind the counter again and create some new cocktails, so that customers can join in the happy task of coming up with some suitably peaceful names for them.

29.06.2023

The Role of Culture after the War

During the first months of the new Russian invasion in February 2022, alongside discussions about combat operations, there was active debate in Ukrainian society about the country's future reconstruction. Activists announced the establishment of foundations to raise funds for reconstruction. Foreign architects presented their visions and projects. Western European cities and even entire countries announced which areas of Ukraine they would "take under their wing" to assist with the restoration of infrastructure, roads, and buildings.

Since then the war has dragged on. The toll of destruction has mounted and discussions about Ukraine's post-war reconstruction have receded into the background. Local reconstruction work continues in Kyiv region, where Russian rockets and artillery fire have laid waste to the towns of Borodianka, Bucha, Irpin, Hostomel and Vorzel, among others. While several high-rise apartment buildings damaged by Russian rockets in Kyiv have been restored, it seems that Ukraine will face a gargantuan, almost insurmountable task after the war: to physically rebuild a country that Russia has ravaged, twenty per cent. of which remains under occupation today.

Physically rebuilding Ukraine means reviving areas of the country that have been destroyed and left in ruins. Former residents will only return once conditions for normal life have been restored. In rural areas, many Ukrainians will probably want to rebuild their own houses and homesteads. However, we must not disregard the psychological and physical state of all those who will be returning to the newly rebuilt cities, towns and villages. Ukraine is a country of traumatised people. The scope of the trauma can vary greatly. Many have lost not only their homes but also loved ones and relatives. Many have witnessed death up close and narrowly escaped death themselves. Many Ukrainians living far from the front lines have heard the explosions of rockets and drones and seen the consequences of air strikes. All of this can be summed up in a single word – pain. This pain accumulates in the soul of every single Ukrainian and it must not be ignored because it needs comfort and healing. It will resurface time and time again long after the war is over.

Reconstructing cities, towns and villages will require building materials, construction machinery, tools and labour – but very different tools are needed to rebalance a traumatised person's mind. One of the most important "tools" to help a person's return to normal life is culture.

This word encompasses many concepts. It is not only about the arts, but it is also about being able to return to a community where there is a familiar culture of communication, a culture of being good neighbours and exhibiting traditional Ukrainian tolerance, something especially important in the border regions that are home to various national minorities.

In recent months, I have often thought back to my childhood in the 1960s and 1970s. Although fifteen or twenty years had already passed, World War II was omnipresent for me. Kyiv had been rebuilt and restored and if there were still ruins in the city, they were often those preserved as memorial sites, as reminders of the war. One example of this is the Dormition Cathedral at Kyiv-Pechersk Lavra, Kyiv's most important monastery.

Despite the seemingly peaceful life of the 1960s and 1970s, the war nevertheless had a day-to-day presence, constantly reminding us of itself and retelling its stories. The war had been made the main theme of Soviet culture after 1945. War films were aired on television every day and veterans came to schools and recounted their heroic deeds. Bookshops sold numerous novels about heroic Soviet soldiers. We children "played war" in our front yards. When we went to school, it was the teachers who organised the war games. In what now strikes me as something more akin to military drills for children, they would take us to the countryside and arrange "games" known as *zarnitsa* (meaning summer lightning). Such games were played regularly throughout the Soviet Union. Field trips to war museums and the battlefields of World War II also played an important role in our education.

These memories lead me to think that after this current war, Ukrainian childhoods should not be stamped with war. Culture, music, film and literature have special responsibilities. Ukrainian culture should guide Ukrainians out of the state of war and help them cope with their trauma. While fostering freedom of expression and championing diversity, Ukrainian culture needs to become a unifying force for all Ukrainians; it should unite them on their road in a post-war future.

The voices of this war will nonetheless remain audible. They will play an important patriotic role. The books by writers who defended Ukraine with weapons in their hands will become new classics: Anatoliy Dnistrovy, Artem Chekh, Artem Chapay, Markiyan Kamysh and many others, will form a new generation of frontline writers. However, they should not share the fate of Soviet frontline writers who were obliged by the Communist Party to write books about the war for the rest of their lives.

History imposes patterns, but we live in a more dynamic age and, above all, a more democratic one. This means that the state cannot dictate to artists, writers and musicians what they ought to be singing and writing about. The state does not tell architects what style suits the moment. During more than 30 years of independence, a culture independent of the political climate has emerged in Ukraine. Ukrainian culture has managed to become self-sufficient. Ukrainian cultural figures have been responding to Ukrainians' own cultural needs. When Ukrainians wanted to know more about the history of their country and their people, new academic books and works of fiction were published on the subject. When Ukrainians wanted to know more about their historical figures, biographical novels and studies about Hetman Ivan Mazepa, Pavlo Skoropadskyi and Nestor Makhno were written.

Right now, books about the history of Ukraine are very popular at the front. Ukrainian soldiers ask friends to send them such books. Meanwhile, in the occupied territories, Russian soldiers are destroying books on the same topics. A people's history and culture are part and parcel of its national identity. One of the chief objectives of Russian aggression against Ukraine is to destroy Ukrainian identity, to assimilate Ukrainians into Russia. This is precisely why Russian missiles have destroyed places such as the museum near Kharkiv that was dedicated to the well-known Ukrainian philosopher Hryhoriy Skovoroda and the museum about the artist Maria Pryimachenko, also not far from Kyiv.

Ukrainian culture, like Ukrainian society as a whole, has suffered heavy losses in this war. Yet this war also demonstrates the enormous role culture plays in defence of a country's independence. Today, Ukrainian culture is as well, if not better represented in Europe than within Ukraine itself. This is happening mainly through a new generation of Ukrainian cultural managers, exhibition curators, playwrights and writers. Thanks to their educational and diplomatic work abroad, the world understands Ukraine and Ukrainians better and is supporting them more strongly.

After the war, the main burden of restoring cultural life will also rest on this new generation's shoulders. Nevertheless, I very much hope that the cultural institutions of Europe and other continents will not step aside. The special cultural relations that have developed between Ukraine and other European countries before and during the war should be further intensified once it is over, allowing us to speak of Ukraine's complete cultural integration into Europe in the near future.

For me, an exhibition of Gustav Klimt in Kharkiv, say, or of Egon Schiele in Kyiv, would be a meaningful and symbolic milestone in the revival of normal cultural life in Ukraine. This would immediately give me and all Ukrainians hope and faith in the future, in Ukraine's European future.

03.07.2023

Prigozhin's Window of Opportunity

It might seem that a new era has begun in Russia – the era of a weak Putin and a strong Lukashenko. At least that is the view you get from Belarusian television news where it was reported that Lukashenko himself offered to stop the rebellion and, in one day of telephone conversations with Prigozhin, saved Putin's Russia from sliding into civil war.

In the first days after the suddenly aborted march of Prigozhin's private army on Moscow, no-one in Russia contradicted these statements. However, the other day Russian journalists voiced the version that it was Putin who instructed Lukashenko to negotiate with Prigozhin. The exact details of the agreements with Prigozhin are not known. In a comment Prigozhin gave to his supporters a few days later, he said that the "march of justice", as he calls his uprising, was provoked by his conflict with Defence Minister Shoigu and Chief of General Staff Gerasimov and by the desire of the Ministry of Defence to physically and legally destroy the Wagner private army. Lukashenko had guaranteed that the Wagner forces would remain intact and that they would be able to continue activities with the same legal status as the mercenary armies enjoyed in Russia.

The strangest thing about all this, perhaps, is that the Wagner private army cannot have any legal status in Russia because the existence of mercenary groups is prohibited in law in the Russian Federation. Russian laws clearly do not apply to the Wagner group, just as they do not apply to dozens of other private military companies, including that of Gazprom, which, in early February, announced the creation of its own private army "to protect gas pipelines and other assets". There are already 30 such private armies in Russia today. Among them, there is even one that is registered as a public organisation to further the upbringing of patriotic youth. Members of this private army, E.N.O.T, are fighting in Ukraine, Syria and other countries.

At least one of the private armies, known as Patriot, is connected directly to the Russian Defence Minister Shoigu. Why a minister of defence would have two armies under his command is not clear, but Patriot fighters have been spotted in Ukraine and are fighting in Donbas. Apparently, this army is not as combat-ready as the Wagner group. Shoigu might otherwise have used it against Prigozhin from the very beginning of their conflict. Instead, he tried to use the Russian Army, which resulted in the humiliation of some Russian officers who were taken as prisoners of war by Prigozhin's soldiers. On the other hand, pushing two private armies head-to-head on the front line of the war with Ukraine could provoke loud discontent among the Russian ultra-nationalist public.

The more private armies there are in Russia, the more likely it is that there will be clashes between them and Russia's national army, as happened during Prigozhin's march on Moscow via Rostov and Voronezh. Wagner units shot down six helicopters and one military transport plane of the Russian army command, killing twelve Russian military pilots. Up to twenty Russian soldiers were also killed in armed skirmishes.

Since then, in the cemeteries where both soldiers of the Russian army and Wagnerites are buried near to each other, someone has removed the Wagner flags flying from poles above the graves. However, the relatives of dead Wagner fighters may be even more upset about the closure of Wagner offices, which used to give out large sums in compensation to families when a Wagner soldier was killed.

After Lukashenko's triumph as the man who stopped the civil war, Prigozhin's private jet flies regularly and unhindered between Belarus and St Petersburg, the city where Prigozhin befriended Putin more than twenty years ago. Is it possible that Prigozhin is transporting furniture from his St Petersburg apartment to his new one in Minsk? Or is he wrapping up his business and transporting cash to Minsk? During searches in and around his offices following the mutiny, F.S.B. officers found a minivan loaded with boxes full of cash. Prigozhin confirmed that it was his money. How many more of these purses on wheels he has is not known.

The Wagner fighters now in Minsk may think that they will simply have a new base, from which they will be allowed to fly to Syria, Mali, the Central African Republic, Sudan and other countries where the Wagner group has long been involved in internal conflicts. Moreover, in the past, they also flew to Africa via Minsk. However, it seems likely that there may be some surprises awaiting these fighters in Belarus. It is no secret that sections of the Belarusian military leadership would rather stay out of the war in Ukraine. With the help of blackmail, or very high pay, Lukashenko might think he has his own small but well-trained army, ready to carry out any task that is unpopular with the Belarusian military. On the other hand, Putin has often expressed dissatisfaction with the speed of Belarus' unification with Russia. If Putin demands it, the Wagner forces could be ordered to seize Minsk.

The location of Prigozhin and his fighters in Belarus is also already creating tension on the border of Belarus with Poland and Lithuania. Depending on the number of Wagner fighters eventually stationed there, the level of threat to neighbouring N.A.T.O. member states could be very high, requiring additional defence spending from the governments of Poland and the Baltic states.

Today, many journalists are sure that Putin will not forgive Prigozhin and that the commander and owner of the Wagner group will sooner or later be killed. The head of Ukrainian military intelligence, Budanov, has even said that the Russian F.S.B. has already received an order to eliminate Prigozhin. This is possible, of course. After all, it was not for nothing that Putin said that the Wagner army was fully funded from the Russian budget and not from Prigozhin's pocket. *De facto*, this suggests that the real "Prigozhin" is Putin and that the Prigozhin we know is a hired manager who simply went out of control – like so many other managers, who have recently begun to fall out of the windows of hospitals, expensive apartments and even Spanish villas and Thai hotels.

So, it is quite possible that sooner or later Prigozhin will be faced with a choice: to seize Belarus or fall out of the window. What is more, Prigozhin will be aware that, even if he does as he is told by Putin, it does not mean that the "window of negative opportunities" will be closed for ever.

"Oh Sport, You Are Peace"

When Ukraine's top tennis player, Elina Svitolina, defeated the Belarusian Victoria Azarenko at Wimbledon recently, she as usual refused to shake hands with her Belarusian opponent. "I have repeated many times: until the Russian troops leave Ukraine, until we take back our territories, we will not shake hands," she said. Journalists at Wimbledon immediately approached Victoria Azarenko and asked if she felt like a victim.

"Victim?" Victoria answered. "Victim because someone didn't shake hands with me? Oh, no! She does not want to shake hands with Russians and Belarusians. I respect her decision!"

"Oh sport, you are peace!" Pierre de Coubertin wrote in his "Ode to Sport". "You establish good, kind, friendly relations between peoples." I would like to agree with Pierre de Coubertin, but the reality appears to be somewhat different. When the Wimbledon stands booed Victoria Azarenko, the noise was, of course, aimed not at her but at Lukashenko and Putin.

Svitolina's run at Wimbledon came to an end in the semi-finals, but we are very proud of her. The pressure and responsibility that she must feel, especially when playing against Belarusian or Russian athletes, can only be compared with the state of the Ukrainian soldiers during the battle. "Oh sport, you are a battleground!" sounds closer to reality.

While I am proud of Svitolina, I feel ashamed that I was once proud of some other Ukrainian champions who have changed sides, betraying their country, not in the sports arena but in a more serious way. How should sports historians evaluate the contribution to the development of Ukrainian sport of certain figures, like the former long-term chairman of the National

Olympic Committee and Olympic pole-vaulting champion, "Hero of Ukraine" and politician Serhiy Bubka, or the four-times Olympic swimming champion, also a "Hero of Ukraine", Yana Klochkova?

At the very beginning of the war, Klochkova went to annexed Crimea, to her parents' home, and once there deleted her Facebook and Instagram accounts. Now she communicates with her fans only on the pages of Russian social networks. Nobody has managed to get a comment from her about Russia's war against Ukraine. For her, there is no war, which means that she has chosen to side with Russia.

Bubka became a refugee in the first days of the new Russian invasion, going first to Switzerland and then to Italy. Later, he resigned as chairman of the National Olympic Committee of Ukraine and passed his responsibilities to the Minister for Youth and Sports, Vadim Gutsait. However, Bubka has remained on the International Olympic Committee. There, he came up with the idea of giving Ukrainian passports to Russian athletes who cannot or do not want to compete on behalf of Russia. The suggestion was not supported by the Ukrainian government.

The International Olympic Committee, headed by Thomas Bach, decided at the beginning of the year to allow Russian and Belarusian athletes to take part in the 2024 Olympics. This drew protests from many countries and a final decision was postponed until the summer of 2023. However, it is already clear that Russian and Belarusian athletes will take part, albeit without the Russian flag or anthem.

Both of these famous athletes, Bubka and Klochkova, were supporters of the pro-Russian Party of Regions and its leader, former Ukrainian President Viktor Yanukovych, who has lived in Moscow since he fled Ukraine after the Revolution of Dignity in 2014. If Yana Klochkova is slowly fading out of the

Ukrainian consciousness, then Serhiy Bubka is still remembered and even sought out. He has businesses registered both in Kyiv and Donetsk (in Donetsk they are registered under Russian law) and these businesses attract close attention from both journalists and detectives. His most famous company, Mont Blanc, which until 2018 participated in tenders for the sale of fuel, food and much more besides to the Ukrainian state, recently signed contracts with the Donetsk occupation administration for the supply of fuel. True, these contracts are signed not by Serhiy Bubka himself but by his brother Vasily, also a former athlete – a pole vaulter who now lives in Donetsk. However, the list of the company's founders includes the name Serhiy Bubka.

Other recent news that has succeeded in diverting Ukrainians' attention from events at the front also has some sporting elements. Ihor Kushnir, the head of the Kyivvmiskbud Construction Holding, which is 80 per cent. owned by the Kyiv City Council, has gone into mountaineering. He and his wife Oksana paid $150,000 for the chance to climb Everest. They reached the summit and took photographs of themselves with the Ukrainian flag and that of their construction company. All this might be laudable, if it were not for the fact that in order to leave Ukraine, Ihor Kushnir presented the Ukrainian border guards with a disability certificate. Further investigations have shown that since the start of the war, Kushnir has spent 240 days abroad.

Equally interesting is the fact that Kushnir demanded and received one billion hryvnias (nineteen million euros) from the Ukrainian government to restart Kyivmiskbud and complete construction projects that were frozen when the war started in February 2022. At the same time, Kushnir and his wife have spent a significant part of the war in a luxury villa located in a secure area near Nice in France. The villa is registered with

Oksana's Cypriot company and has an estimated value similar to the sum Kushnir received from the government to restart Kyivmiskbud, that is, about nineteen to twenty million euros.

On July 6, the mayor of Kyiv, world boxing champion Vitali Klitschko, temporarily removed Ihor Kushnir from his duties as head of the board of the construction company and ordered a financial audit to be carried out by a well-known international firm. It seems that Kushnir will now have more worries.

The rest of us can meanwhile remember how Elina Svitolina's performance at Wimbledon sent waves of happiness around Ukraine.

20.08.2023

Quiet Roads and Heroism

In summertime, Ukraine's most popular highway was always the one connecting Kyiv to Odesa – the road to the seaside. This August, this road is eerily empty in both directions. Gone are the kilometre-long traffic jams and the queues at petrol stations. You only need to slow down at the occasional military check-points. As you drive, you get the feeling that everyone has left and gone somewhere else. Only the carefully cultivated fields of sunflowers and wheat on both sides of the road indicate that life goes on here.

"Our fuel sales are one fifth of what they were at the begin-ning of the war," a petrol station attendant complained. At the next station, already near Odesa, three employees were sitting looking bored without any work to do.

As soon as you enter Odesa region, you receive an S.M.S. from the regional military administration, reminding you that because of mines and bacteriological danger, walking along the coastline, swimming and fishing in the Black Sea is prohibited, except at the beaches officially open for bathing inside Odesa. We are not going to the Black Sea. Instead, we turn west towards the fortress town of Bilgorod-Dnestrovsky and then north-west, towards Moldova, into the Bessarabia steppe.

In the spring and summer of last year, Bilgorod-Dnestrovsky and surrounding resort villages, were targets for Russian drone and missile attacks. The Ukrainian military shot down a Russian aircraft that was trying to destroy the local power plant.

These days the city is quieter – perhaps too quiet. Economic life has all but come to a standstill. There is little activity at the Bilgorod-Dniester seaport, one of the city's main industrial enterprises. The port is state-owned but is up for sale to private bidders. Since March of this year, the State Property Fund has tried to sell it five times, although no-one wants to buy it. Now it is up for auction again and the starting price has been halved.

There is another port nearby which, so far, seems to be more fortunate. This is the Ust-Danube seaport near the town of Kiliya. It was recently sold at auction for three times the starting price. The buyer, Elixir Ukraine, a fertiliser company, took out a six-million-euro bank loan for the purchase. However, the State Property Fund is delaying the registration of ownership, fearing that Elixir Ukraine could refuse to process the cargo of other companies. Why were these issues not resolved and specified in the contract prior to the purchase? Does the State Property Fund lack good lawyers, or have all its best people been mobilised?

Elixir Ukraine's management is considering terminating the deal and returning the loan to the bank. Some of the seaport equipment included in the auction documentation, for example, two floating cranes, has already been sunk by Russian artillery and missiles. The buyer was planning to raise and restore the submerged equipment. Taking on an operation like this during war must surely count as heroic – albeit not the same type of heroism as shown by the tens of thousands of Ukrainian soldiers who have already received medals, many thousands of them posthumously – but heroic, nonetheless.

Recently, the talk among Ukrainian civilians has been less about soldier heroes and more about the previously little-known businessman and blogger Oleksiy Tolkachev. "You can kick me, but I will say it! Ukrainians deserved this war with Russia and it is a consequence of the previous thirty years of independence – a period of mismanagement, selfishness, theft and sloppiness," he wrote on his Facebook page. "We don't have a culture of cooperation and gratitude. We have a cult of hate. We have a toxic social environment . . . Unfortunately, so far only a small part of society is demonstrating change. It's as if some Atlanteans are holding the country on their shoulders."

Interestingly, in his statement Tolkachev never mentioned the word "corruption" and focused his criticism on the "national qualities of the Ukrainian people" rather than on the country's political elite. Tolkachev's verbose cry from the heart has clearly touched a nerve in the thinking portion of Ukrainian society and as predicted by Tolkachev himself has caused a wave of criticism and hate against him. However, a considerable number of Ukrainians support his views. Indeed, the idea that Ukrainians need to show gratitude for help received has become a separate discussion, with activists already proposing a gratitude rally to honour countries that are helping Ukraine with weapons and finance. They suggest it should be held on Ukrainian Independence Day, August 24.

I am not sure that the idea of "Gratitude Rallies" will take root in the minds of Ukraine's political elite. This Independence

Day will, more likely, be remembered for the fact that on Ukraine's largest monument, the "Motherland" statue erected in 1982, the coat of arms of the Soviet Union has finally been removed and replaced by the coat of arms of Ukraine – the trident. Now we can say that the 102-metre steel and titanium statue of a warlike woman turned with her face, sword, and shield towards Moscow, has finally been Ukrainianised. Yes, we love monumental symbolism.

06.09.2023

Dungeon Kids, Stray Dogs and Frozen Shrimp

In Kharkiv, in the first week of September, 34 new bus routes appeared. Each route starts near a school and ends near one of the city's metro stations. These are bus routes for the "children of the underground" – the city's school pupils. The children will gather near their regular school and then go with their teachers to a classroom at a metro station.

By the beginning of the school year, 60 classrooms had been equipped for teaching at five stations. Classes are organised into two shifts, so that as many pupils as possible can enjoy live communication with each other and with their teachers. The first shift is from nine in the morning to midday, the second is from one to four o'clock. To enable as many pupils as possible to study with others, each class will only study underground two to three days a week. They will have online lessons for the rest of the week. Psychologists will be on duty in the underground schools. Free meals and medical assistance will also be organised.

Kharkiv's Mayor, Ihor Terekhov, proudly showed off the

metro schools, which have brand new furniture and relaxation spaces for the children. If it were not for the huge ventilation pipes under the rather low ceilings, one might think that the classrooms were those of an ordinary, newly built school. The pipes are decorated with school posters and portraits of Ukrainian writers. Cheerful children's drawings enliven the cold, marble walls. "The metro school is a temporary measure," says Terekhov. Everyone avoids making these measures sound long term, let alone permanent, but it is clear that the war is here for the foreseeable future.

In Kharkiv, 108 schools have suffered war damage. Some have been destroyed by Russian missiles and will have to be rebuilt from scratch. Parents want their children to learn as much as possible in a classroom, not online. Even the opportunity for their children to study underground is seen as a great way out of a difficult situation. Perhaps that is why groups of security specialists are surveying other metro stations, hoping to find more spaces that can be equipped as classrooms.

On September 5, the mayor announced that they had managed to open another class underground, the sixty-first. However, this number still represents a drop in the ocean. Before February 24, 2022, Kharkiv had more than 120,000 schoolchildren. Many families have since gone abroad or moved to safer regions of Ukraine, but there are still about 50,000 children in the city, among them many internally displaced children from Donbas and Kharkiv regions.

About 7000 Kharkiv first-graders have gone to school for the first time this year. They "went" but mostly stayed at home. No more than a hundred of them can be accommodated in the underground classrooms. The rest will have to study solely online. While there are school buildings in Kharkiv that have not been affected by the war and possess properly equipped bomb shelters, even they have not reopened this September. It takes 48 seconds for a S-300 missile to fly to Kharkiv from Bilgorod, just over the border. That is not enough time to reach the bomb shelter even from the ground floor of a school, so online learning remains the only option. What is more, 5000 Kharkiv schoolchildren who left the city with their parents expect to study online with their Kharkiv school friends and teachers, from wherever they are.

Soon the construction of an underground bunker school for 450 pupils will begin in an industrial district of Kharkiv. The Ukrainian education system is adapting to the conditions of permanent war. At the same time, adverts have appeared on various Kharkiv websites for boarding schools in England. The cost of tuition is advertised as £450 per month, plus board and lodging, of course.

No schools are functioning in the city of Izyum in Kharkiv region, which was under occupation for five months last year. The settlements that were under Russian control are recovering very slowly. Izyum was liberated by the Ukrainian army in early September 2022 and electricity, gas and water were reinstalled quite quickly, but the atmosphere there remains tense. Many people who died during the Russian shelling of the city have not yet been identified. Residents who have lost their loved ones have been asked to donate D.N.A. samples. No more than 10,000 of the original population of about 50,000 have returned to the city. The residents who have returned are served by only a few small shops, although you can already buy brand new coloured souvenir magnets depicting the iconic views of the city from before the war.

A key challenge for the town of Izyum is the large population of aggressive, stray dogs that have settled on the territory of a partially destroyed and abandoned machine-tool plant. Six people were recently attacked and have been vaccinated against rabies. Residents have appealed to Izyum's military administration for help, but the army is overloaded with responsibilities and its priority is demining the city and its environs. A year after Izyum's liberation, mines and unexploded shells are still being discovered. From time to time, the military detonates one of them and, at these moments, the dogs run to hide in the plant and temporarily cease to terrorise the local population.

Life in the east and south-east of Ukraine is very different from life in the west of the country. Previously, the Kharkiv and Donbas regions were the most densely populated areas of the country, while western Ukraine suffered from a sparsity of population. Now it seems, all activity and a huge number of people have moved west. Ukraine's border with the European Union cannot deal with the increase in traffic. Bus passengers must wait for up to ten hours to cross the border into or out of Ukraine. Train passengers get across more quickly. Truck drivers wait longer than anybody else.

The trucks travelling into Ukraine are carrying humanitarian aid, building materials, windows, and everything else needed to rebuild the devastated territories. However, new cars, designer clothes, Spanish *jamon* and Norwegian salmon are also being imported. In large areas of the country, life goes on as usual and international brands continue to operate shops and present new collections.

Sometimes Ukrainian businesspeople try to use the war to make more money, or maybe cover their losses associated with the war, for example, by trying to import luxury brand clothes under the guise of humanitarian aid for war victims. They also try to negotiate with customs officials to bring in more and pay less. Sometimes they succeed, sometimes they do not. Judging by how often the heads of western border customs stations are fired each year, we can assume that a good many cargoes are imported into Ukraine without full payment of customs duties. Since February last year, the number of customs officials arrested for corruption has increased dramatically. At the same time, however, state revenues from customs fees have also increased.

One of the most curious cases of goods being imported under the guise of humanitarian aid came to light at the end of last year. During a routine check at a customs post in Odesa, a truck was found to be carrying 22 tons of frozen shrimp from Ecuador. According to the documentation, the cargo was humanitarian aid on its way to a Ukrainian charity that helps victims of the war. When the charity mentioned in the documents was contacted by customs officials, they expressed great surprise about the many tons of frozen shrimp that appeared to be heading their way. The charity had no industrial freezers and was engaged in a completely different type of assistance.

During a search of the truck's cab, customs officers found another package of accompanying documents for the shrimp, this time the real ones: they indicated that the shrimp were imported for a commercial entity that sells frozen seafood. As a result, 22 tons of shrimp were confiscated by the state.

The fate of the cargo of shrimp is not known, but we do have information about some confiscated jackets and suits from Armani, Brioni, Chanel, Hugo Boss, Louis Vuitton, Prada and Versace. According to a statement from the Odesa customs, these products, also imported under the guise of humanitarian aid, were handed over to the military personnel of the 122nd Territorial Defence Brigade. However, nobody remembers seeing the brigade's fighters in Hugo Boss jackets. Later, Odesa customs amended its statement, adding that the illegally imported products were cheap fakes. I suppose this story will be investigated by literary detectives later, after the war, but at least we have some official statements by customs to be going on with.

It is true that nowadays a lot depends on customs officials. It depends on them whether the residents of cities and towns near the front line, as well as those far from it, receive new German-made windows before the onset of freezing temperatures, whether the residents of the Kherson and Kharkiv regions receive humanitarian aid and medicines, whether Izyum receives equipment to restore mobile communications. This all depends on customs officials.

Everything important that is happening today in Ukraine and around Ukraine will become a chapter in the school history textbooks of tomorrow. I hope that by the time these textbooks appear, the war will be over and the children will go to regular schools, not underground ones.

The convoluted stories of frozen shrimp and real or fake Brioni suits are likely to end up in novels. After the war, Ukrainians will require literature full of humour and laced with a sense of irony. This will help us learn to laugh again, at first through tears, but eventually with relief and joy.

Surely, every foreign truck driver who has reached Izyum will remember the trip for the rest of his life, with or without the souvenir magnets from that ruined city.

19.09.2023

Hide and Seek – Mobilisation in Ukraine

Recently, in Lviv, a car full of military registration and enlistment officers drove up to a group of young men who were waiting at a bus stop. The officers jumped out, grabbed one of the men and began to drag him into the car. He resisted. The officers started beating him and he fell to the ground. Passersby demanded that they leave the man alone. Eventually, he broke away and ran off down the street. The officers did not pursue him.

I suspect that similar scenes are occurring in other cities. I know the same thing happened in Odesa a couple of months ago. Someone captured the incident on video and it went viral across Ukraine, sparking controversy about mobilisation practices. Frightened men have stopped going out to public places and avoid travelling to other regions of the country because they might be "mobilised" at road checkpoints during document checks.

A paradox has arisen: Ukrainian soldiers fighting at the front are adored and declared heroes, while military registration and enlistment employees, who are also military personnel, are scolded, often despised and even attacked.

Russian intelligence services have launched an Internet campaign designed to disrupt mobilisation in Ukraine and provoke fear among potential conscripts. From specially created accounts on Facebook, TikTok, and Instagram, Russian bots teach Ukrainian men how to avoid mobilisation.

At the same time, frontline officers complain about a lack of personnel. It is clear to everyone that losses during the counter-offensive have been heavy. There are many killed and wounded; if they are not replaced the counter-offensive may stall. This is a war of attrition, the grinding down of manpower, artillery, missiles and drones. If, at the beginning of the war, the Ukrainian army responded to 50,000 Russian shells with one or two thousand, now both armies have equal artillery power and each side fires 40,000 shells a day at enemy positions.

Despite facing heavy losses, Russian generals feel confident.

They say that Russia has 40 million human resources for the war and Ukraine has only four million. Meanwhile, the Ukrainian Parliament is discussing several new bills, the adoption of which could affect mobilisation and the country's defence capability in general.

The main bill, which more than a hundred Members of Parliament have been working on, concerns the introduction of electronic registration of military personnel.

After Zelensky came to power, electronic documentation became all the rage, especially among young people. A government application called Diya (meaning action) was installed by the majority of Ukrainians on their smartphones. This app allows you to receive certificates and documents without visiting state offices. Thanks to Diya you can receive your electronic driver's licence and electronic internal passport on your smartphone.

The proposed bill involves the collection, from existing government databases, of the personal details of all men liable for military service between eighteen and 60 years of age. This super-database will contain not only the names and addresses of persons liable for military service but all the information known about them, including their mobile phone numbers and email addresses. Here the question arises, will the Diya system, which Ukrainians love so much, use a smartphone's G.P.S. to tell military registration and enlistment offices where potential conscripts are located? The government says that it will not, but it has already increased the fines for those who do not live at their official address and have not informed the authorities about their current place of residence.

A relatively humane bill among those prepared for discussion in Parliament is number 9566, tabled by Heorhiy Mazurashu, a Member of Parliament from President Zelensky's Servant of the People party. The bill would allow Ukrainians who do not want to go to war to refuse mobilisation and, instead, to work in defence enterprises. Mazurashu believes that this law will reduce societal tension. It might also reduce the number of men who want to leave the country, legally or illegally. However, most likely it will not be adopted by Parliament since it contradicts the policy of general mobilisation.

Ukraine's military medical commissions now operate under close scrutiny. The commissions determine the suitability of a potential conscript for military service based on their health and physical condition. Initial checks showed that some members of these commissions sold certificates of "unfitness" to those who did not want to go to the front and were ready to pay $4,000 –$5,000 for such a fictitious diagnosis.

The State Bureau of Investigation is compiling lists of those citizens who may have received illegal exemption certificates. These men will be called back for repeat medical check-ups. I can only imagine the "societal tension" they are experiencing right now.

A week ago, Ukrainian news outlets published a list of 372 N.G.O.s and volunteer organisations that, for a fee, have been helping men to go abroad. These organisations produced letters with which men could leave Ukraine for a few days to carry out work connected with humanitarian assistance and volunteer projects in support of the Ukrainian army. Thousands of men who left the country using such letters have never returned. Instead, they have asked for temporary protection status in neighbouring countries.

Ukrainian Member of Parliament David Arakhamia has suggested that recently strengthened international co-operation will solve the problem. "In any country in the world, except Russia, our law enforcement agencies can request the extradition of such people. They can be brought back to Ukraine so that they suffer the appropriate punishment," he stated. However, representatives of the Austrian, German and Hungarian governments have already said that they will not extradite those who left Ukraine because they did not want to end up in the Ukrainian army. There are now officially about 200,000 Ukrainian men of military age in Germany alone and it is unlikely that the German police will get involved in finding out which of them left Ukraine in contravention of the country's wartime laws.

From October 1 of this year, women aged eighteen to 60 who are medical professionals are also required to register for military service. They can be drafted into the army as doctors and nurses. Only pregnant female medics and those on maternity leave are exempt from such registration. Women who have other skills that could be useful to the army can register with the military voluntarily. Politicians have also raised the idea of making all women in Ukraine liable for military service, citing the Israeli army, in which men and women serve on equal terms. This idea has not found popular support.

Currently, more than 60,000 women serve in the Ukrainian army. Among this number, about 7,500 are female officers. This is two and a half times the number in 2014, at the beginning of the war with Russia. The most senior-ranking female is Colonel Larisa Yakobchuk, a deputy brigade commander. "First of all, I am an officer, then a woman, and only after that, a blonde," she says smiling about herself. Since February last year, more than one hundred female soldiers have died at the front and more than 500 have been wounded.

The Ukrainian army is slowly being transformed from an almost exclusively male establishment. In the early days of the transition, female soldiers had to alter men's military uniforms. This issue is now largely resolved.

The problem of motivating newly mobilised men remains. The Ministry of Defence has ordered several motivational videos for use on social media networks. The Ministry of Education offers free university education to young men after military service, but this is not enough to change attitudes towards mobilisation. Many experts believe that the best motivation would be higher salaries for military personnel, providing $5,000 to $10,000 a month. At the moment, the standard salary is 100,000 hryvnias a month (equivalent to little over $2,600 at the time of publication) for frontline service, or 30,000 hryvnias if you are serving at the rear.

In Russia, much higher salaries motivate people to join up. A large percentage of Russian soldiers enter military service because of money problems and unpaid debt. At the same time, despite international sanctions, Russia still has the financial reserves to maintain high salaries. Ukrainians tend to have less debt and the Ukrainian state is functioning mainly thanks to assistance from the European Union and the United States of America. The government will therefore have to come up with something other than financial incentives to motivate conscripts as it continues the general mobilisation over the next two to three months.

02.10.2023

Ukraine and Poland – Friends or Just Neighbours?

Kyiv resident Olga Vyazenko, a lawyer and journalist, moved with her husband to New Zealand just before the war and immediately became a prominent figure in the Ukrainian diaspora. As Russian missiles rained down on Kyiv, Olga spent days clutching her smartphone, trying to persuade her mother Lyudmila and her mother-in-law, Natalia, to leave Ukraine. Eventually, she succeeded and they left, taking with them Lyudmila's dog, a toy terrier called Patrick.

Olga had also been busy posting requests for help on the Internet, mostly addressing Poles because of the warm welcome Ukrainian refugees were receiving in Poland. In the end, it was Michał and Gosia, a Polish couple living in America, who offered to help. As soon as they heard of the two ladies' plight, these total strangers bought plane tickets and flew to Poland to meet Lyudmila and Natalia and to take them and the toy terrier to their house in Kraków, which was standing empty.

The plan was for the two Ukrainian refugees to stay in Poland while they applied for a New Zealand visa, but that process took much longer than anyone expected. When Michał and Gosia had to return to America, they paid for their Ukrainian guests to stay in a hotel for a month and at the end of that period, Pavel, another Polish stranger, offered to house the two ladies in his village home, free of charge. He looked after them for six months until, eventually, the New Zealand visa arrived, and Lyudmila and Natalia flew to be with Olga. Now you can see a toy terrier named Patrick running about in Pavel's yard because the dog was not allowed to enter New Zealand. At least the pet does not live as far from his native Ukraine as its owner.

There must be thousands of stories like this, examples of hard work, determination and solidarity. Polish publishers collected and sent hundreds of thousands of euros to their colleagues in Ukraine. At their own expense, they have printed children's books in Ukrainian and distributed them to young refugees, free of charge. All over Poland, people collected clothes, food, toys and furniture for Ukrainians driven out of their homes by the war. Polish volunteers regularly deliver humanitarian and military aid to Ukrainian cities and villages. Millions of Ukrainians will remember with gratitude everything that the Polish people have done for them during this Russian aggression.

The same can be said for the Polish state, which organised logistics hubs on its territory to provide military assistance to the Ukrainian army, gave Ukraine large quantities of ammunition and weapons, and opened the country's borders for Ukrainian exports and the transit of grain and other goods. Polish politicians and members of the government regularly risk missile attacks to visit Kyiv and express their support for Ukraine's government and its President.

In recent months, however, conflict over Ukrainian grain has somewhat marred bilateral relations. Back in March of this year, Polish farmers blocked roads to protest against the import of Ukrainian grain into Poland. Officially, grain was imported only for transit to Polish seaports on the Baltic Sea because Russian attacks had made the use of Ukraine's Black Sea ports impossible. However, once the flow of Ukrainian grain started, Polish grain prices paid to the farmers started first to fluctuate and then fall, indicating that some of the Ukrainian grain, rather than being in transit, was finding its way onto the domestic market.

In April 2023, the Polish government announced a new mechanism for the transit of Ukrainian grain that would prevent these leakages and promised their farmers that Polish grain silos would be emptied of Ukrainian grain before the start of the new harvest. However, the Minister of Agriculture, Henryk Kowalczyk, later resigned, saying that he could not manage the grain crisis. Poland is now blocking the transit and export of Ukrainian grain and the tensions over Ukraine's grain shipments show no sign of cooling. The upcoming parliamentary elections in Poland are key to this, with farmers' votes likely to affect the outcome.

In August, when Zelensky rather bluntly accused the Polish government of "preparing the stage for a Moscow actor", Poland's Prime Minister Morawiecki called on Zelensky to "never offend the Polish people again!" He then stated that Poland could no longer provide Ukraine with any weapons since it must arm itself.

Morawiecki admitted that these arguments between Warsaw and Kyiv only serve to make Russia happy.

While the Polish and Ukrainian governments try to douse the flames of this conflict, grain is not the only issue souring Polish–Ukrainian relations. There remains little historical reconciliation between the two countries regarding the Volyn Massacre and other tragic episodes in Polish–Ukrainian history.

From the spring of 1943, the Ukrainian Insurgent Army actively exterminated ethnic Poles living in Volyn, an area where Polish and Ukrainian communities had resided in close proximity. In response, the Polish Home Army destroyed Ukrainian villages and killed their inhabitants. Everyone was slaughtered, including the elderly, women and children. Village residents were reportedly herded into houses or churches and then burned alive. Neither Poland nor Ukraine wants to admit guilt in these massacres.

The history of Polish–Ukrainian relations is not always written in blood. There are also many positive episodes that politicians seem slow to remember. One of Ukraine's early heroes, the bishop, writer and thinker, Meletiy Smotrytsky (1577–1633), wrote his works exclusively in Polish, while the Polish writer Wacław Lipiński (1882–1931) wrote in Ukrainian. The much-admired Ukrainian author, Ivan Franko (1856–1916), wrote in Ukrainian, Polish and German.

Today, as before the war, the main foreign market for Ukrainian literature is the Polish market, where books by Ukrainian authors translated into Polish sell better than in Ukraine. This can be explained partly by shortcomings in the Ukrainian book market but also by the enormous interest in Ukraine that exists in Poland.

Interest in Polish literature inside Ukraine is not as great or as stable, although this does not appear to upset Poles. The vast majority have a very positive attitude towards Ukrainians. This has been proved by the Polish people time and time again since the beginning of the war. If he could talk, Patrick the toy terrier, who is running about in a Polish yard, would no doubt also testify to this.

17.10.2023

A Matter of Trust –
Who and What Do Ukrainians Believe in?

More than 600 days have passed since the Russian army's all-out attack on Ukraine. Soon two sad dates will be engraved on the country's modern history: it is ten years since the annexation of Crimea and the start of the war in Donbas and two years since Russia started to target everyone, anywhere in Ukraine. I do not expect these dates will be marked in any special way, but for most Ukrainians February 2024 will bring a new reason to contemplate the recent past, the present and the future.

It is no secret that optimism regarding an imminent end to the war has waned since last year when even those who did not vote for President Zelensky believed that his unbridled energy would help Ukraine obtain the weapons necessary to expel the enemy from the occupied territory. It did not seem to worry anybody that reports about the supply of weapons only ever mentioned very small quantities: "Slovakia gave Ukraine two Zuzanna howitzers and Germany gave two Iris air defence systems," and such like.

There were rumours that our allies were giving much more in secret, not wanting to irritate Russia. If Ukrainians once expected a miracle from Western weapons, now talk of H.I.M.A.R.S. and Storm Shadow missiles has become something familiar, almost banal.

Many people worry about what will happen if the occupied territories are liberated but Russia continues to fire missiles and drones at the entire territory of Ukraine. Could this be considered a victory or only a partial victory? What should Ukraine do in response to such attacks? Bombard Russian territory? Would Ukraine be forced to keep spending money on weapons when so much costly restoration work will need to be done? These questions provoke melancholy thoughts about more months or even years of war and this has prompted Ukraine's leadership to focus squarely on the issue of national unity and like-mindedness, highlighting sociological studies that confirm this to be the case.

Before the war, the main split in Ukrainian society was between Poroshenko supporters and Zelensky supporters. 75 per cent. of Ukrainians still support Zelensky. However, surveys on a range of themes do show divergence in Ukrainians' attitudes and beliefs. The results often show contradictory attitudes existing in one individual. This is not surprising: we are a war-traumatised society, torn between belief in miracles and the not-so-inspiring reality.

President Zelensky's trust rating reached 90 per cent. last year, before it dropped to today's level. While he is still at the top of the list of popularity for public figures, this summer, 78 per cent. of Ukrainians consider President Zelensky personally responsible for corruption in the government and regional military administrations. In the ranking of institutional and personal trustworthiness, the Ukrainian army takes first place among national institutions, trusted by 93–94 per cent. of Ukrainians, followed by the volunteer military formations and volunteers in general. The President is in seventh place, with a rating of 72 per cent.

Looking at who and what is not considered trustworthy, political parties are least trusted, with 74 per cent. of Ukrainians saying they do not trust them. 72 per cent. of respondents do not trust Ukrainian civil servants either. The government of Ukraine is not trusted by 60 per cent. of Ukrainians. Among the current politicians in President Zelensky's camp, the least trusted are the head of the Office of the President, Andriy Yermak, the Speaker of the Parliament, Ruslan Stefanchuk and the Prime Minister, Denis Shmygal.

Ukrainians are not looking at Ukraine's situation through rose-tinted spectacles. While there is unconditional support for the armed forces of Ukraine, this is not a consolidating factor for Ukrainian society as a whole. Discussions about possible presidential elections, which are heard increasingly often in the Ukrainian media, could further split society.

Zelensky said recently in an interview with foreign journalists that if the war continued, he would run for a second term, but if the war ended, he would not seek an additional five years as President. This is probably the most concrete signal regarding his intentions that we have received, as it is clear to most Ukrainians that the war will continue. Elections during a war, when about eight million Ukrainians have become refugees abroad and more than half a million are on the front line, would hardly be considered fair or legitimate. For some reason, opinion polls have not been conducted on this matter.

Meanwhile, attacks by opponents on the presidential camp have intensified. In traditional Ukrainian style, one of the leaders of these attacks is a former adviser to the Head of the Office of the President, Olexiy Arestovich. Last year, while working for Zelensky's team, Arestovich, a blogger and former military intelligence officer, broke all records in the popularity polls. Today, according to the sociological service of the Razumkov Centre, 71 per cent. of Ukrainians do not trust him at all, although this does seem not to upset him. He clearly has presidential ambitions and appears intent on regaining most of his lost popularity by criticising Zelensky and his government.

In recent days, President Zelensky provoked displeasure among Ukrainian journalists by gathering a narrow circle of loyal journalists in his office for an informal chat during which he asked them to stop writing about corruption in Ukraine until the end of the war.

In the meantime, a survey of how many Ukrainians would be willing to accept territorial losses in exchange for an end to the war should be of interest to journalists. This number has grown by four per cent. over the past six months: overall, fourteen per cent. of the total population would accept territorial losses in exchange for peace. However, if we consider the results by region, we will see that in the south of Ukraine the number of those who are ready to compromise has increased from eight to 21 per cent. and in the east of Ukraine from thirteen to 22 per cent. Talk about territorial compromises carries the assumption that the Ukrainian army cannot win this war; respondents may feel that a lack of faith in victory is unpatriotic. So, it is possible that some respondents may shy away from being honest when answering this question.

Meanwhile, the Ukrainian counter-offensive in the south is proceeding very slowly. In the east, Russian troops have again launched an offensive around Avdiivka, Marjinka, and Kupiansk. It looks like the winter on the front line will be hot and Ukrainian soldiers will again celebrate the New Year in the trenches and under fire.

24.10.2023

Ukraine Gets Tough on the Moscow Patriarchate

Autumn fogs have descended on Ukraine. It is getting colder. Russia is once again launching drones in all directions across Ukraine. Explosions were recently heard in many parts of Kyiv region. This was the sound of our defence systems working effectively.

Now that life depends on heating, electricity and water, people fear an intensification of attacks on Ukrainian power plants and infrastructure. However, Ukraine's leadership is confident that our anti-aircraft systems are ready for whatever Russia throws at our cities this winter. European countries are renting out additional air defence systems to Ukraine for the cold season. As well as highlighting the commercial nature of the relationship between allies, the idea of renting out equipment indicates that European countries are afraid of being left without weapons.

Winter is freezing the front line. There is less and less talk about the counter-offensive in Ukrainian media, but the Russian army still tries the occasional offensive manoeuvre in the regions of Kharkiv and Donbas. A recent attack on the Avdiivka area, very close to Donetsk, involved hundreds of tanks and thousands of soldiers. It was timed to coincide with President Putin's arrival in Rostov-on-Don, near Ukraine's eastern border with Russia, where he was to hold a meeting with the Chief of Staff of the Russian army, General Gerasimov.

The Russian military command was apparently hoping to present Putin with a gift on his arrival, the capture of Avdiivka, which has been controlled by Ukraine since 2014. As a result of this offensive, more than fifty Russian tanks were destroyed and thousands of Russian soldiers died or went missing. The Generals had no "royal gift" to offer up to their leader. Russian media played down Putin's trip towards the front line, showing only nocturnal photographs of General Gerasimov and President Putin, in which both resembled figures from Madame Tussauds.

While the Russian command is licking its wounds and sending more reinforcements to Donetsk and Kharkiv regions, the Ukrainian Parliament has launched another offensive against the Orthodox Church of the Moscow Patriarchate in Ukraine.

For many months now, despite court and parliamentary decisions, the Church of the Moscow Patriarchate has refused to vacate the premises of Ukraine's most important monastery, the Kyiv Pechersk Lavra. Some of the buildings in the monastery complex have long been part of a state-run museum, but the monks and priests of the Moscow Patriarchate continue to hold out in other buildings, not allowing the police or the bailiffs to evict them. To everyone's surprise, last week the Ukrainian Parliament voted to approve a bill that would ban religious organisations with centres in Russia or which are affiliated with that country. Though the Ukrainian authorities were clearly in no hurry to introduce this bill, a group of active Members of Parliament collected 240 signatures of their fellow deputies, which was sufficient to bring the bill before Parliament. At the first reading, 267 voted in favour of it.

Before the vote, a tempestuous conflict arose within the

largest parliamentary faction, President Zelensky's Servant of the People Party. Its deputy head, Artem Kultenko, turned out to be a key defender of the Moscow Patriarchate. Kultenko sent out text messages to other Members of Parliament who supported the bill with the words "I want to save your soul!" Many deputies perceived these messages as something of a threat. Together with Artem Kultenko, the infamous bishop of the Moscow Patriarchate Church, Abbot of the Ionin Monastery, Ion Cherepanov, sent similar messages to deputies: "Save your souls! We will all perish!"

Artem Kultenko assured his fellow party members that more than 80 deputies from the Servant of the People faction would vote against this bill. The Speaker of the Parliament, Ruslan Stefanchuk, stated that there would not be a vote on the bill and the head of the faction of the presidential party, David Arakhamia, said that such a bill would distract Parliament from voting on the key issue of the budget. Nonetheless, the bill has already passed its first reading. After some editing and a second vote, the President would be expected sign it into law. It is not clear how long these procedures will take, but Ukrainian society has enthusiastically welcomed the initial moves.

Liquidating religious organisations associated with Russia will be very complicated for one simple reason: the Ukrainian Church of the Moscow Patriarchate is not legally registered in Ukraine as one integral organisation. There is the Kyiv metropolitanate, several episcopates and more than 9000 church communities, each of which is registered separately. According to the new law, each case must be investigated to prove a connection with Russia. Each legal entity must then be given time to correct the situation by bringing to an end its connection with Russia. The Moscow Patriarchate is unlikely to give up control of its Ukrainian churches without a struggle, so long court proceedings can be expected.

The Moscow Patriarchate has already begun a defence campaign, using international platforms to make declarations about the persecution of religious communities in Ukraine. Not surprisingly, they do not mention any of the priests who collaborated with Russian forces during the invasion and who helped the Russian army to occupy Ukrainian territories. Nor do they mention the rapid re-registration of church communities in the occupied territories, where Ukrainian churches of the Moscow Patriarchate automatically became churches of the Russian Orthodox Church. The same thing happened in Crimea after the annexation in 2014. Many Ukrainian politicians prefer not to talk about how quickly the Ukrainian churches of the Moscow Patriarchate in Crimea transferred allegiance to the Russian Orthodox Church.

The Ukrainian Autocephalous Church is following these events in great anticipation. The adoption and implementation of the new law will mean that it will become the main church in Ukraine. Actively patriotic Ukrainians expect this too, seeing the Ukrainian Autocephalous Church as more progressive and democratic and, of course, less politicised than the Moscow Patriarchate Church.

While deputies in Kyiv debate about the Moscow Patriarchate, something of a scandal has broken out in Lviv in the west of Ukraine. The rector of one of Lviv's ancient churches, the Church of St Andrew the First-Called, allowed the cult poet and rock singer Serhiy Zhadan to film a music video inside the church. The well-known Lviv singer Khristina Solovey also sang in the video. It is rumoured that Serhiy Zhadan, who recently filed for a divorce from his wife, is in a romantic relationship with Solovey.

When the video was released, the rector of the church declared it immoral and demanded that it be removed from public access. The video shows same-sex couples kissing, although these clips were not shot in the church. Khristina Solovey has expressed fears that if she returned to her native Lviv, she would be burned in public. There have been pleas from other priests that everyone should forget about this clip, so as not to turn glorious Lviv into the centre for some kind of Ukrainian inquisition. Meanwhile, the rector of St Andrew the First-Called has cancelled all the non-liturgical events that were to take place in the church, including a charity auction for the Ukrainian army. A logical continuation of this story would be the ritual of cleansing the temple from the defilement of the video clip. This episode might be merely amusing if it had not harmed the fundraising efforts for the Ukrainian army.

Meanwhile, Moscow has provided something else for Ukrainians to laugh at. During one of his speeches, Patriarch Kirill, the main voice of the Moscow Church and Putin's closest ally, stated that Soviet scientists had created atomic weapons with the help and protection of the Russian Orthodox Saint, Seraphim of Sarov, and that it is only thanks to these atomic weapons that Russia continues to exist.

31.10.2023

Funerals and Weddings, Tears and Joy

The cold weather and snow that affect tactics along the front line also bring new reasons for anxiety at the rear. Winter will postpone many construction projects, including the plan to create a National Military Cemetery as a resting place for the military heroes of this war.

It is no secret that the families of many fallen Ukrainian soldiers keep the urns with the ashes of their loved ones at home, or stored in crematoria, in anticipation of the creation of the National Military Cemetery that Parliament approved in May 2022. However, the plan has not moved forward since then. Indeed, the bill has not yet been signed by President Zelensky.

Initially, it was decided that the location of the new Pantheon would be discussed with the families of the victims. In March the N.G.O. Heart Out was registered in Ukraine to unite the relatives of fallen Ukrainian soldiers. Its founder and leader is Vira Litvinenko, the mother of Vladislav Litvinenko, who died fighting in Mariupol. As the number of dead increases, Heart Out has become more active and Vira Litvinenko's public statements have increased in intensity.

State and city authorities first considered four locations in Kyiv for the memorial complex, including an area near the Holocaust Memorial Centre at Babyn Yar. Each of these locations was later ruled out. Next, an area on the very edge of Kyiv, near the village of Bykovnya, was discussed. This place was notorious, in Soviet times, as the execution and burial site of "enemies of the people" during 1937–40. Many of those killed were representatives of the Ukrainian intelligentsia, including writers, journalists, teachers and scientists.

Heart Out members considered Bykovnya an acceptable location for the cemetery, but government officials once again changed their minds and decided to locate the cemetery further from Kyiv within the boundaries of the village of Gatne in Fastiv district. The official explanation for the change of plan was that Bykovnya already had a memorial complex dedicated to the victims of Stalin's repressions and that the location offered too little space. From the outset, it was thought that 100 hectares would be required, but the proposed site in Bykovnya offered only 50 hectares.

The authorities believe that Gatne is the best place for the cemetery because there is plenty of land there and restrictions on construction projects are less strict than within Kyiv city limits. However, the relatives of fallen soldiers are unhappy. Kyiv's largest public cemetery, Pivdenne, is located near Gatne and traffic is always heavy. Secondly, there is also a German cemetery nearby, where German soldiers from World War II are buried, as well as those German prisoners of war who died in the post-war years while being used as forced labour to rebuild Kyiv. Olena Tolkacheva, a well-known volunteer, politician and veteran of this war, commented, "The relatives of the victims perceive the proposal to create a cemetery in Gatne instead of Bykovnya as an insult."

The regulations regarding the future National Military Cemetery have been drafted. It is already clear who will have the right to be buried in this cemetery and that funerals there will be paid for by the state. For the relatives of fallen soldiers, the cost is probably not the most important thing. However, the fact that military personnel already buried in other cemeteries cannot be reburied at the National Military Cemetery is a serious restriction and explains why many relatives are keeping the urns with the ashes of their dead at home or in storage in crematoria.

A number of family members have lost patience and faith in the project. On Saturday, October 28, the ashes of the fighter Oleksandr Gryanik were buried at Kyiv's Lukyanivske cemetery. He was missing, presumed dead, for eight months before his remains were eventually identified through D.N.A. tests. He was cremated in January 2023 and the family had been hoping later to bury his ashes at the National Military Cemetery.

Speaking after the farewell ceremony for his son, Gryanik's father said, "It makes my heart feel better because now we can come here, bring flowers and talk to our son."

As Ukraine repels increasingly fierce attacks along the front line, funeral music is heard in every region of Ukraine. However, the military conflict has not stopped people wanting to get married. The war has also expanded the geographical scope of Ukraine's wedding agencies. Occasionally, weddings take place on the front line. Certain agencies organise ceremonies for military personnel, which are conducted with unusual speed and for free. One such agency was created by Olena Yaroshenko from Zaporizhzhia. Her brainchild is called Love Wins. Last year, when Zaporizhzhia was under constant attack, Olena moved to Khmelnytsky, further from the front line. She continues to organise weddings for military personnel throughout Ukraine, including in settlements very close to the front line.

Sometimes both the bride and groom are soldiers, but more often it is only the groom. They will be given only a couple of days' leave for their wedding. Olena convinces such couples, who usually envisage a quick signing of the register with minimal ceremony and no celebration, to have a proper wedding. She finds wedding outfits for them, provided free of charge, and an appropriate venue where the couple can enjoy a traditional Ukrainian wedding celebration. Over the past seven years, Olena has organised more than fifty weddings for military personnel. "This is our way of saying 'Thank you!' to the guys for risking their lives. We want to give them the best day of their lives," she says.

Since February 2022, much has changed in Ukrainian legislation on marriage. Couples no longer have to wait a month after applying to marry. You can now complete the process in a single day. Military personnel can even marry online; a soldier's immediate commander is now permitted to draw up a marriage certificate and marry the couple in this manner, if necessary.

While the changes in legislation around marriage are making life easier for families in this time of war, the controversy over the creation of the National Military Cemetery is not helping them.

The cold and the snow of winter lie ahead. At this time of year, emotions subside. I hope that by spring a solution will be found that suits everyone and, above all, suits the families of the fallen Ukrainian soldiers.

06.11.2023

Bullets Flying in All Directions

Last winter, in his studio on Lukyanivska Street, Matviy Weisberg – one of Kyiv's best-known artists – began work on his painting "Blackout". He worked by candlelight because attacks by Russian missiles had left the city without electricity. The painting is still in his workshop, but it no longer reminds him of last winter.

Rather, it reflects a new reality.

Weisberg's workshop is in a five-storey block of artists' studios which was designed as a creative space in the Soviet era. As many as 80 artists work in the building, which is administered by the National Ukrainian Academy of Fine Arts and Architecture. Recently, the Academy's president – an artist who worked in the same building on Lukyanivska Street for ten years – gave the order to disconnect the electricity supply, saying that a number of the artists owed money for amenities and that it was his job to look after the Academy's students and not to pay the debts of professional artists.

However, some of the studio tenants donate earnings from the sale of their work to the Ukrainian army. Weisberg recently donated 20,000€. Now he has to "fight" on two fronts, continuing to help the Ukrainian army while battling for reasonable conditions in his workspace.

It remains impossible to predict how this internal battle will end. Ukraine is still without a Minister of Culture, which makes resolving the conflict through official channels difficult. Artists get a lot of moral support and sympathy from the public, but this is not the time for mass demonstrations in defence of workshops. War sets its own priorities. In the newsfeed, information about the artists' struggle is lost among more dramatic stories.

———

The war against the Ukrainian Church of the Moscow Patriarchate continues, but with no significant developments, it has dropped out of the news. That battle has been replaced in the media by the Special Services' fight against the "charismatic sect" AllatRa, whose offices in twenty cities of Ukraine were recently raided. Until recently, the organisation had drawn little attention to itself, and the raids have unearthed some surprises, including the fact that some Ukrainian deputies and government officials were affiliated with it.

During the searches, explosives, weapons and pro-Russian literature were discovered, as well as strange pyramid-shaped, mirror-clad cabins – like something out of a science fiction film. These one-person pyramids make me think of telephone booths for communicating with outer space.

The sect's leader, Igor Danilov, was born in Donbas, where he began treating spinal problems in the 1990s. In his free time, he translated English-language detective stories and science

259

fiction into Russian. In 2002, he moved to Kyiv and opened a private clinic for the treatment of spinal diseases and injuries on the land belonging to Ukraine's most prestigious monastery, the Kyiv-Pechersk Lavra.

At the very beginning of the war, he escaped abroad, presenting forged disability documents to the border guards. From elsewhere in Europe, he continues to direct AllatRa, which has branches in many countries of the former U.S.S.R., as well as in the E.U. and the U.S.A.

A key message preached by the sect is "the friendship of the Slavic peoples" and the unification of all Russian-speaking people in a "creative society", under the leadership of Tsar Nomo, whose biography is reminiscent of Vladimir Putin's.

In August, the sect was banned in Russia. AllatRa was accused of establishing ties with political opposition groups and spreading "fake news" about the Russian army. The Russian prosecutor's office did not present any evidence for these accusations, which indicates that the real reason for the ban was the Kremlin's lack of control over the sect's activities or the impression that Igor Danilov was making money using the Russian President's image and the idea of the "Russian World".

For now, AllatRa's Ukrainian offices and mirror pyramids are sealed and under police supervision.

———

Meanwhile, the real war continues in the south and east of the country. As Ukraine knocked out the newly built battleship *Askold* which was moored in Kerch, Crimea, Russian missiles struck targets in Odesa. One missile landed right in front of the Central Art Museum, shattering the windows and seriously damaging the facade.

Social media posts by Ukrainian intellectuals suggest that

each attack on Russian-speaking Odesa will encourage more citizens to switch to speaking Ukrainian. But it is worth noting that Odesa is a commercial city – full of sellers and buyers – where people are used to responding in the buyer's language if they know it. At the central market, in addition to Ukrainian and Russian, you will hear Moldavian, Bulgarian and Gagauz. Hatred of Russia, which is evident at every step around the city, has not transposed into hatred of the Russian language.

Before the war, tension around the language question appeared to be a figment of individual politicians' imaginations, but now a very real internal conflict has flared up. Over the past ten days, attacks against speakers of Russian have increased public interest in the issue and gleaned some strong reactions from the military.

First, two women in Kyiv ordered a Bolt taxi (the equivalent of Uber) and demanded that the taxi driver who came to pick them up speak to them only in Ukrainian. The taxi driver turned out to be a refugee from Crimea who did not speak any Ukrainian. He called the women "sick" and suggested they call another taxi. One of the passengers recorded the conversation and posted it on Facebook as evidence of a violation of "the Law on the State Language", which says that the default language for all service providers is Ukrainian unless the client asks for another language to be used.

Bolt immediately revoked the driver's permit to use their platform. Language Ombudsman Taras Kremin announced that he would report the matter to the police and that the driver would face a huge fine for violating the language law.

Then the Ukrainian singer Svitlana Loboda, who, it must be said, is very popular in Russia, offered the taxi driver a job as her chauffeur. Both Yuri Boyko, a Member of Parliament from the now outlawed pro-Russian party Opposition Bloc for Life and Oleksiy Arestovich, the former adviser to the Office of the President, publicly supported the driver.

Alongside this scandal, a court in Lviv sentenced an internally displaced person from Donbas to seven years in prison for stabbing his colleague – a native of Lviv. The drama occurred when the two men were renovating an apartment. During a lunch break, tempers flared when the worker from Lviv suggested that his Russian-speaking colleague should switch to Ukrainian and asked him why he had not joined the army. As a result, an apartment remains unrenovated, one worker is in prison, and another is in hospital.

The climax of this round of the fight over language was a statement from the infamous anti-Russian-language crusader and former Member of Parliament, Iryna Farion, who declared that Russian-speaking Ukrainian soldiers should not call themselves Ukrainians. Feedback from both Russian- and Ukrainian-speaking soldiers was not long in coming.

Ukrainian soldier Ekaterina Polishchuk – known throughout the country by her call sign Ptashka (Birdie) – who fought in Mariupol and survived Russian captivity, said: "Your position is not pro-Ukrainian and I consider you a project of the Kremlin. You are an enemy, promoting poisonous narratives. Your position and statements are complete shit. I say this as someone who spoke Ukrainian in captivity and who has been defending Ukraine for three years side by side with heroes who speak Ukrainian, Russian, Georgian, Belarusian, Polish, dozens of dialects, English, and dozens of other languages . . ."

Major Maxim Zhorin, deputy commander of the 3rd Joint Assault Brigade, responded with the same message, but in words that nobody is likely to print. Yegor Chernev, Member of Parliament and Deputy Chairman of the Parliamentary Committee on Security, Defence and Intelligence, commented on Farion's statement, emphasising that there cannot be a division of Ukrainians into first- and second-class citizens along linguistic lines. He also asked the Special Services to investigate Iryna Farion's statements for evidence of incitement to ethnic hatred – a criminal offence.

After all that, we can predict that the fight over language will subside for a while and other hot topics will appear. For myself, I would like to see Kyiv's artists working in their workshops on Lukyanivska Street, with the heating and lights on.

I also hope that the Odesa Art Museum can be renovated and reopened to the public. Perhaps Weisberg's "Blackout" can be acquired and put on display there. Through their works, Ukrainian cultural practitioners can ensure that what happens to us today remains not only in our memories but also in art, literature, music and cinema. The reality that kills can become a story that keeps our brains and hearts alive.

14.11.2023

Kherson – City without Music

A few days ago, the city of Kherson celebrated the first anniversary of its liberation from Russian occupation. The date was marked more online than in person and there were no fireworks. President Zelensky, however, announced awards for the defenders of Kherson and for those residents who displayed heroism while under occupation.

One of those awarded was Ihor Dryuk, a surgeon from the city hospital who continued to operate on townspeople while refusing to treat Russian military personnel. How he managed to stay alive and keep working is a mystery, but we know that the Russian military distrusts Ukrainian doctors, especially surgeons. They lure Russian specialists to the occupied territories with very high salaries and travel allowances.

President Zelensky did not visit Kherson on the occasion of the anniversary. The city and the surrounding towns and villages are under constant shelling from the still-occupied left bank of the Dnipro River and to call the mood in the city celebratory would be untrue. The date was, however, marked by the opening of a new underground public space Svoï (Ours) – the result of cooperation between local businesses, social workers and activists. Svoye is a well-equipped bomb shelter, made to look like a club. It will serve as a venue for cultural events and training courses, including sessions for children which focus on safety.

Security is a key issue for Kherson. The city's population used to be 350,000 before the war. Now it's only about 55,000, and that includes about 5,000 children. All schools operate online because of the daily shelling and because most school buildings have been damaged or destroyed. Kindergartens also work online, but in reality parents look after their children while kindergarten teachers attend online pedagogical conferences for which they are paid two-thirds of their salaries, just so that they have something to live on.

Since liberation, more than 800 people, including more than 30 children living in or near the city, have been killed by Russian shells and missiles.

A Military Writers' forum was held in Kherson on the anniversary of liberation. Events took place both under- and overground. Participants had to register in advance on a special website and were informed about the exact location of meetings only shortly before they started.

Attendance was good despite the danger. There is not

much intellectual entertainment in the city. The drama theatre only performs in its small underground auditorium which seats 50 people. Cinemas are closed.

The star of this year's Military Writers' forum was Olena Mokrenchuk, a major in the Ukrainian army and Press Officer for the operational command of the North Group. Before the war, she lived in Donbas, but after her city of Snezhnoye was occupied, she moved to western Ukraine and then joined the army. Before that, she worked as a journalist, a teacher and also as a church choir conductor.

Now, in her off-duty moments, she writes children's stories about the war. One of her books, *Aliska – the Front-line Fox*, was published in two versions: for primary-age and secondary-age children. Serviceman Oleksandr Olshinsky spent time between battles creating a computer game based on the book.

Mokrenchuk's talk at the forum was attended mainly by adults, including military personnel stationed near Kherson who were given special leave for the event.

Russia monitors activity in Ukraine very closely. They are especially interested in what is happening in Kherson. On the very day of the writers' forum, they dropped a guided bomb on the city's main library – the Oles Gonchar Regional Library.

The building had already been shelled by Russian artillery several times but each time repairs were made and windows and doors replaced so that the library could remain open. This time, the bomb destroyed most of the building, and tens of thousands of books were destroyed in the ensuing fire.

As firefighters were trying to bring the blaze under control, Russia attacked the library again, this time trying to kill the firefighters and destroy their equipment. Some of the firefighters were injured, but the fire was extinguished after a few hours.

The library will not be reopening any time soon. It needs major restoration and a new stock of books.

On the left bank of the Dnipro, the Russian administration has also organised literary festivals. "Ivan Turgenev Day" was celebrated almost simultaneously with the anniversary of the liberation of Kherson. The meetings and exhibitions dedicated to the Russian classic writer's life and work carried pompous titles like "Strings of the Russian Soul", "All My Thoughts about Russia" and "Singer of the Russian Word". Photographs used in press releases show only Turgenev's books and no crowds of participants. Perhaps nobody was invited, or nobody wanted to be caught on camera for fear of compromising themselves.

Russia has already proudly announced that it has brought to the occupied territories more than three million copies of books by Russian writers, including Turgenev, Dostoevsky and Pushkin. Ukrainians, meanwhile, are posting announcements on Facebook and Instagram offering to give away volumes of Russian classics to anyone who wants them. Many more people are getting rid of these books than are taking them. Families who read would have possessed volumes of Tolstoy, Chekhov and Dostoevsky from Soviet times.

In the morning and early afternoon, civilians whom you meet on Kherson's streets will be wearing bulletproof vests. They will be civil servants, officials of all ranks and communal services personnel – janitors, plumbers and electricians – who are all required to wear an extra ten kilograms of "clothes" every day. There are a lot of vacancies for these positions, and residents say that it is precisely because of the mandatory wearing of body armour that people do not want these jobs. The heavy kit makes the work too tiring.

The curfew in Kherson starts at 8 p.m., but you will hardly see anyone on the streets after 4 p.m., which is when city transport stops working. Taxi drivers serve citizens only until lunchtime and usually refuse to go to the suburbs that are most often shelled from the left bank. Given all this, the city's residents tend to spend their days inside their apartments and houses, going out only to visit the shops.

Despite the ongoing shelling, shops are reopening in the city and neighbouring villages. Over the past ten months, businesses in the Ukrainian-controlled areas of Kherson region have received more than 800 licences to sell alcohol and tobacco.

All basic goods are available, but life in liberated Kherson remains far from normal, and stress levels must be much higher than in towns and cities further away from the front line. Nonetheless, even in Bukovina, in western Ukraine, local authorities see the need to distract their residents and displaced people from thoughts of war. The mayors of the mountain towns of Putyla and Vyzhnytsia are attempting to achieve this through music.

In Putyla, every day at noon, Petro Semashko comes out to the central square to play the trembita, a Hutsul folk instrument, similar to an Alpine horn. The trembita can be up to eight metres long and its sound can be heard at a distance of up to ten kilometres. Residents and visitors converge on the town centre at noon for the daily ritual.

In the neighbouring town of Vyzhnytsia, Ihor Luchik, a violinist and teacher at the music school, comes out to the central square at noon to play a song about the Carpathian Mountains that is well known to all Ukrainians.

"There were comments that, since there's a war going on, it's not the time for this," says Ganna Vatamanyuk, Ihor Luchik's colleague from the music school. "But it seems to me that culture, history, and art are always appropriate. What's more, thank God, it's calm here!"

Unfortunately, things are never calm in Kherson and the

only musical event to occur recently was the shooting of a video clip in which Kyrylo Boridko, a former student of one of the city's now-defunct music schools, played the piano in the ruins of the city's oldest gymnasium. Kherson residents share the video clip link with friends and relatives who have left the city and together they cry over a past that will never return.

21.11.2023

War, Winter and Ski Jackets

In the popular Ukrainian ski resort of Bukovel, snow ploughs are clearing the streets as restaurant owners put the finishing touches to their menus and negotiate with suppliers of fresh produce. The profitable season is about to begin, and although Russian missiles and drones are bound to affect their plans, businesses are determined to entertain guests and make money.

Hotel prices have come down a little and less wealthy Ukrainians may be able to afford a winter holiday this year. However, if the crowded restaurants in Odesa and Kyiv and reported sales figures for new cars (almost at their pre-war level) are anything to go by, there are still plenty of people in Ukraine who will not be too worried about how much their ski trip costs.

The real issue for resort managers is staffing. There is a serious shortage of personnel in Bukovel: some 275 vacancies for hotel administrators, cooks, waiters, housekeepers, electricians and plumbers. For the less specialised posts, employers are ready to take people with no experience and train them on the job. Employees get free meals, accommodation and reasonable wages. However, many men are simply too afraid to go to this "mountain mousetrap", where military enlistment officers can arrive at any moment on one of their mobilisation campaigns. It would not surprise me if some of the restaurants and cafés are turned into self-service food courts this winter.

Hostilities continue, especially around Avdiivka, a town that the Russian army has been trying to capture for several months. Thousands of Russian soldiers have died there already, but their commanders are forever sending in reinforcements, often without the support of tanks or armoured personnel carriers. Each day, a new swathe of Russian soldiers crawls towards Ukrainian positions through muddy fields strewn with the bodies of their compatriots. At the same time, Russian artillery is diligently wiping the city off the face of the earth. More than a thousand residents are still living in the basements of Avdiivka's apartment blocks. The population shrank further recently when a hundred people finally agreed to evacuate. They were taken to the rear by Ukrainian police.

Together with volunteers from a Kharkiv animal rescue organisation, the police have been helping with another special operation in the area. In the spring, the Russians bombed a stud farm in the suburbs of Avdiivka, killing some 300 horses. Two horses escaped into the town, where they have been living among the ruins ever since, traumatised and frightened of people. Animal rescue volunteers brought a professional groom and his horse to Avdiivka. As expected, the feral animals were put at ease seeing the visiting horse and the groom was able to lead them into an enclosure, from which they will be transported far from the front line.

A new batch of Russian prisoners of war is also waiting to be sent west. They are easier to transport than horses, but those who are not wounded first undergo a series of interrogations to determine whether they have committed war crimes. After the verification process, a long journey awaits them. It usually ends in western Ukraine, at the only functioning prisoner-of-war camp, Zahid-1, where some commentators say life is a little too comfortable. Inmates rise at six, exercise and then have breakfast. On their way to the dining hall, they pass portraits of historical Ukrainian figures, including Taras Shevchenko, the poet. To cure prisoners of the effects of Kremlin propaganda, they are obliged to attend lectures on Ukrainian history. The lectures get mixed reviews. Some prisoners of war perceive them merely as Ukrainian propaganda.

Since Russia froze the prisoner exchange process several months ago, there are more and more prisoners in Ukraine, as there are Ukrainian prisoners in Russia.

For now, Russian prisoners are set to work performing simple tasks, like dismantling wooden pallets and turning them into other wooden products. In their free time, they can read or watch Ukrainian television channels, including the Russian-language state channel Dom. Sometimes they talk to their relatives in Russia on the telephone. There is also a library, for the most part stocked with Soviet editions of Russian and Soviet authors.

In exchange for their work, the P.O.W.s receive a symbolic wage, the equivalent to about seven euros a month. There is a shop in the camp where they can spend this money. The most popular product is said to be Coca-Cola, which is no longer available in Russia.

Among the Russian prisoners, there are ordinary, mobilised soldiers, contract soldiers, and former criminals who were released from prison in exchange for a commitment to fight against Ukraine. The last group of "professional" prisoners have tried to establish the same systems they had in Russian prisons, where inmates and not the administration set the rules and where less experienced prisoners are abused. The Ukrainian camp staff have had to work hard to maintain control. Some of these P.O.W.s have been transferred to civilian prisons and they can now be found at 50 prisons around Ukraine.

As Zahid-1 reaches capacity, a new camp is being built in Vinnytsia region in the south-west of the country, and the construction of a further camp is being discussed. No-one knows when Russia will unfreeze the exchange of prisoners.

Not all Russian prisoners are eager to return home. If they do, they know that they will be sent back to the front. They feel safe in Ukraine and, according to information on the Ukrainian Government website, their living conditions are reasonable. Recently, one of the Russian P.O.W.s even had a visit from his wife.

Indeed, the tender for the purchase of food for P.O.W.s, which was announced by the state, has caused outrage among many Ukrainians. A Member of Parliament, Serhiy Rudyk, a historian and lieutenant colonel in the Ukrainian army, addressed the Minister of Justice saying, "We purchased more than one hundred thousand hryvnias' (about 2,900€) worth of sweets and chocolates alone. And I only looked at the first few pages of government procurement for September . . . Dozens of varieties of expensive sausage, cheese, coffee . . . People, are you crazy? Is this how you feed Russian prisoners of war, or are you just stupidly and cynically stealing?" No response has been forthcoming from the Minister of Justice, although Rudyk probably did not expect one. His was a cry from the heart.

Some Ukrainians joke morosely that soon prisoners of war will be taken out on excursions and theatre trips, while there is evidence that Ukrainian P.O.W.s in Russia are being kept on starvation rations and are bullied and subjected to torture. All Ukrainians remember the film of the exchange event when a thin, exhausted Ukrainian soldier wept after being given an apple by people who greeted him.

Life in the Zahid-1 camp cannot be compared to life at the Bukovel ski resort, but the Russian inmates may be surprised to know that some of the jackets for their national ski team were produced not so far away, in Zakarpattia. The Russian ski team's kit, with the double-headed eagle on the left sleeve of a bright red jacket, is fairly conspicuous and you might think it would be impossible to produce such a garment in Ukraine right now, but as we have seen many times, in Ukraine nothing is impossible.

The ski kits are produced by the Italian brand Vist and the job of making the jackets was given to a clothing factory near Uzhhorod that is owned by an Italian citizen. Most of the factory employees did not know about this "special operation". The ski jackets were made in an isolated area of the factory and five seamstresses who had a reputation for being able to keep quiet were selected to work on the project. Despite these precautions, word got out about the order and the factory was raided by the police and the S.B.U., but not before 40 batches of the ski jackets had already been sent to Russia by way of Italy. While part of the factory's Ukrainian management is under investigation, workers continue to make clothes for the domestic market and for export to Europe.

Keeping people in work and occupied is important as fears increase about the winter and the continuing attacks on Ukraine's infrastructure. Fortunately, the meteorologists are promising that this winter will be two to three degrees warmer than last year, with no severe frosts. But there will be plenty of snow – enough to satisfy the holidaymakers in Bukovel and the children of all ages throughout the country who are eagerly awaiting the chance to take to their sledges.

28.11.2023

A Place Where You Can Choose Your Family Name but Not What to Remember

The weather has made a dramatic entry into the war. First, a storm raged over the Black Sea, the like of which had not been seen for a hundred years. The waves rose to a height of nine metres, washing away Russian fortifications and trenches from the beaches of Crimea. A Russian Raptor-class military patrol vessel was split in two by the force of the waves. In the Azov Sea, the storm destroyed all the floating defence structures that Russia had placed to protect the bridge between Kerch and Russia. At the same time, heavy snowfall in Odesa region blocked roads. Ten Ukrainian citizens died in the snowstorms and accompanying strong winds, and tens of thousands of people were left without electricity for some time.

The extreme weather began after the Holodomor Remembrance Day, which marks the death by starvation of millions of Ukrainians during 1932–3 following the confiscation of all food stocks from Ukraine's peasants, including any seed grain, by special units of the Red Army. To remember this tragedy, we place lighted candles in our windows.

Although the last Saturday in November was established as Holodomor Memorial Day in 1998, lighting candles only became a broadly accepted practice after the Orange Revolution of 2004–5. As the nation's awareness of this tragedy has grown, Russian politicians have become increasingly hysterical in their ridicule of it. Russia has never admitted its part in the Holodomor or in Ukraine's post-war famine of 1947. According to Putin, no-one organised the famines. "It was just a bad harvest." To underline his attitude, on the night of Holodomor Memorial

Day, Saturday, November 25, Iranian drones attacked the capital in the most intensive bombing of Kyiv for many months, preventing the city's three million residents from getting any sleep. Seventy-five drones were fired at the city, of which 74 were shot down. In the morning, the people of Kyiv got up and went about their business as usual, tired but resolute.

For collaborators and representatives of the occupation authorities in the town of Oleshki, Kherson region, November 26 was also a busy day. Their task was to destroy the town's monument to the victims of the Holodomor. No monuments to these events now remain in the occupied part of Kherson region. The Russian government calls them "instruments of manipulation" by which "the Ukrainian government incites hatred of Russia among its citizens". From Russia's point of view, the destruction of these monuments is about "dismantling symbols of disinformation".

In addition to removing everything Ukrainian, the occupation administrations are pushing forward with other processes that were launched as soon as they took power, such as the distribution of Russian passports. This process is, however, going more slowly than at first. While most people refused to take the Russian passports, all the pro-Russian Ukrainians took Russian passports early on, thereby becoming eligible for Russian pensions and other state benefits. For residents who continue to refuse, meanwhile, new barriers are being thrown up at every step. For example, medical care is now provided only to holders of Russian passports and only Russian citizens have the right to work as taxi drivers.

In every occupied town or village, the "authorities" have lists of residents who have refused to exchange their Ukrainian passport for a Russian one. From time to time, representatives of Russia's secret services visit these "troublemakers" for "a chat", while collaborators are asked to watch them and report on their activities. At school, children of such families often have their mobile phones checked for evidence that they are working for the Ukrainian army.

Despite these efforts, Russia has not achieved great success in destroying Ukrainian identity in the occupied territories. On the contrary, many parents have submitted petitions to school directors demanding that classes be taught in Ukrainian. They are making use of a Russian law which determines how the language of instruction should be decided in the territories of "national minorities". Since many Ukrainian-speaking teachers left Kherson and Zaporizhzhia regions as the occupying forces moved in, teachers from Russia have been brought in to replace them. As a result, few teachers in the occupied territories are able to conduct lessons in Ukrainian.

There is also the problem of Ukrainian language textbooks, although the Russian Ministry of Education is working to solve this. Last summer, a textbook on the "classical Ukrainian language" was developed for elementary schools in the occupied territories. The book contains texts in Ukrainian about all that is beautiful in Russia and wonderful about Moscow. The preparation of "classical Ukrainian language" textbooks for high school students is a work in progress. "We teach in Russian, but teach Ukrainian as a native language, as well as other languages of the peoples of Russia. We will create all the conditions for this," said the Russian Deputy Minister of Education, Aleksandr Bugaev.

While school textbooks in Ukrainian are being prepared for printing in Russia, Russian representatives in Zaporizhia region have come up with an additional device to encourage the switch to Russian passports. Residents with Ukrainian surnames who wish to receive a Russian passport can change their surnames so that they sound more Russian. Posters advertising this service read: "Changing your passport? Change your last name too! Let's cleanse ourselves of imposed Ukrainian Nazism!"

Ukrainian surnames have a number of traditional endings, such as ending in "ko" – such as Shevchenko, Petrenko, and the like. If you add the single letter "v" to these surnames, they immediately sound more "Russian" because many familiar Russian surnames end in "ov". To illustrate the possibilities, the poster offers an example of how the "discordant" Ukrainian surname Halushko can suddenly become the "beautiful" Russian surname Glushkov. (There is also no equivalent to the letter H in Russian.)

In response to the call to Russify Ukrainian surnames, Ukrainian activists, remembering how many Ukrainians still live with surnames that were Russified during the Soviet era, have called on people to remove these extra letters from their surnames. All this reminds me of a conversation I once had with the Ukrainian poet Pavlo Movchan. In the early '90s, he tried to prove to me that my real name was not Kurkov but Kurko, and that my ancestors were Russified Ukrainians.

It is unlikely that Ukrainian citizens will engage in the de-Russification of their surnames while the war goes on. There are millions of ethnic Russians in Ukraine with common Russian surnames. After the war, however, ethnic Russians may be first in line to register for a change. They will not want to be reminded of their origins and a Ukrainian name may smooth their career path and prevent their children from being called "Muscovites" at school.

Mind you, given how multicultural Ukrainian society is today, I am not sure that Ukrainians should worry too much about having a typical Russian surname. After all, one of the main ideologues of Ukrainian nationalism from the beginning of the twentieth century bore a typical Russian surname that is associated with the Don River. His name was Dmitriy Dontsov; he is thus associated with the toponym for Donetsk and Donbas.

Residents of the village of Sartana, near Mariupol, also in Donbas, mostly have Greek surnames. They are Azov Greeks and they have always had a special sympathy for Russia. In 2014, they lay down in front of Ukrainian armoured vehicles, preventing them from driving towards the Ukrainian border with Russia and so helping the Russian army capture the city of Novoazovsk. In 2015, a Ukrainian officer serving in Donbas told me how Azov Greeks were helping the Russian military, but he asked me not to write about it. "There is no need to provoke ethnic hatred," he said wisely. Nine years have passed and people now talk openly about the Azov Greeks – how they became the most active collaborators and how quickly they joined the Russian Society of Ethnic Greeks.

Recently some completely unexpected news has arrived from Sartana. The Russian occupation authorities issued summonses to all men in the village demanding that they come to the military registration and enlistment office. It seems that mobilisation in the occupied territories is gaining momentum and soon many new citizens of the Russian Federation will be asked to fight against the Ukrainian army. Residents of Donetsk and Luhansk have been fighting against the Ukrainian army for a long time and, when they are taken prisoner, they claim that they were forced to join up.

What do the Azov Greeks from Sartana, Mariupol, Novoazovsk and other coastal towns say when they fall into Ukrainian captivity? They took Russian passports voluntarily and were among the first to do so. They may not want to fight but men who have already taken a Russian passport cannot refuse mobilisation.

In the meantime, Ukraine is posting instructions to Azov Greeks about how to surrender correctly. This knowledge could very well save their lives.

05.12.2023

Flight and Flights of Fancy

Whenever a wave of pessimism rises in Ukrainian society, the media turns to the topic of resuming air transport links with the rest of the world. Since articles started to appear analysing the reasons for the failed summer counter-offensive, politicians are again saying that Ukraine is about to re-launch civil aviation. Recently, the Head of the Office of the President, Andriy Ermak, summoned foreign diplomats to a meeting at Kyiv's Boryspil airport. Invitations to ambassadors were sent in the form of boarding passes, on which the flight destination was the Ukrainian peace formula.

Photographs of the meeting showing a hundred participants, including representatives of 83 foreign states, sitting around a huge round table in the large hall of Terminal D. Foreign participants in the meeting spoke about supporting the Ukrainian peace formula. The photographs were calculated to restore optimism and faith in the imminent end of the war. The airport terminal sparkled and looked ready for action. Even the flight departure board glowed, showing optimism in its indication of destinations to which there were previously no direct flights – Buenos Aires, Jakarta, Panama City, Reykjavik and Washington.

The choice of venue was not accidental. The country's main airport symbolises readiness for decisive diplomatic action to promote the Ukrainian peace formula.

As the meeting was taking place, Ukrainian journalists noticed that advertisements for vacancies at Boryspil airport appeared on job sites. The airport is looking for pilots for an Airbus and an An-148 plane, flight attendants, an aviation ornithologist and specialists in pre-flight aircraft maintenance. At the same time, there was an announcement from the Office of the President that Boryspil would be the first Ukrainian airport to restart operations. Admittedly, the statement included a line about how the airport will only open when civil aviation flights are one hundred per cent. safe, so we should not hold our breath.

Discussions on the same topic held earlier in the autumn were more pragmatic. Experts analysed which airport in Ukraine might be safest and suggested that at least one of them, that in Uzhhorod, could start operating without waiting for the end of hostilities. The runway of Uzhhorod's airport ends right at the border with Slovakia. As soon as planes leave the runway, they find themselves in European Union airspace.

Planes are still flying, even if there are no commercial passenger flights. During my time as an internally displaced person in the far west of Ukraine in Zakarpatsky city, I would see small planes taking off and landing there. They were not ordinary passenger planes, although the airport remains in working order and still has some personnel.

The Ukrainian airline SkyUP, whose eleven Boeings have been operating on lease outside Ukraine since the beginning of the war, recently reminded Ukraine about its existence in an unexpected manner. The company has published a children's book in Ukrainian on how to prepare for air travel. The book aims in particular to support children with autism, for whom any trip is associated with stress. It describes, step by step, a passenger's preparations for a flight.

It has to be said that for most children in Ukraine, the sky is

279

now a dangerous place, from which comes devastation. Few Ukrainians will look up at the stars over Christmas and imagine Santa Claus' sleigh sparkling overhead.

Plenty of children will be hoping to at least spend the festive season with both their parents. Sadly, even this simple wish is out of reach for many. The catastrophic shortage of soldiers on the front line that stretches for more than a thousand kilometres is forcing military registration and enlistment offices to take ever more decisive action to strengthen the mobilisation campaign. Enlistment officers, together with the police, now stop vehicles on highways and are taking drivers straight to military training camps, leaving their cars abandoned by the roadside. These highway mobilisation events can be startling in their cinematic absurdity.

In November of this year, a children's taekwondo team travelled by bus from Vinnytsia to Uzhhorod for a competition. At night, military enlistment officers blocked off the hotel where the bus driver was sleeping. The driver and other men staying in the hotel were woken up and taken off to a military training camp. As a result, this group of young athletes from Vinnytsia was stranded in Uzhhorod until their trainer could find a new driver and the mobilised driver was able to send the keys back to Uzhhorod, which he did with the help of some obliging strangers.

A couple of days ago, also in Uzhhorod, military enlistment officers, working alongside the police, blocked off the exits of three fitness centres and handed enlistment papers to all the men who were exercising inside.

Judging by a recent interview with President Zelensky's wife, even she is not sure that her husband will be with the family for Christmas. Mrs Zelensky also said that she was categorically against her husband running for a second presidential term. She sounded quite sincere. However, President Zelensky's first term could easily stretch into two terms. It has already been decided that neither presidential nor parliamentary elections can take place while the war continues. How indeed could elections be held when eight million citizens are living as refugees abroad, millions of others do not live where they are registered as voters and hundreds of thousands of voters are fighting at the front?

As Christmas approaches, we must spare a thought for the people in the occupied areas of Ukraine, especially the children in the cities of Lysychans'k and Rubizhne, in Luhansk region, for whom the festive season will be overshadowed by a figure from their nightmares, the Babai, the night-time bogeyman.

Putin has instructed the Republic of Tatarstan to take over the patronage of these cities, which once had a combined population of approximately 200,000 people. The figure is now probably only a quarter of that. Products from Tatarstan have since appeared in the shops and doctors, electricians, musicians, plumbers and public administrators from that far-away republic have been brought to work in these cities. As a result, you can now hear Tatar spoken on the streets of Lysychans'k and Rubizhne.

Money from the Tatarstan budget is being used to help rebuild the two cities, which were all but destroyed by the Russian army. On top, Kysh Babai, the Tatar Father Frost, is about to fly in for the holidays. The trouble is, that since the time of the Tatar-Mongol invasion, children in both Russia and Ukraine have been told that if they behave badly the Babai will come and take them to a terrible, dark world. While Kysh Babai looks and behaves very like Russia's Father Frost, and is no doubt loved by children in Tatarstan, Putin's imposition of his name on celebrations in occupied territories of Ukraine carries a grotesque irony that should not go unnoticed.

A Prisoner Exchange and Other Things
You Cannot Laugh about

At the beginning of January, news came to the village of Solovyivka about the death of soldier Yuri Yakovenko. Yuri's family put on mourning clothes. A grave was dug in the cemetery and neighbours and friends prepared to greet the vehicle which would bring the body to the village the next morning. The funeral did not take place, however. No-one recognised the body in the coffin. It was not Yuri. Everyone perked up. Perhaps Yuri was still alive? After all, "missing" might mean that he had been captured.

In the first days of January, Russia and Ukraine exchanged prisoners of war for the first time in six months. Ukraine saw the return of 230 of its citizens, both military and civilian. Among them were 48 military personnel who had been considered "missing in action". This exchange brought joy to the relatives and friends of those released, but the hearts of those still waiting for news of their loved ones grew heavier. More than 15,000 soldiers are reported missing. There are about 6000 Ukrainian prisoners of war in Russia. Most of them have been identified and are not on the missing persons list.

Among those who returned from captivity in early January was Halina Fedyshyn, a Marine and nurse. She took part in the defence of Mariupol and was captured along with fellow Marine Mykola Gritsenyak. While Mykola was released in the September 2022 prisoner exchange, Halina remained in captivity for almost two years. As soon as Halina was released, Mykola proposed to her and she agreed to become his wife.

While the war continues, this story cannot be considered to

have had a happy ending – not yet. Many military personnel who returned from captivity strive to go back to the front. We will only be able to count happy endings when the war is over. No-one knows when that will be or who will live to see it.

The aggressor is forcing Ukraine to play Russian roulette. The entire country is bombarded with rockets and kamikaze drones every night. What do people think about when they go to bed? They know that tonight someone will die, someone will be injured, someone's house will be destroyed. In the morning, the survivors will survey the news to find out who was unlucky.

For a long time, Ukrainians were mystified by drone videos showing wounded or surrounded Russian soldiers killing themselves. They would blow themselves up with grenades or shoot themselves with machine guns. "Why don't they just surrender?" people asked.

One answer to this question was provided by a prisoner captured last week near the village of Rabotino in Donbas: "Aren't you going to pour polyurethane foam into our mouths?" he asked in terror. It turns out that the Russian officers instil fear into their soldiers with tales of the terrible and painful death that awaits them in Ukrainian captivity.

There were also leaflets campaigning against surrender found in the pockets of Russian soldiers captured near Rabotino. "Soldier! If you want to live, dig a trench and fight! Outside the trench, there is only death or Ukrainian captivity, where death is the best thing that awaits you! If you are not killed immediately, you face inhuman torture: broken ribs, gouged-out eyes, castration, rape, punctured lungs, starvation, your fingers and ears cut off. You will be beaten to death and quartered."

Some of these tortures are practised on Ukrainian prisoners of war; Russian soldiers are easily persuaded, therefore, that similar treatment awaits them in captivity in Ukraine.

Meanwhile, the temperature in Ukraine has dropped to −20°C. Sitting in trenches in freezing conditions can be deadly. Ukrainian soldiers are being admitted to hospital with frost-bitten fingers and toes. They cannot light fires in their dugouts because the smoke would immediately attract the enemy's attention. If they fall asleep at these temperatures, they might never wake up. They need to keep moving. The cold may also explain why Russian soldiers go on the attack so often. Death from hypothermia may seem more likely than death from a bullet, or perhaps they think it preferable to die in battle so that their relatives can call them "heroes".

The frequency of the Russian attacks forces Ukrainian soldiers to be on full alert all the time. It is exhausting but action keeps you warm. Wounded soldiers who cannot move are in as much danger from the cold as from their injuries. Military doctors have much less time to act than in warmer weather. Sometimes they simply give up trying to save a life because it takes too long to evacuate the wounded from the combat zone. In the snowy landscape, vehicles transporting the wounded are easily spotted, even at night. They immediately become targets for Russian artillery and drones.

Military medic Alina Mikhailova could tell you a lot about this, but she keeps quiet. She is the widow of the legendary volunteer fighter with the call sign "Da Vinci" who died last spring. Now she has to fight "on two fronts" – in the trenches and at the rear, against comedy shows on television and You-Tube. In a recent episode of "Alcomics", stand-up comedian Victoria Taran, who writes her own scripts, caused a storm of indignation with one of her jokes, "What are women with money called? Widows!"

"You are dirt and rot that deserves to be cancelled by society. You can go to hell with your apology! Today you spat in the faces of thousands of Ukrainian widows, thousands of children who have become orphans, thousands of mothers," said Mikhailova in response to the joke. In her video apology, Victoria Taran promised to be more careful in writing her texts. At the same time, some fellow stand-up comedians came to her defence.

This is the second scandal in two weeks involving dubious jokes. The first was associated with Ukraine's best-known comedy show, "Kvartal-95", of which Volodymyr Zelensky was the founder and former producer. The show, broadcast on the 1+1 television channel and the Kvartal-95 YouTube channel, has a massive audience. A recent episode included a skit that made fun of a fictional female refugee from the occupied city of Skadovsk, a predominantly Russian-speaking town. The humour was based on the refugee's inaccurate use of the Ukrainian language. Residents of Skadovsk, including the mayor of this seaside resort, were offended by the skit and they complained about it in perfectly good Ukrainian. The video apology recorded by the actress who played the refugee sounded more like a parody of an apology than a sincere plea for forgiveness and only added fuel to the fire.

Ukrainians are enjoying a good deal of humour accessible on platforms where budding stand-up comedians show off their talents. There is also a busy exchange of information about new stand-up YouTube channels, but the recent scandals have sparked a debate about wartime humour. Psychologists and sociologists are supporting the discussion with articles that facilitate serious analysis and reflection about what can and cannot be laughed about in wartime.

While the debate continues, the scandals have brought to my attention another trend that leaves me feeling uneasy: "video apologies" created under pressure from the offended party. They are becoming a common phenomenon in Ukraine.

Such apologies already have an unhealthy history. The authoritarian leader of Chechnya, Kadyrov, made offenders say sorry in this way as a form of punishment. Russian comedians who allowed themselves to joke about the Chechen leadership were so intimidated by Kadyrov that they recorded tearful video apologies, promising never to offend again. In Russia, the police and intelligence services began to use the same method to silence less dangerous dissidents and youth who exhibit "wrong thinking".

Recently, a young Ukrainian woman posted an emotional video monologue on Facebook. She described how, on a road in Transcarpathia, police and enlistment officers had grabbed her husband out of their car, leaving her with their small child cold and alone in the vehicle. Two days later, a video apology appeared on social media networks in which the same woman – only now with a frightened look on her face – explained that things had not happened exactly the way she had said in the first video. Commenting on the incident, representatives of the enlistment office said that they had released her husband after three hours, having given him a summons to appear at the enlistment office at his place of residence in the city of Dnipro.

During the coming week, Parliament will discuss five draft laws concerning mobilisation, including one submitted by the Cabinet of Ministers which would make roadside incidents like the one in Transcarpathia impossible. Fortunately, laws to regulate what we should and should not laugh about are not being considered and the scandals and debates about this on social media will continue.

13.12.2023

Back to the U.S.S.R.

On Monday night and into early Tuesday morning, Russia and Ukraine exchanged cyber attacks. Ukrainian hackers disrupted Russia's tax administration, while a Russian cyber attack on Ukraine's Monobank was successfully repelled. The Russian hackers did succeed in blocking the work of Kyivstar, however, one of Ukraine's three main mobile telephone operators. The blow to Kyivstar was very serious. It paralysed the provider's mobile telephone communications and financial transaction systems across the country and left many cash machines out of service. Several regions of Ukraine lost air raid warning services, including Boryspil city near Kyiv, where police drove around announcing air raid warnings through loudspeakers.

The cyber attacks followed another emergency which Russia had nothing to do with. A branch of Kyiv's metro system has been partially closed owing to depressurisation problems in an underground tunnel. Repairs will take several months. Already the roads in the areas affected are hopelessly jammed with traffic.

As soon as the cyber attacks occurred, Kyivstar subscribers queued up to buy starter packages from other providers. These quickly sold out. Now Kyivstar's competitor, Vodafone, is facing its own problems due to the surge in users.

Ukrainians started posting their new phone numbers in open chat on Facebook, oblivious seemingly to the fact that in doing so they were advertising their numbers to scammers the world over.

While experts are trying to understand why Kyivstar proved to be so vulnerable, questions are being asked about a possible connection between the cyber attack and the discovery of Kyivstar S.I.M. cards inside the targeting systems of Russian attack drones shot down recently. Experts have suggested that Ukrainian S.I.M. cards were being built into the drone guidance systems to increase their accuracy.

Meanwhile, Russia is bringing payphones to the occupied territories and installing a cable telephone system in the cities of Luhansk region. Many residents are just about old enough to remember Soviet payphones, so they will not have to learn how to use them. To date, it is not clear which currency of coins the payphones will accept, or who you will be able to call from them. We can assume that it will not be possible to use these payphones to call relatives in free Ukraine. Perhaps someone in Lysychans'k, for example, might be able to call another payphone located in Donetsk? To do so, they will only need to think of a way to warn friends or relatives in advance, so that they are waiting at the right payphone at the right time.

Street payphones are now being installed in occupied Sieverodonetsk. The city's pre-war population of 100,000 people has shrunk to 15,000. Russian civilians and military personnel are moving into any inhabitable apartments and houses that were left empty by former residents who evacuated the city. There are now more Russians than local residents in Sieverodonetsk.

It is not just apartments that are being occupied. The occupation authorities have reopened a war-damaged kindergarten, albeit without repairing it, bothering only to hang a portrait of Putin on the wall. In the building of the former trolleybus depot, a new café is also preparing to open. The U.S.S.R. Canteen is looking for a cook and other employees. The menu will include "home-cooked dishes" which will be served in a "retro-style" space. If the U.S.S.R. Canteen intends to give clients a Soviet experience, excessive comfort or particularly tasty food should not be expected.

The majority of indigenous residents remaining in Sieverodonetsk are pensioners for whom survival meant taking a Russian passport so that they could receive a Russian state pension. Once a month they go to the so-called "Luhansk Peoples Republic" (L.P.R.) post office to collect their pension, before going shopping for groceries at one of the two supermarkets now operating.

L.P.R. Post is another island of late Soviet life. Here you can subscribe to newspapers and magazines that are printed in Luhansk. They contain crossword puzzles and advice for agricultural enthusiasts.

The most interesting goods at the post office are L.P.R. stamps. Since 2015, the Luhansk and Donetsk separatist authorities have been issuing stamps that are very similar to the Soviet stamps of the 1960s, although not as brightly coloured. The stamps sport images of Soviet World War II heroes, Soviet cosmonauts, poets and writers. As in Soviet times, L.P.R. Post issues stamps to mark significant anniversaries, including the birth or death of prominent figures. There are also stamps including the letter Z and images of Russian soldiers and tanks. There is even a series of stamps of birds found in the Luhansk forests. The stamps are very popular among philatelists in Russia and Belarus and are bought for resale by Russian military personnel and even by construction workers and officials on business trips in the area.

Stamps issued in Luhansk in 2015–21 have disappeared from the post offices in the separatist republics. You can now only buy them from online Russian philately stores. Stamps without pictures that only indicate their value are more easily available. Apparently, these stamps are designed to be unattractive, so that collectors will not buy them. However, because they resemble Soviet stamps of the 1920s and 1930s, these plain stamps are nonetheless also attracting the attention of collectors.

The poor quality of the L.P.R. postage stamps sets them apart from those produced in real countries. It would seem there is not a single professional or talented artist remaining in the territory.

Meanwhile, in the free part of Ukraine, for the wives and mothers of fallen Ukrainian soldiers, public activists have launched a project called "Alive: Real love stories". The project, as a kind of art therapy, involves painting classes, during which professional artists teach the bereaved to express their feelings about their lost loved ones through paint.

The most recent class in this series took place in Lutsk, not far from the border with Belarus. One of the participants in the master class was Lyudmila Kaminska, the mother of serviceman Maris Kaminsky, who died in Donbas. She came to paint a picture as a gift for his widow Yana and his little daughter, Samira. Maris was Lyudmila Kaminsky's younger son. His older brother is at the front.

"I know from my own experience that art heals," says artist Zoryana Ruban-Golovchuk, who conducted the master class in Lutsk. Zoryana believes that you can free yourself from pain and overcome difficult experiences through the process of artistic creativity. At the same time, you can imbue a painting with a story that expresses your love for those who are no longer with you.

The paintings produced by the widows and mothers of fallen soldiers most often use bright colours and positive imagery, which seems to indicate that for these women, their sons and husbands remain alive and much loved. Several exhibitions generated in the "Alive" project have already been held in cities around Ukraine. There is one currently taking place in Vinnytsia.

As Christmas approaches, museums and art exhibitions in Ukraine receive many more visitors. People are looking for positive emotions to take their minds off their worries about the future.

Another popular place for urban dwellers to visit is the railway station. The "Christmas Flame of Bethlehem" has arrived. In the past, the flame was flown to Kyiv from Israel but this year this unusual cargo crossed into Ukraine from Slovakia, over land. It was then handed to Ukrainian scouts, who have travelled with it by rail throughout the country, so that believers can light their candles from it and bring the Bethlehem flame home for Christmas.

The flame has just reached Kramatorsk, a city in Donbas where, last year, near the same railway station, a Russian missile killed dozens of people waiting for a train that would take them away from Donbas. Now people again hurry to the train stations, not with suitcases but with candles. I imagine this flame burning in the homes of Kyivstar employees while they do overtime, fighting to eliminate the consequences of the Russian hacker attack.

This was the most serious cyber attack yet experienced by Ukraine. While services were being restored many local authorities deployed Starlink systems. Despite Elon Musk's unhelpful statements, Ukrainians continue to be grateful to him and wish him and everyone who has acted to help our country happiness and peace for Christmas and the New Year.

19.12.2023

Three Grenades for Christmas

The distance from this war's current hotspot, the town of Avdiivka, to the Transcarpathian village of Keretsky is 1,300 kilometres. That makes Keretsky as far away from the front line as you can get without leaving Ukraine. Yet this is where three grenades exploded the other day, killing one person and injuring 24. The explosions occurred during a meeting of the village council at which the budget for 2024 was being discussed. The head of the council, Mykhailo Mushka, had tabled a motion to increase his salary and award himself an end-of-year bonus. While these proposals were being discussed, Serhiy Batrin, a member of the council from the Servant of the People party, left the hall. He went home, wrote a suicide note and returned to the meeting taking three grenades with him. This event was video recorded and so the moment when Batrin re-entered the hall and detonated the grenades is fully documented.

The first thing local journalists remembered when they learned about the explosions was that the head of the village council, Mykhailo Mushka, had been a member of the pro-Russian party Opposition Bloc for Life until it was banned in September 2022. He had refused to remove the village's monument to a Soviet soldier, for which he received praise on Russian television. Not long ago, Mushka was detained by the police on suspicion of taking a bribe, but he was not charged and he continued to chair the village council.

In the community, Serhiy Batrin had a reputation as an idealist and warrior for justice. He built a children's playground and organised the restoration of the village cemetery on his own initiative. Batrin was once involved in the transport business, although at the time of the incident he had given that up some-time previously. At the fateful meeting of the village council, he had put forward his candidacy for Secretary. However, his name had not been put on the agenda and another deputy, also from the Servant of the People party, was elected as Secretary instead.

Among the victims of the explosions was council member and veteran of the war in Donbas, Vasyl Shtefko. He had lost both his lower legs in an accident twenty years earlier, but this did not stop him from volunteering as a driver at the start of the all-out invasion. He transported ammunition to Ukrainian forces. At the Keretsky Village Council meeting two grenades exploded under Shtefko's chair. If he had had legs, he probably would have lost them. One of his prosthetic legs was torn off and will have to be replaced once he has been discharged from hospital. For now, doctors are dealing with the many grenade fragments lodged in his body.

Immediately after the incident, someone posted a meme on social networks showing a grenade with the caption, "A bonus from Serhiy Batrin". The meme appeared in local authority chat groups in several regions of Ukraine and seemed to be calling for action against people in authority who were raising their own salaries and issuing bonuses for themselves. Although the cyber security service removed the material from social networks before it could go viral, other examples of the meme appeared almost immediately, along with images of grenades and the inscription, "A wartime bonus".

It is strange that in the comments and articles about the incident in Keretsky, no-one mentioned the climax of the tele-vision series "Servant of the People", in which Goloborodko, a simple Ukrainian teacher, played by Zelensky, machineguns the Ukrainian Parliament because he is fed up with high-level cor-ruption. The Russian mass media, even openly propagandistic channels, were restrained in their comments about the events in Keretsky, only hinting at the huge number of unregistered weapons in the hands of Ukrainian civilians.

A great many weapons are indeed circulating in Ukraine away from the front. The trial of a priest from the Ukrainian Orthodox Church of the Moscow Patriarchate will shortly take place. He was arrested while trying to sell two anti-aircraft missile systems. He had hidden other weapons in a half-built church and in the basement of a multi-storey apartment building in his hometown of Kherson. The stash included grenades and grenade launchers, 7,000 cartridges for Kalashnikov assault rifles, and a machine gun. According to the priest, he had found these weapons in Kherson after the Russian army had retreated.

The sound of shooting from legally held hunting rifles can now be heard around the town of Radekhiv, in Lviv region, where the authorities, with the approval of the Regional Military Administration, have announced the culling of animals in the nearby forests. Along with wolves and foxes, stray dogs and cats were also on the original list of animals to be shot. The war has forced them to migrate to the west of Ukraine and tens of thousands of both wild and domestic animals are now living in relatively confined spaces close to populated areas. This has given rise to a fear that cases of rabies will increase. Animal rights activists protested at the culling and the Radekhiv administration finally agreed to exclude dogs and cats from the list of animals to be culled.

Meanwhile, the hunt continues for men who are fit for the army. This is creating considerable problems for urban transport services. Bus drivers were among the first men to be mobilised, not only because the army needed professional drivers but also because it was easy to find them at their place of work. As a result, bus schedules have been disrupted and remote towns and villages are sometimes left with no public transport services at all. In the Vasylivka district of the city of Sumy, near the border with Russia, residents complain that it is impossible to get back home later than six o'clock after visiting the city centre and while the first bus into town in the morning is supposed to come at six-thirty, it rarely arrives at all.

"It is now very difficult to provide transport links in the city," said Serhiy Yakovenko, head of Sumy's Department of Transport. "We regularly receive complaints from Vasylivka residents, but it is simply impossible to resolve this issue . . . There is a catastrophic shortage of drivers since so many have been mobilised. The owner of the bus company says that if they continue to take away his men, he will close the business altogether because there will be no-one left to work. This is the situation for all businesses and it will only get worse in the future."

While residents of city suburbs await their buses, the Ministry of Internal Affairs has announced measures to increase security in public areas. Metal detectors will soon be installed at train stations and shopping centres, as well as in schools. The metal detectors will be staffed by specially trained police. However, there is not yet any talk of installing metal detectors in village and city council buildings where next year's budgets are being discussed. No-one talks about the need for police to be on duty at such meetings.

Not all local councillors in Ukraine have been voting to give themselves bonuses. The behaviour of most indicates that they understand that the country is fighting for its very existence. The town council of Yavoriv, in Lviv region, voted recently to give the Ukrainian army 143m. hryvnias from the city budget (3.5 million euros) for the purchase of drones and other military equipment. Ordinary Ukrainians also regularly donate whatever they can to the Ukrainian army. They understand the quote attributed to Napoleon: "He who does not feed his army will feed someone else's."

01.01.2024

Ukraine 2024 – Food for Thought

Two days before the New Year, Ukraine experienced its biggest ever Russian missile and drone attack, one even larger than that of November 25. This new sad date will go down in the history of the capital, with at least 25 civilians killed and many more wounded. The missile and drone attack lasted all night and the entire city again stayed awake until the all-clear sounded in the early morning.

The following night, afraid of further attacks, Iryna Khazina, the widow of my first publisher, sat in the corridor. In the morning, she had some tea and took the metro to one of the capital's best-known flea markets, Petrivka, where you can buy everything, from books and antiques to exotic foodstuffs. "I simply wanted to be among people," she explained. To justify the trip for herself, Iryna came up with a specific goal. For two decades now, she has been buying spices from the same stall at the Petrivka market. Iryna went straight to the spice trader and was pleased to see the familiar saleswoman behind the counter. Her very presence had a calming effect and gave Iryna strength. She bought spices, including some from Yemen to add to her coffee. The two women chatted about life and the war. Iryna then went to have breakfast in a Crimean Tatar café across the way from the market. She ordered lamb pasties and sat there for a long while, enjoying her breakfast in this quiet space.

"There were fewer people at the market than usual," Iryna said, "but the Crimean Tatars have added Ukrainian pancakes to their menu. There's even a notice on the door announcing it."

Iryna celebrated the New Year with her daughter's family. For the first time since her youth, Iryna did not prepare any food for the festive table. Alena and her husband Taras did all the cooking.

While the citizens of Ukraine were seeking hope in the dawn of a new year, Russian drones were flying over the country. In Kyiv New Year's night passed without any explosions, but in Odesa debris from a Russian drone hit a multi-storey building. One resident was killed and several others were injured.

At the very end of December a special kitchen train called "The Food Train" visited the frontline cities of Kramatorsk, Sloviansk, Zaporizhzhia, Kherson and Mykolaiv. The special train was sponsored by the American billionaire Howard Buffett, the son of Warren Buffet. Its task was to deliver meals to Ukrainians who did not have the opportunity to prepare festive food for themselves. The 8,000 meals and one thousand New Year's gifts for children delivered by the train allowed many families living under constant Russian fire to feel something of the holiday spirit. I do not suppose their minds were taken off the war, even for a moment, but at least the train provided them with a sign that they had not been forgotten.

On December 31, 1,200 Kharkiv residents received free food from Fuminori Tsuchiko, a 75-year-old Japanese pensioner who has gained hero status throughout Ukraine. On February 24, 2022, he was in Poland, having spent most of January in Kyiv studying the war crimes committed by the German fascists during World War II. When Ukrainian refugees started arriving in Poland, Tsuchiko returned to Kyiv and then went to Kharkiv. Throughout the brutal attacks on that city he lived in a metro station with ordinary residents. It was during those difficult days that he decided to stay in Ukraine and help its citizens.

Tsuchiko sold his house in Japan and opened a free food café in the most dangerous district of Kharkiv, Saltovka. Together with Ukrainian volunteers, he began preparing food every day to feed all the needy residents of the city. The Fumi café does not offer Japanese cuisine, but there is always borscht, pasta, pies, garlic dumplings, buns and tea.

Tsuchiko's efforts are in part funded by well-wishers in Japan. Every day, he uses social media to report on the work of the café and to show how Kharkiv is managing to survive. With more and more people coming to eat at his free café, Tsuchiko has now started collecting money from Kharkiv residents on the streets of the city. Just before the New Year, he was standing with his donation box at Kharkiv's Nikolsky shopping centre. The management called the police and demanded that they remove the Japanese beggar from the mall. Kharkiv residents immediately protested against the mistreatment of the city's benefactor. The question was discussed throughout Ukraine and the mayor of Kharkiv, Ihor Terekhov, had to intervene. The story has a happy ending, however, with the Nikolsky shopping centre offering to donate a large supply of food to the Fumi café.

A year ago, Tsuchiko decided to go to Poland for a few days to take a little break from volunteering. Ukrainian border guards removed him from the bus and all the other passengers had to wait for several hours until the Japanese pensioner had paid the fine for exceeding his visa-free period in Ukraine. Tsuchiko paid the fine, left for Poland and spent his holiday obtaining permission from the Ukrainian authorities to re-enter the country. Now, one year later, Tsuchiko is better known in Ukraine than Mother Teresa. Recently, President Zelensky awarded him the state prize of the National Legend of Ukraine.

Feeding the hungry has become a national pastime. Every few weeks, volunteers in our village collect *smakoliki* (tasty morsels) for the military. They usually ask locals to donate cookies, canned and bottled products, and anything that can be stored for a long time. It is difficult to calculate how much food Ukrainians sent to the army in the run-up to the new year, but the military leadership often looks askance at such donations and regularly claims that soldiers are already given adequate food. Although this is probably at least 90 per cent. true, in a country that has lived through two man-made famines, people are almost programmed genetically to think that help with food is aid of the highest value.

This feeling can result in some "gastronomic volunteer" programmes reaching the point of absurdity. In December 2023, a group of Ukrainian volunteers prepared eleven tons of olive salad for frontline soldiers. The salad is made using diced potatoes and carrots, peas, sausage and gherkins and was a traditional dish on the Soviet festive table. News reports about the eleven tons of salad were shown proudly on television programmes. Thirty-six cars packed with plastic buckets of the salad set off towards various points of the front line. The reaction from the military was unexpected.

"This olivie salad will not reach the hottest spots on the front, where there may be problems with food," said serviceman Ilya Krotenko. "The military is provided with food at a perfectly decent level. These headlines about volunteers preparing eleven tons of salad for the Ukrainian army could be interpreted as saying that volunteers threw more than one million hryvnias into the rubbish bin. All these buckets of dumplings, salads, pies, meatballs and other homemade food spoil on their way to the front. Some units have already reported cases of food poisoning. Officers no longer allow their subordinates to eat such home-cooked food provided by volunteers. So, if any of your friends have the brilliant idea of sending buckets of salad to the front again, slap them on the wrist! The money would be better spent on purchasing drones!"

Over the past two years, Ukraine and Russia have become the main buyers of drones on the world market and they will soon become the main manufacturers of drones too. Produced for battle, these essential tools will have a short life and so production must be on a huge scale. By the end of 2023, Ukraine was producing 50,000 drones per month. Russia produces about 300,000. Recently, President Zelensky promised that Ukraine would produce one million drones per year. And this is possible. A year ago, there were only seven drone production companies in Ukraine. Now there are 70. How many will there be in twelve months? Secrecy around the subject makes it impossible to gather statistics, but Ukraine is gradually shifting its economy fully onto a war footing.

The last two years have revealed so much talent and goodwill inside Ukraine. This has attracted more of both from outside the country, as our Japanese National Legend proves. The country has become synonymous with ingenuity, although I still cannot help worrying about how much of that olivie salad reached soldiers' festive tables before it went bad. Could they have used drones to get it to the front line more quickly?

16.01.2024

Keep Breathing and Listen to the Crows

As I was driving along the Zhytomyr highway recently, I passed two supermarkets that were destroyed and looted by the Russian army during the offensive against Kyiv in the spring of 2022. Both shops have been rebuilt and now are open for business.

The Zhytomyr highway, the main road from Kyiv to the west of Ukraine, was repaired in the autumn and is now easy to drive along. That cannot be said for the minor roads in the region. Some are almost impassable by anything other than a Jeep or a tank.

The administration of the occupied Donbas has lately boasted about the quality of their roads. They proudly explained how these roads had been repaired. Their explanations made me feel uneasy. I was reminded of how in the 1990s the American horror films that appeared in the cinemas in newly independent Ukraine failed at the box office. These films did not attract viewers because Hollywood horror looked like a set of ridiculous misunderstandings compared to the real-life horror experienced by the inhabitants of Ukraine during the Soviet era. Deportations, the Holodomor of 1932–3, the Holocaust, the Gulag: this historical experience set the standard for Ukrainians as far as horror is concerned. As an entertainment genre, it aroused little interest.

The details given in Russian reports about the road engineering in Donetsk remind me of those Soviet horrors. The roads in the Donbas, we are told, were repaired using more than 100,000 tons of "construction waste" from Mariupol. This means that Russia crushed and removed from the ruined city the debris of

301

apartment blocks and private houses destroyed by Russian missiles and artillery, along with the bodies, or fragments of the bodies, of residents who had died in their homes. This "construction waste", soaked in the blood of murdered Ukrainians, now forms the roads along which travel private cars, public buses and Russian military vehicles.

For parents in the rest of Ukraine, dealing with horror and fear – their own and their children's – is a daily preoccupation. Parents are concerned about how the experience of war affects the young psyche and the child's perception of life. Parents want to know how best to talk to their children about war and death, how to calm their children's nerves during attacks and how to distract them from feelings of fear and anxiety.

Several children's books designed to help parents with this task have appeared in bookshops and are selling well. Newspaper and magazine columns written by child psychologists are also popular, and social networks are full of messages from parents about what they have learned. It occurs to me that this is useful knowledge for all adults in Ukraine today. For example, when you are in a bomb shelter with a child and there are explosions outside, you need to make sure that the child is breathing normally. There are games you can play to help, like blowing soap bubbles or getting the child to make the sound of air being let out of a balloon. If the explosions are very close, it is important to maintain tactile contact with the child: massage their ears and stroke their cheeks. From time to time, you need to ask the child to pretend to be very tired, to give a big yawn and stretch.

Once the all-clear is sounded, be sure to praise the child for their courage. Tell them, "It's over! We're safe! Thank you for being so brave and strong! We heard so many explosions, but we made it through! We weren't scared!"

After these words, you need to invite the child to suggest what they want to do in the hours following the air raid. Making plans for the future is the best way to distract children from the war.

For adults, thinking about the future is complicated. We may have made plans for the year but their fulfilment is shrouded in doubt. When I think about the future, I look to the sky. Over Kyiv these days the sky is grey-blue. Sometimes snow falls onto the streets and there are the usual noises of the city and the crying of crows. The crow is, in fact, Kyiv's unofficial ornithological symbol. Our crows do not fly away for the winter. They patronise the city all year round. Their cawing is not a pleasant sound. In peacetime, it seemed they were always warning each other about something. Now they seem to warn the residents of Kyiv.

A couple of days ago, several crows on Lviv Square screamed so loudly and excitedly that I stopped along with other passersby and for a long time we watched the crows in the crowns of the bare trees, from where the large black birds were making their raucous speeches. In the past, these crows would have irritated me, but now I found myself listening to them with pleasure. They distracted me for a short time from the reality in which I live, from the reality in which all of Ukraine lives today.

Like a little child, I suppose part of me is waiting for someone to say, "It's over! We're safe! Thank you for being so brave and strong! We heard so many explosions, but we made it through! We weren't scared!"

Passports and the War

The Russian economy is working for the war. This is no longer a secret. Russian factories producing explosives, rockets, shells and tanks operate around the clock. The Russian propaganda machine also works 24/7 and the same can be said apparently of the printing houses that produce official documents. There is great demand for special forms to register the deaths of military personnel and for application forms for Russian Federation passports.

Russian passports have become a powerful weapon. The seizure of Ukrainian territory, together with its inhabitants, is only the first stage of a take-over strategy that aims to turn Ukrainians into "Russians". Passports play a key role.

It has become almost impossible to survive under occupation if you do not accept the obligation to have a Russian passport. Pensioners do not have access to their Ukrainian pensions and so are left without money. They are told: "Take a Russian passport, and we will issue you with a Russian pension." Car owners are not allowed to drive with a Ukrainian driver's licence or with Ukrainian licence plates. They must get a Russian passport, then a Russian licence, then Russian number plates. If you get sick, access to medical care will depend on your having a Russian passport.

Residents of the occupied territories understand the risks that come with Russian citizenship. It is especially dangerous for men under 60 because they are simultaneously registered with the Russian enlistment office. Sometimes, along with a Russian passport, Ukrainian men receive a summons from the occupiers to join the Russian army. Very soon they end up at the front.

The Ukrainian government's position on imposed Russian citizenship was made clear even before the 2022 invasion. Residents of Crimea or Donbas and Luhansk regions who take Russian Federation passports in order to survive are not considered traitors. For Ukraine, only collaboration – that is, voluntary and pro-active cooperation with the occupiers – is illegal. Holding a Russian Federation passport is not in itself a crime. As Russian "passportisation" of Ukrainians continues, however, it aggravates the situation both at the front and in the occupied territories. If a person takes a Russian passport, even if they do so under duress, they may still consider themselves as traitors at some level. A sense of guilt can make them fear their homeland, just as they fear Russia.

As things stand, Ukraine does not recognise dual citizenship. By law, a citizen of Ukraine cannot hold a passport of another country. In 2021, President Zelensky announced the preparation of a bill that would allow dual citizenship. It is possible that the motivation behind this was the need to make legal an existing situation. Many Ukrainian businesspeople, politicians and government officials illegally hold passports of other countries. While passports from Israel, America and Cyprus are popular among Ukrainian politicians and businesspeople, passports from the Russian Federation were more common among civil servants. This became obvious when, immediately after the occupation of their cities, former Ukrainian civil servants joined the Russian Federation occupation authorities. This happened in Crimea after the annexation in 2014 and it happened again in 2022.

President Zelensky has now submitted to Parliament another bill on dual citizenship. One clause in the new bill, which was also included in the 2021 bill, states that citizens of Ukraine who have a passport of another state cannot participate in the political process, work as civil servants, have access to state secrets, or manage state property. It seems that it was because of this clause that the 2021 version of the bill was never discussed in Parliament. In an anonymous interview with *Forbes Ukraine*, a legal consultant to the Office of the President said that the bill was not discussed because there were many people with illegal dual citizenship in the Servant of the People party, including among President Zelensky's inner circle. If this law had been adopted, they would have lost their positions.

It would appear that the President's party is now ready to vote for this bill. The law clearly states that dual citizenship with the Russian Federation is prohibited, but Ukrainians will now be able to obtain passports from other countries. Citizens of other countries will also be able to apply for Ukrainian passports without giving up their primary citizenship.

Why has President Zelensky decided to return to this bill during a full-scale war? One reason could be Ukraine's demographic crisis. Experts predict that after the war, the population of Ukraine will have shrunk to between 25 and 35 million. More precise forecasts are impossible because, although the country's pre-war population was thought to be around 43 million, there are no accurate statistics. On top of this, the forecasts are based partly on the number of Ukrainian refugees currently living outside the country. This data is also only approximate.

Researchers estimate that one-third of refugees will return home. In Germany there are 1,100,000 and approximately one million in Poland. In Canada 210,000 are officially registered and about 60,000 in Norway. In recent days, Polish authorities have hinted that they expect new Russian offensives against Kyiv, Kharkiv and other cities and that Poland must be prepared to accept a new wave of refugees from Ukraine.

At the same time, the German government is proposing major changes to the procedure for acquiring German citizenship. The naturalisation process will be faster and easier and there will be no need to renounce any other citizenship that the applicant holds. Once the law has been adopted, foreigners will be able to apply for German citizenship after a five-year stay in the country and in some cases, after only three years. Previously, only people who had lived in Germany for at least eight years could begin the naturalisation process. News of these changes has no doubt cheered many Ukrainian refugees in Germany. I suppose they will apply for citizenship after three years in the country and they will be issued with German passports.

As the bill on dual citizenship was being submitted to Parliament in Kyiv, voices from the Office of the President began calling on European states to reduce assistance to Ukrainian refugees. In an interview, the politician, journalist and adviser to the President, Serhiy Leshchenko, appealed to Western governments to facilitate the return of Ukrainian refugees to their homeland. He talked about the widening gulf between refugees and their compatriots in Ukraine. "Because people who left Ukraine will never understand the people who stayed, I believe that host countries should stop helping refugees so that they will return home," he said.

Surely these words from a representative of President Zelensky's narrow circle of friends were not uttered by accident. Ukraine's demographic crisis affects everything, but first and foremost, it affects the economy. Making Ukrainian citizenship a possible option for foreigners is only one of many policies that could improve the situation, but even if the law on dual citizenship is adopted the procedure to obtain a Ukrainian passport is likely to be complicated and slow. Nor is it likely that the war makes the country appealing to potential second-passport holders. The printing houses where Ukrainian state documents are produced will not need to work around the clock. Their usual rhythm will suffice.

30.01.2024

A Hard Monday and a Military Secret

Last Monday evening was difficult for Ukrainians. Not because, again, like every day, flocks of Iranian-Russian drones were flying from annexed Crimea. Not because Russia fired missiles at Donetsk, Kharkiv, Sumy and other regions from the occupied territories. Nor because news of these attacks reminded us of the monotonously precarious situation at the front and elsewhere in the country. Monday evening was tough because reliable sources of information reported that President Zelensky had fired the head of the Ukrainian army General Zaluzhny. This was enough for social media to boil over and overload the mobile networks.

"What's going on?" Ukrainians wanted to know. "Only this morning the two of them were laying wreaths at the monument to heroes who died for independent Ukraine in 1918!"

The unconfirmed information about Zaluzhny's dismissal was picked up by the media in Europe and, of course, in Russia, where one of Russia's main propagandists, Margarita Simonyan, said that even if it is not true, the rumours highlight the chaos that currently reigns in Ukraine.

Only a couple of hours later, the Ukrainian Ministry of Defence posted on its website a very short message: "No, it's not true!" This could hardly be considered an official statement, but the words bounced across the waves of social media networks, relieving the tension in Ukrainian society. President Zelensky himself did not comment. His press secretary, however, later confirmed that Zelensky had not fired Zaluzhny.

It is tempting to blame the stress experienced by Ukrainians that evening on a successful Russian media provocation. However, public figures in Ukraine and one of the main online publications in the country, *Ukrainska Pravda*, would not have spread the rumour without triple-checking its accuracy – that is, they would not have risked going public with such statements without first confirming the information with the Office of the President.

Ukrainians' frustration expressed itself in the form of criticism of Zelensky, while civil society and politicians, including the previous president Petro Poroshenko, came out in defence of Zaluzhny, who had not been fired.

For two years, Ukrainians have not only been living in a physical warzone, they have also been living in a media battleground, where the enemy's weapons are designed to spread doubt and confusion. Ukrainians are also feeling their way in the dark zone of poor communication between state authorities and society. What is more, Ukrainians often forget where they are living. They forget about the perils and assume that the information they see all around is correct.

Russian disinformation operations daily attempt to break Ukrainians' unity and convince them that the country's leadership is incompetent and corrupt, that the army is demoralised, that the soldiers do not have enough ammunition or food while generals are buying villas for themselves in Spain and Italy. When such information is placed on top of what Ukrainians already know about corruption and the lack of transparency in their country, almost any fake information can be perceived as truth. Ukrainians become easy channels for Russian propaganda, further spreading false information among their friends and acquaintances.

Last week, Russia organised the mass distribution of emails to Ukrainians that purported to be sent from the Office of the President. The emails contained a statement from Zelensky about his readiness to give up occupied and annexed territories to Russia. Before this, "Zelensky's statement of surrender" had been spread on Ukrainian social media networks by anonymous users. With two years' experience of Russian fake news and psychological provocations, Ukrainians might have learned to identify and ignore them, yet these provocations continue to send powerful tremors through Ukrainian society. Our authorities are partially to blame for this. They have not learned to respond quickly and effectively to false information. The pauses between the appearance of fake news and its refutation are too long, allowing the fallacies to become topics of discussion on social media.

Perhaps most surprising of all is the way that important and true information does not become the main topic of discussion in Ukraine. This too must be the fault of the authorities, who either do not know how to distribute information or do not wish to convey this information to our society.

Recently, searches and arrests took place in Lviv, the main city in western Ukraine. The police action was related to a high-profile case of corruption in the supply of ammunition to the Ukrainian army at the very beginning of hostilities, in February–March 2022. The Ukrainian government allocated huge sums for the purchase of shells. The largest contract was awarded to the Lviv Arsenal company, which undertook to provide the Ukrainian army with 100,000 mortar shells. The Ministry of Defence paid the supplier 97 per cent. of the contract amount in advance.

The Ukrainian army did not receive any of the shells but an active investigation into the matter has begun only now, two years later. The number of Ministry of Defence officials and businesspeople associated with this case is rising. One of those arrested is the former deputy Minister of Defence.

Information about the theft of the budgeted money and other criminal cases related to corruption in the military supply chain appears in the public domain in very measured doses and in a form that does not greatly attract the attention of the general public. It seems that the Ukrainian authorities are more satisfied when society discusses fake news than when they grapple with genuine issues. Perhaps this is true. Fake news is always, sooner or later, followed by a refutation and then everyone breathes a sigh of relief. In contrast, information about real corruption cases must constantly be updated with new details. Legal processes must be got under way and followed through. Court verdicts in major corruption cases are rare. Could this be because society does not follow either the investigations or the trials?

Today, a mass audit, under way at the Ministry of Defence, has already found financial irregularities amounting to more than ten billion hryvnias (approximately $265 m.). Closer public attention could motivate the authorities to fight more actively against corruption.

The new Minister of Defence, Rustam Umerov, has already replaced many ministry officials. He is also creating separate agencies for the purchase of lethal and non-lethal goods. In the country's 33 years of independence, a purge of this nature has never been carried out in the Ministry. Ukrainians would like to believe that the Ministry of Defence will no longer purchase eggs and potatoes for the army at a price three times higher than in the supermarket. They would like to believe that Ukrainian businesspeople who sign contracts with the ministry will fulfil their obligations honestly and that the regime of "military secrecy" necessitated by the war will not be used by corrupt officials to hide their crimes from the public.

It was precisely this regime of "military secrecy" that facilitated the theft of billions of hryvnias from the budget of the Ministry of Defence at the start of the all-out invasion. In any country, the purchase of arms may be carried out in secrecy and journalists who try to find out the details of these transactions could be accused of espionage. For the unscrupulous, wartime remains a golden moment in which to do business.

The good news is that the American audit team that monitors America's military aid to Ukraine has so far found no wrongdoing and Ukraine has started to lift the cloak of secrecy that veiled investigations into corruption within the Ministry of Defence. Suppliers have been replaced. These developments could improve both the image of the ministry and its ability to fulfil its function as the army's organ of supply.

Although the fight against corruption in the Ministry of Defence has not become the main focus of attention among ordinary Ukrainians, it has nonetheless pushed them towards some unexpected conclusions. Historically, Lviv, the capital of western Ukraine, was considered the cradle of Ukrainian culture and patriotism. There was a common perception that eastern Ukraine was a pro-Russian territory, with high levels of crime and corruption, while western Ukraine was a territory of sincere patriots – a haven of the Ukrainian language, honesty and religious morality. Recent events in the Ministry of Defence have rather dented these stereotypes, while the eastern city of Kharkiv, 40 kilometres from the Russian border and subject to daily mortar and missile attacks, has become a new symbol of Ukrainian patriotism and resilience.

The story of General Zaluzhny's possible dismissal, which made Ukrainians nervous last Monday, continues. By Wednesday, several media outlets published materials confirming that there had been, after all, an attempt by the Office of the President to fire the general. The Ukrainian publication *Dzerkalo Tyzhnia* (Mirror of the Week) published a summary of an interview with an anonymous source in the Office of the President. From this conversation, it appears that the President invited the General to resign voluntarily. General Zaluzhny refused and made it clear that President Zelensky, as Commander-in-Chief, could dismiss him by decree.

There is no longer any doubt that the Office of the President is preparing important changes in the army's leadership, but the dismissal of General Zaluzhny by presidential decree could impact Zelensky's ratings negatively. More thought will be required by Zelensky and his team.

04.02.2024

Early Spring

While Putin is trying to bolster his unnecessary presidential campaign and demanding some hint of victory from the Russian army, Ukraine has delivered several strong blows against Russian oil industry infrastructure in St Petersburg and Volgograd and against Russian aviation and naval forces in Crimea. Ukrainians were especially pleased with the six naval drones that sank the *Ivanovets*, a Russian missile attack vessel. Each drone recorded a video of its assault on the ship and Ukrainians were able to enjoy the sight of the *Ivanovets* being hit by the blows that took it to the bottom of the Black Sea.

It does look as though spring will be early this year and perhaps it has already begun. In central areas, we have seen the temperature rise to 12°C. A warm winter has its advantages. Less gas is used for heating residential and public buildings and Ukrainians pay less to heat their homes. The government has already announced triumphantly that no imported gas has been used this winter and that reserves of Ukrainian gas will last until the end of the central heating season.

There are things that the government would rather not talk about. For example, the fact that a transit gas pipeline still runs from Russia across Ukraine carrying Russian gas to European clients. The pipeline, however, plays a somewhat positive role for Ukraine. Russia wants to keep it intact, so towns and villages located along the pipeline's route are not exposed to the attacks suffered by the rest of the country.

As during last winter, Russia has aimed to damage Ukraine's electricity and heating infrastructure, especially during the cold snaps, but the attacks focus on installations in the east of the country which can be reached in a matter of minutes. Further west, our air defence systems have time to bring down most of the enemy's missiles and drones.

———

Now that the sun occasionally peeps through the clouds and temperatures are rising, Ukraine's anticipation of spring has become an important factor in sustaining optimism. Along the main roads, there are billboards advertising loans to farmers for the sowing campaign. Many of the loans are proposed by private banks, but the state-owned Oschadbank is also offering farmers low-interest credit to finance the clearing of fields.

The front line has been relatively stationary for a while now. This has allowed demining work to continue. Last year more than 275,000 hectares of land were surveyed. Of these about 200,000 hectares were "returned" to agriculture. Demining goes on even in winter. More than 21,000 hectares were cleared of explosive objects in January alone. Kherson region has been the focus of attention. Cereals and vegetables will be sown there in the spring. Ukraine will certainly produce a harvest this year. The question is what will become of the produce if the harvest is too big for the domestic market. The agricultural war with European farmers continues. Since September 15 last year, it has become difficult to export produce through Poland, Slovakia, or Hungary. Polish farmers have set up a blockade at the Polish–Ukrainian border and Hungarian farmers are planning to do the same. They consider that the preferential conditions for Ukrainian produce introduced by the European Union are a threat to their businesses.

———

The Kremlin has opened a new front in their very special war. This time the targets are Russians. Nobody inside Russia speaks out against the war anymore. There is no-one to fight with there. However, intellectual Russian émigrés in Europe are gaining confidence and becoming more active. As happened after the Bolshevik Revolution of 1917, we could soon see Russian émigré publishing houses and clubs operating in Europe. Émigré, anti-Putin online publications are already attracting new readers and this is probably what prompted the Kremlin to attack Dmitriy Bykov and Boris Akunin – the best-known Russian writers living abroad. Their books can no longer be published or sold in Russia and this could be a serious financial blow to the authors. Akunin's plays are still shown in Russian theatres, but he will no longer be paid royalties on ticket sales and his name has already been removed from theatre posters.

The Academic Aleksandrinsky Theatre in St Petersburg will continue to perform its production of "1881", which is based on Akunin's play of the same title. But now the production's artistic director will be named and paid as the author.

It is not yet clear whether Putin's cultural special forces will succeed in persuading millions of Russians to abandon their favourite writers. But the effort to combat dissenting cultural celebrities will continue. Books by another iconic Russian writer, one tipped to win the Nobel Prize for Literature, Lyudmila Ulitskaya, are being withdrawn from sale. Russian universities have revoked her honorary professorships, while media channels are working diligently to portray her as one of Russia's greatest enemies.

Writers are not the only group to suffer from the Kremlin's new campaign. The cult Russian rock band BI-2 recently arrived in Thailand to perform for the many Russian citizens who now live there. The musicians, however, did not ask the Thai authorities for permission to hold a concert. They were detained for that infringement and for failing to pay taxes on ticket sales. Russian diplomats demanded the immediate deportation of the musicians to Russia where they would face prison sentences for their anti-war speeches. Fortunately, the musicians hold Israeli as well as Russian passports and the sharp deterioration in Israeli–Russian relations since the Kremlin sided with Hamas worked in the musicians' favour. After intervention by Israeli diplomats, they were sent to Tel Aviv instead of Moscow. Now they will enjoy an early Israeli spring, rather than the ongoing, Kremlin-induced, cultural winter that is bound to continue in Russia even after the warmer weather arrives.

While nobody inside Russia openly opposes the war with Ukraine, the authorities still see fit to fight against the wives and mothers of Russian soldiers who "had the audacity" to unite in an organisation called The Way Home. These women demand that their menfolk be demobilised and others mobilised in their place. They are not against the war or Putin. They do not make public statements, only placing carnations tied with white ribbons on monuments to the unknown soldier. They then take photographs of these carnations and post them on social networks. They also write letters to Putin begging for the demobilisation of their menfolk. For these peaceful actions, they are detained and fined.

Russia's chief propagandists denounce these women on television, calling them traitors and accomplices of Ukraine. The police also detain journalists who come to photograph the "protest" laying of carnations. The authorities do not want information about this movement to provoke other wives and mothers into doing the same. Mobilisation in Russia will continue and there will be no demobilisation any time soon.

There is no demobilisation in Ukraine either and the law proposed to regulate this difficult area has yet to pass through Parliament. Here too, the wives and mothers of soldiers are protesting, but they demonstrate openly and are not persecuted. They try to make sure that their protests are not confused with those of the relatives of prisoners of war. Society views the demobilisation cause with sympathy, but the protests have no effect. Those who were drafted into the army many months ago continue to fight unless they have been killed, captured, or left disabled.

Defending Freedom of the Press

The era of General Zaluzhny, Commander-in-Chief of the army, has ended surprisingly peacefully and without causing the split in society that political analysts predicted as inevitable if he were to be pushed aside. For two days a crowd gathered on the Maidan with "Bring Zaluzhny Back!" posters, but these peaceful rallies were small and hardly attracted the attention of journalists.

Ukrainian society had grown tired of speculating about an undefined conflict between General Zaluzhny and President Zelensky and its possible consequences. When, the day after the general's dismissal, a video report appeared from the Office of the President announcing that General Zaluzhny and General Budanov had been awarded the title of "Hero of Ukraine" all controversy subsided and for the first time some Ukrainians expressed disappointment in Zaluzhny. After receiving the "Hero of Ukraine" star, Zaluzhny hugged the President with apparent genuine friendliness. In contrast, General Budanov – the chief military intelligence officer – was restrained. Having received the award from the President, he simply nodded and stepped aside.

The new Commander-in-Chief, General Syrsky, is a well-known personality in Ukraine. He commanded the military operation in Donbas after the annexation of Crimea. An ethnic Russian; his parents and brother still live in Russia and they support Putin. General Syrsky's father is a retired colonel. His 82-year-old mother sings in a veterans' choir. His brother works as a security guard in a shopping centre and posts Russian flags and the words "I love Russia" on his social media page.

Now General Syrsky's parents are hiding from journalists and the wave of hatred that has risen against them in Russia. They are referred to as "the parents of a traitor", but they should not have been very surprised by the son's stance because he linked his fate and military career with Ukraine immediately after the collapse of the Soviet Union, learning the Ukrainian language as a young man.

Some military experts predicted that he would be less concerned about the lives of Ukrainian soldiers than Zaluzhny, and would send them on bloody assaults in order to maintain Ukrainian positions in the Donbas. But he began his work as Commander-in-Chief of the Army by auditing military units and subunits and, together with Defence Minister Rustem Umerov, he made a statement about the need to pay more attention to unit rotations and rest and recovery for military personnel.

The situation at the front cannot be called quiet, but owing to the lack of big news, Ukrainians behind the lines are taking a closer look at political life in the country – a theatre of manoeuvres that can resemble military operations. The other day, the latest round in a fight between Ukraine's security services and a well-known team of investigative journalists called BIHUS.INFO ended in a draw. The security services started their "war" against anti-corruption journalists on orders from above.

Denis Bigus, who created BIHUS.INFO more than ten years ago, is hated by many politicians and officials because he and his team, which includes experienced specialist lawyers, seek to uncover corruption among officials and representatives of Ukraine's political elite. Their investigations have spurred government anti-corruption agencies to open criminal cases against senior civil servants and politicians.

The security services started monitoring the journalists' activities and were able to make a video that compromised two members of Bigus's team – not journalists, but cameramen. The video, secretly recorded during a New Year's party, showed the two young men preparing to indulge in drugs. It was leaked to the public via a media channel linked to the Office of the President.

Immediately after the video appeared, the two cameramen were fired, and Denis Bigus's team began to investigate the security service's undercover activities against them. Their investigations revealed that the monitoring operation had lasted about a month and occupied 30 officers, all at the taxpayer's expense.

As well as raising the issue of press freedom in Ukraine, these revelations caused an international scandal because BIHUS. INFO projects are supported by dozens of international organisations, including the European Commission. The leadership of Ukraine's Security Service had to publicly explain why it had been spying on journalists. President Zelensky fired the Head of the Department of National Statehood, Roman Semenchenko, under whose leadership the operation against the journalists was carried out. For the time being there is a fragile truce between the anti-corruption journalists and the security services.

Ukrainians are willing to try new things, even new generals. They are frustrated by the lack of transparency in the government of the country and they are certainly not prepared to return to the old prison of Moscow's autocratic regime.

Acts of Resistance

I had a strange dream recently. A younger me was standing on the street in Soviet Kyiv with my classmate, Leonid Shterenberg, who, owing to the anti-Semitism of that time, later took a more Ukrainian-sounding family name. In my dream, Leonid is busy with something. He has a shovel and I'm standing next to him on a dry road, but I feel water filling my boots. I take them off, pour out the water and put them on again. My feet remain dry and yet, time and time again, water appears in my boots.

For two years after serving in the Soviet army, I kept wearing my military footwear. Perhaps I thought it was fashionable, or perhaps it was some kind of psychological inertia – I was still in the army's grip, although already at home and living as a free person, as far as that was possible in 1980s Kyiv.

This dream brought to mind others I have had recently – all startlingly graphic and all imprinted in great detail on my day-time memory. They may not be about the current war, but I am sure it is because of this that I remember these dreams. My sleep is different now – unstable, anxious and intermittent. I seem to be listening to the silence, and if I hear an air raid signal I get up easily. I go into the hallway and sit down on our small upholstered bench. I look at the clock to decide whether I should put some bedding down on the floor, or wash my face and make coffee.

I am not alone in experiencing powerful dreams these days. Even if our bodies have not been captured by the enemy, our minds have been. "In a recent dream, I ended up in a filtration camp in occupied territory," my friend Oksana Tsyupa told me. Oksana was not exposed to Russia's gruesome methods of uncovering pro-Ukrainian civilians in the occupied territories, but she is from Irpin, one of the towns on the edge of Kyiv that were controlled and ravaged by Russians at the beginning of the war. She escaped just in time, along the road that a day later became a killing field.

Journalists from all around the world are pouring into Ukraine. From Khreshchatyk, Kyiv's main street, from cafés and pubs, they will report on the second anniversary of the full-scale Russian invasion on February 24. It is a good reason to remind the world about Ukraine. The cheerful and dynamic journalists interview passers-by. Their respondents answer slowly, perhaps reluctantly. They seem tired – tired of uncertainty, tired of the vacillating support from our European and American partners.

But perhaps it is our partners who are tired. Perhaps it is they who are imposing their fatigue on Ukraine. Are they trying to wear away Ukraine's appetite for a just outcome – for the free-ing of all territories occupied by Russia?

We have always known that victory for Ukraine depends on Western aid, but during the past few months, with funds blocked in the U.S. and a lack of unity in Europe, it has become increasingly difficult to maintain our hope in this support.

Ukrainians may be responding to journalists less optimistically than they did a year ago, but there is no pessimism either. The time has come for realism – an understanding that this war will last for a long time, that we must learn to live with it. The effort to keep on "keeping on" that has been a form of resistance for civilians since the all-out invasion now requires a little more energy. For those Ukrainians who are not at the front, the war has become the background of life, and the daily air raid alerts are noted alongside the weather forecast.

Almost all Ukrainians have an app on their phones that alerts them to the possibility of missile or drone attacks. The air raids are a regular variable in plans for the day, with hours spent in bomb shelters or in the corridors of apartments and offices.

The end of February means the end of winter. Spring will be early this year – at least, that is the prediction made by Timko, our national groundhog, who lives in a research facility of Karazin Kharkiv National University. Timko was woken as usual on February 2 but he remained sleepy and showed no interest in studying his own shadow, the process by which he "predicts" spring's arrival. I am afraid he barely slept during the winter, with Russian ballistic missiles and drones raining down on Kharkiv. Ukrainian Groundhog Day was nonetheless shown on national television, which means Timko's forecast is official. The two dozen people who came to the weather centre for the event clapped joyfully and smiled at the employee who held the sleepy groundhog in her arms and interpreted Timko's reaction. For a moment, those present could put the war aside and think about the spring.

In Ukraine, spring begins in earnest with the return of the white storks – the country's ornithological symbol. They fly to north Africa in the autumn and in the spring they return to Ukrainian villages, to their nests on telegraph poles, on the chimneys of abandoned houses or on the branches of tall, dried-up trees. The nests on telegraph poles are often less stable and the electrical cables pose a threat.

This year, Ukraine's largest energy provider, DTEK, has launched the Lelechenki project, which aims to strengthen any nests at risk. Villagers who notice an unstable nest can call a team of electricians who will move it to a metal platform higher above the live cables. Time is of the essence. The nests must be moved before the storks return. So, while some Ukrainian electricians are restoring power lines destroyed by Russian missiles, others are shoring up the habitats of the country's storks.

Refusing to hide in bomb shelters, or to put their lives on hold until the end of the war, Ukraine's farmers continue preparing their fields and allotments for the sowing season. Of course, those who were mobilised into the army can only dream of returning to their former life. They may come back on short leave – barely enough time to see family and friends. Those with light or moderate injuries can spend a little more time at home after treatment, and may even be able to arrange a temporary return to their pre-war activities.

While the fight against corruption inside Ukraine continues, in every sphere of the country's life, forces are working to counteract Russia's aggression. In culture and sport, the struggle is relatively high profile, but the fight goes on in other less noticeable areas. The National Association of Sommeliers, which is a member of the International Association, is able to exert an influence on the global wine industry. Since the annexation of Crimea in 2014, Russia has not for a moment stopped trying to legitimise its control over the peninsula. Political attempts to gain recognition of Crimea as Russian territory have largely failed. However, Russia has tried to gain "economic recognition" that would give Crimea access to international trade.

In 2014, the most famous winery in Crimea, Massandra, was transferred illegally to Russian management under the Administration of President Putin. In 2016, the winery started "exporting" wine to the separatist "republics" of Donetsk and Luhansk, as well as to Belarus. Since then, Taiwan and Kazakhstan have appeared on the list of importers of this wine.

One of Ukraine's top sommeliers, Ivan Perchekliy, a Ukrainian with Bulgarian roots, volunteered for the front in April 2022. After only a short period of training, his brigade, number 241, was sent to the front near the now destroyed city of Bakhmut in the Donbas. He was stationed there for many months, fighting alongside his comrades. During a battle last year, a shell exploded next to him and a fragment hit him in the face. He was sent to the hospital and, following treatment, was given a temporary barracks position in Kyiv. In two months, he will return to the front, but while in Kyiv Perchekliy has been catching up on his duties as vice-president of the Ukrainian Sommelier Association.

The association is busier than ever. Many members have been mobilised, but the industry is trying to stay afloat and supervise export contracts. One of the association's main tasks is the promotion of Ukrainian wine, the quality of which soared in the ten years before the all-out invasion.

"At the beginning of the war, we sent a container of the best Ukrainian wine to Great Britain," Perchekliy told me. "The British are doing their best to help – 'If you want to support Ukraine, drink Ukrainian wine!' was our British partners' favourite phrase. We are now arranging a second container for the UK and preparing for the participation of Ukrainian winemakers in international exhibitions."

Perchekliy and I sat for more than an hour in the Boulangerie café on the corner of Olesia Honchara Street and Yaroslaviv Val, in Kyiv's historic centre. We drank sea buckthorn tea and talked about wine and the war. We did not talk about the looted and wrecked wineries in Kherson region or the destroyed vineyards. I was interested in how the Ukrainian Sommelier Association achieved the suspension of its Russian counterpart from the international association, and how Ukrainian sommeliers prevented Russian sommeliers from participating in tasting competitions under the Russian flag.

The next national exhibition, "Wine and Spirits 2024", takes place in Kyiv on April 26 in Natalka Park on the Dnipro embankment. It is not clear whether Perchekliy will be able to attend. By then his treatment and rehabilitation should be complete. Most likely, he will have returned to the front.

"After the war, I will pay more attention to small craft wineries, especially those in Transcarpathia!" Perchekliy said with an enthusiastic grin. "There is a lot of interesting, good wine there! If you're in Berehove, be sure to visit Krisztián Sass. He's definitely one of the future stars of our winemaking industry."

I am very fond of Transcarpathia, but I know little about its wine. My wife Elizabeth and I spent the first four months of the all-out war as "internally displaced persons" in this westernmost region of Ukraine. And we visited Berehove to see other I.D.P. friends. The town's population is largely ethnic Hungarian and you see and hear Hungarian on the streets.

The next time I go to Transcarpathia, I will make a stop in the city of Vinnytsia on the way and visit a recently opened bookshop called Heroes. As many as a dozen new bookshops have opened in Kyiv during the past year, and soon the largest bookshop in Ukraine will open its doors on Kyiv's main street. The capital's bookshops follow a pattern. You can enjoy a coffee while leafing through a book before buying it or putting it back on the shelf. The story of the new bookshop in Vinnytsia is more unusual, although you can drink good coffee there too.

Vinnytsia journalist and poet Mykola Rachok dreamt of opening a bookshop. Before the war, he worked as editor of the cultural magazine *Kunsht* and also edited an internet site for vintage car enthusiasts. When the war began, he immediately went to the front as a volunteer and, in July 2022, he died in the Donbas during a battle against Wagner forces. His parents and sister decided to open a bookshop in his memory. None of them had any experience in the book trade, nor any other business for that matter. They had to learn everything as they went along.

To give the bookshop the best possible chance of survival,

the family decided to buy premises rather than rent them. The money received by Mykola's parents in compensation after his death was not enough to buy a property; they had to sell their apartment as well. Then they designed and renovated the premises and, at the end of January this year, Heroes opened. Customers are happy to have the shop's logo stamped on the inside cover of the books they buy. It shows Mykola in silhouette, wearing a helmet and sitting on a pile of books, holding a volume in his hands.

The memory of fallen Ukrainian soldiers is a painful topic. The government has said that it will give no statistics on casualties until the end of the war, but foreign intelligence sources estimate that at least 70,000 have been killed. In cemeteries throughout the country, Ukrainian flags fly over soldiers' graves. In some cemeteries, such as the Lychakiv cemetery in Lviv, the sight of so many flags fluttering in the wind is appalling.

The mournful music of military funerals does not drown out the daily music of life in big cities. Dozens of new rock groups and solo artists have appeared and are making a name for themselves in bars, pubs, concert halls and even military hospitals. I recently heard the song "Be Patient, Cossack" performed by a young singer and was surprised to learn that the lyrics had been written by world heavyweight boxing champion Oleksandr Usyk. It turns out that Usyk, who is Crimean born and bred and grew up speaking only Russian, and who previously publicly defended the Russian Orthodox Church, is now writing patriotic poems in Ukrainian.

At the same time, Kyiv's well-known Checkpoint Drum School is busier than ever, with more than a hundred students. It closed on February 24, 2022, but reopened that April and has been operating continuously since then. "It is a rather interesting moment to study the behaviour of people who want to learn percussion," says Yuri Ryabchuk, the school's founder and director. "The fact that we don't know what awaits us tomorrow plays an important role here. Playing the drums is something many people have always wanted to do, but put off. They understand that it could be now or never, and they go for it."

The school is located in the basement of a five-storey residential building. The neighbours don't complain about the noise from the drum school. Hundreds of people spent long hours huddling in the underground premises, surrounded by drum kits and other musical equipment, and listening to explosions from Russian missiles and Ukrainian air defence gunfire.

Riabchuk is trying to organise a free "rehabilitation through percussion" course for war veterans. The organisation Veteran Hub helped him make contact with potential participants, but even after a powerful advertising campaign through veterans' groups and on social media, not a single war veteran came to Checkpoint Drum School for the course. I assume that veterans are often reluctant to think about their mental health. I would like to hope that the second attempt at this musical project will be more successful. We all believe we are O.K., and this could be the greatest weakness both for former soldiers and ordinary civilians. The fact is, we are all traumatised by this war and the trauma will remain a feature of our society for a long time to come.

Beyond the "Anniversary"

Why is the world not marking the tenth anniversary of the Russian aggression, preferring to talk about the second anniversary of the full-scale phase of the conflict? This war began on February 20, 2014, after the assassination of Maidan demonstrators and following the annexation of Crimea and the emergence of the two separatist entities on Ukrainian soil, the so-called Luhansk and Donetsk "republics". For much of the world, the events of 2014–15 were an "internal" matter for Russia and Ukraine to sort out – something like the Russian aggression against Georgia in 2008, which received little attention beyond the countries of the former Soviet bloc. Until recently, with the notable exceptions of Lithuania, Estonia and Latvia, European politicians saw countries that were previously part of the U.S.S.R. as "one family" in which misunderstandings and scandals were bound to occur, sometimes turning violent.

Two years ago, after the massacres of civilians in Bucha, Vorzel, Irpin and Borodyanka, the world decided to stop considering this war an "internal conflict" and at last took the side of a victim of Russian aggression – Ukraine.

So, for me, February 24 will not be the second or tenth anniversary of Russian aggression but the second anniversary of the moment when the democratic world saw the light, when many states at last acknowledged that such abuse of sovereign territory and its people could not be tolerated by any country that espoused democratic values – and that Putin and the Russian aggression had to be stopped.

On February 18, the anniversary of the date when protesters were killed by snipers on Kyiv's Maidan ten years ago, they were remembered, as was the annexation of Crimea, but it was Avdiivka that was the main topic of conversation. Russian troops had carried out Putin's orders to achieve some kind of victory in time for the presidential elections in March.

The capture of Avdiivka was the direct result of Ukraine's lack of artillery shells and effective air defence systems in the combat area. The city of Avdiivka, already destroyed by thousands of half-ton Russian bombs and hundreds of thousands of artillery shells, has now fallen under the control of the rogue state's army.

The city had resisted the separatists and the Russian army for almost ten years, so the capture of its ruins will not be considered a sufficiently glorious victory for Putin. The Russian army will advance on other sectors of the front, searching for opportunities to break through the Ukrainian lines of defence and to fill the Russian media with photographs of "heroic soldiers" going into battle and dying "for the Motherland, for Putin". Putin needs these messages for his Russian supporters, who need to be fed with reasons to feel proud at regular intervals. Russia has other, different messages for Europe and America. One was delivered on the first day of the Munich Security Conference, the news of Alexei Navalny's death.

———

There are no more "Navalnys" left in Russia. He was one of a kind.

Those who know Putin's Russia understood that he would never leave prison alive. In Russia, it is quite common for prisoners to die in detention. Usually, their bodies are simply taken to the cemetery. But if a death can be used as a message, it must be used to maximum effect. Someone in the Kremlin came up with a plan to change the agenda of the Munich Security

Conference, to force the participants to talk less about Ukraine and more about Russia. This plan would require an event of great significance in the eyes of the international democratic community but one that would mean very little inside Russia. The plan worked. Russia, so terrifyingly cruel, and Navalny, so easily done away with, became the focus of the conference. The shock of the news of Navalny's death in a Russian prison led the participants in Munich to the only reasonable conclusion: more must be done to help Ukraine.

While Navalny was alive, his fate was a trump card that Russia could use in any negotiations. In order to secure his release, the West might have been ready to give up some of the Russian spies and murderers sitting in European and American prisons. The German newspaper *Bild* recently reported that Navalny was about to be exchanged for the Russian agent Vadim Krasikov, who had killed a Chechen political emigrant in Berlin. Releasing Navalny from prison and letting him go abroad, however, would have strengthened the anti-Putin movement among émigrés and this was not on the Kremlin's wish list.

Now Russia will exchange its spies and murderers for *Wall Street Journal* correspondent Evan Gershkovich and other foreign citizens who had the imprudence to find themselves in that dangerous country at a bad time for world order.

The international journalists, who are currently swarming over Ukraine to report on "the anniversary", will soon return to their countries with a sense of accomplishment. The war will continue and the state of the front line will show whether the military aid promised by the European Union and the United States of America finally arrives.

Without military assistance, the front line will gradually be pushed towards the rear. More Ukrainian towns and villages will find themselves within the reach of Russian artillery, setting in motion the mechanisms for the mandatory evacuation of the civilian population.

"Mandatory evacuation" sounds very strict, but the Ukrainian authorities have not learned how to take people out of danger zones by force. It has proved extremely difficult for them even to remove some children from active war zones. Ukrainian police and volunteers had to spend weeks searching for the children hidden by their parents among the ruins in Bakhmut and Avdiivka.

When Avdiivka fell, approximately 900 residents were still hiding in basements. These adults had been offered evacuation to areas further from the front line on dozens of occasions, but they refused to leave. When Russian troops had already captured half the city, the last car to leave, with two tearful women and a dog, was driven out at high speed towards the Ukrainian positions.

Of the people remaining in the ruins, only one resident agreed to give an interview to Russian journalists. "Thank you very much for liberation!" he said. The television journalists could not find anyone else willing to thank the Russian army. No doubt they will find somebody later. Perhaps they will buy another "thank you" for a loaf of bread and a tin of stew. For months, the residents who remained in the battle zone survived on food and water supplied by the Ukrainian military and volunteers, people who risked their lives time and time again so that Avdiivka residents would not go hungry.

What will Ukrainian soldiers do if the West continues to delay the supply of military aid? In what will they put their faith? Support for soldiers' inner selves has become an important issue at the front. Each unit has an officer with training in dealing with mild mental health issues: stress, depression, or aggression. These officers help to the best of their abilities;

studies show that soldiers feel closer to chaplains who are not ranked above them and who fight alongside them if necessary.

Chaplains appeared throughout the Ukrainian army only in October 2022. They are now present on the staffing register of all military units. They receive a salary and take part in both military exercises and combat operations. Many chaplains have been injured and several have died during the past eighteen months. There are now 750 chaplains serving on the front line and in rearguard units. They are mostly young, physically fit people and, on the front line, they often have to put down their Bibles and take up their guns.

Were it not for the war, these chaplains would be preaching peace and love in Ukrainian communities, but military service influences their thoughts and feelings. Sometimes this leads them to make unconventional decisions that might be criticised by other priests. Last year, Chaplain Serhiy Budovy reported that he had got the image of Jesus Christ tattooed on his arm, "So that even my body glorifies the Lord," he explained. This news began a discussion about whether members of the clergy should have tattoos. A variety of sacred texts that mention the subject were remembered, as were the ancient Coptic Christians who put secret tattoos on their wrists to recognise each other. The theological discussion was quietened when Chaplain Budovy explained that he started getting this tattoo in a frontline dugout, in Donetsk region. The tattoo remained unfinished for a long time because the soldier tattoo artist, who was in the dugout with him, was put out of action by severe concussion. Another tattoo artist serving at the front eventually finished the work, allowing Budovy to show off photographs of his Jesus tattoo on social networks.

In St Petersburg, following the death of Alexei Navalny in one of Russia's harshest prisons, only one priest, Father Grigoriy

Mikhnov-Vaitenko, expressed a desire to hold a memorial service for him. He announced this on social media and was soon detained by police. In the police station, he suffered a stroke and was taken to hospital.

Another St Petersburg priest, Father Andrey, stepped in for Grigoriy and conducted a brief ceremony at the memorial to victims of the Gulag. It was attended by a few dozen people, all of whom were immediately arrested. It is not known what happened to Father Andrey.

In Ukraine, Navalny's death did not give rise to a significant reaction. He was considered anti-Ukrainian because of his stance on Crimea. He had said that it would not be returned to Ukraine. "What is Crimea, a sausage sandwich, to be handed back and forth?" he said in October 2014, eight months after its annexation. Ukrainians cannot forgive him for that. Navalny was also slow to recognise Russia's war crimes against Ukraine, although in later statements he did acknowledge the need for Russia to lose this war and for Ukraine to return to its 1991 borders. In the end, Navalny understood that if Russia did not lose there would be no future for the country. There would only be the Russia of the past, the same Russia before which the world now cowers, the Russia which killed Alexei Navalny, Anna Politkovskaya, Boris Nemtsov and many, many others.

Parrots, Propaganda and Puppet Shows –
Keeping our Minds Sharp

In Chernivtsi, near the border with Romania, air raid sirens sound much less often than in the central regions of Ukraine. The reason, of course, is the distance between Bukovina and the front line. The people of this region are more relaxed. They can enjoy the signs of spring and linger over the beautiful sunsets. As the buds on the trees burst into life, residents of Chernivtsi have noticed an exotic addition to the city's flora and fauna – a sizeable population of large green parrots.

Lviv ornithologist Andriy Bokotey believes that, indirectly, this strange phenomenon is due to the war. The birds were released from their cages before their owners fled. Relatively free of anxieties about bombing raids, residents in Chernivtsi feel obliged to take other concerns more seriously and, when the parrots first appeared in November 2023, there were considerable misgivings about whether they would survive the winter. However, these are Kramer's parrots, a very hardy species, and they seem to be thriving in the city. They have their favourite trees and are especially attached to Oktyabrsky Park, where pensioners have hung feeders with apples and lard on the branches. Local ornithologists are wary of the parrots, however, explaining that they are an invasive species and are in danger of crowding out native birds.

The appearance of these feathered guests has prompted city residents, young and old, to update their knowledge of zoology. They now know that Kramer's parrots (*Psittacula krameri*, also known as the rose-ringed parakeet) have, over the past few decades, been gradually occupying western Europe. This "occupation" does not exactly disturb the peace of Europeans, but it has changed the balance of power in Europe's ornithological world and has forced specialists to study the root cause of the invasion.

For the thinking person, everything that happens in the world requires an explanation. We all want to understand where electricity and wind come from and we all want to understand the cause of this war. Could it be this kind of curiosity that spurred the American journalist Tucker Carlson to make his journey to Moscow for an audience with Putin? Carlson already had some fixed ideas about the reasons for the Russian invasion. Was he simply interested in gaining confirmation of his theories directly from Putin's lips? Carlson probably expected that Putin's explanations would be as easy to understand and as logical as the ornithologists' explanations for the appearance of exotic bird species in western Ukraine.

During the interview, Carlson himself looked rather like an exotic bird from warmer climes who had found itself in a land of permafrost. He was clearly indifferent to the information spouted at him by President Putin, the self-styled professor of his own version of history. Carlson did not understand that Putin was giving this interview, or rather his lecture, not for the American television journalist but to the Russian people. What do all these Rurikoviches and Pechenegs mean to the average Tucker Carlson fan? However, just by listening to Putin's historical fantasies, Carlson lent legitimacy to Putin's version of history, which is now being integrated into the school curriculum both in Russia and in the occupied territories of Ukraine.

The Russian non-profit organisation Support for Government Initiatives has already prepared instructions on how to use the text and the video lecture created from the interview. The instructions, prepared for the heads of educational authorities, explain how to discuss the lecture with children and their parents so as to "strengthen their sense of national identity".

"Involving students in research projects related to topics from the interview helps develop skills in collecting and analysing information . . . Discussion about the interview can also help build mutual understanding between the educational institution and the family on issues related to the upbringing of informed and responsible citizens," the document states.

Reading this six-page manual took me back to Soviet times. In the early '80s, all Soviet people, including students like me, had to read, analyse and discuss three comparatively subtle books by the then General Secretary of the Communist Party of the U.S.S.R., Leonid Brezhnev: *Renaissance*, *Malaya Zemlya* and *Virgin Land*. Through these texts, written with the help of professional journalists, Brezhnev addressed, from his point of view, significant events in Soviet history in which he took part. Each of these books was published in editions of fifteen million copies. It appears Brezhnev had some presentiment of his death and tried to leave a "literary monument" to himself and his place in the history of the U.S.S.R. The fact that I still remember the contents of those books suggests that he achieved his goal.

Russian aggression has radically impacted the education system in Russia. The ideological component now occupies centre stage. In addition to openly propagandistic lessons called "Talks about Important Things", there are classes on "life safety", in which children are trained in how to react during terrorist attacks and told that these attacks on Russia are carried out by Ukraine. In recent months, Russia has been discussing the possibility of training schoolchildren to assemble combat drones. It should also prove very easy to reintroduce the "labour lessons" that were abolished in Russian schools in 2010. From September 1 of this year, these lessons will reappear in the school curriculum, sometimes under the heading of "technology", which suggests that, instead of making teapot stands or candlesticks, students will learn about microchips and electronics.

Patriotic education is now a focus in Ukrainian education too. True, in lessons devoted to "The Defence of Ukrainian Statehood", nobody will have to study the speeches and interviews of President Zelensky.

Changes in the school curriculum caused by the Russian aggression are being introduced gradually. The Russian–Ukrainian war itself is studied in history lessons. Deputy Minister of Education Dmytro Zavgorodniy has said that in the near future hundreds of thousands of high school students, as well as college students, will learn to assemble drones. Parents showed mixed reactions to this, with many suggesting that first-aid training was more important for high school students. For the primary school classroom, patriotic computer games and quests have been developed. The war has already, of course, become the theme of children's books and even puppet shows.

The Vinnytsia Puppet Theatre is about to premiere a play about four refugee cats. These feline heroes, each with his or her own personality and biography, live in a bomb shelter. They quarrel and make peace, learn to compromise and create codes of behaviour for refugee cats. One of the play's characters is a semi-paralysed cat called Busya, who has wheels under her motionless hind legs. The authors call this theatre genre "cat therapy". The play has already been staged by theatres in other cities in Ukraine and in Britain, Sweden and Estonia. Children enjoy the story of the four cats whose lives were turned upside down by the war. The messages from the performance become topics of discussion at home.

"It's important to talk to children about the war if only

because they see it and it's important for them to understand what's happening," explained one of the play's authors, Marina Smilyanets. "The idea itself was invented by my co-author Lyuda Timoshenko. Along with her cat Mykola, she became a refugee at the beginning of the war. I was absorbed in the problem of how to tell children about the war, so we combined our efforts and created this story."

During the period 2014–22, Ukrainians who lived far from the Donbas were able to ignore the war, but the full-scale Russian invasion has not left a single corner of the country free of reminders of the aggression. These reminders come more and more often, even in the peaceful domain of Ukrainian restaurants. In addition to traditional tips for the waiters, customers can now leave a percentage of the bill for the Ukrainian army. These extra payments are called "combat tips" and they remind clients, if they needed any reminding, about the relative safety in which they have enjoyed their meal and by whom and at what cost, that safety is provided.

If you are able to put aside fears for the future, you can imagine how, in a matter of weeks, restaurants in Kyiv and Chernivtsi will open their summer terraces, attracting even more diners, who will leave larger tips for the army than for the waiters. Unless, of course, by that time both the waiters and their clients have been mobilised.

22.04.2024

Epilogue

Alas, the war in Ukraine continues. In this book I had hoped to be able to recount how the war ended, to describe Ukraine's rejoicing at the liberation of territories captured by the Russian occupiers. I hoped to report on the start of a massive construction project – the restoration of destroyed cities and villages.

My hopes and the reality do not coincide. The reality is much more complicated and dramatic. It forces Ukrainians to dig deep for additional energy and faith, to remain strong and not to break down. For some it has proved too much.

But Ukraine is holding on. We were taught from childhood that good always triumphs over evil. Only we were not told what the price of such a victory could be. We are learning that now through daily lessons of horror, death and destruction.

Yellow and blue flags flutter over the graves of tens of thousands of Ukrainian soldiers. There is no-one to cry over the graves of tens of thousands of murdered civilians. Hundreds of thousands of families have been broken up – with wives and children living as refugees in Europe and North America, while their menfolk are either at the front or clinging to civilian life but unable to leave the country due to wartime legislation.

Probably the most important event to occur between the completion of this diary and the release date of the book happened on April 20, 2024 – the U.S. Congress' vote in favour of assistance to Ukraine. Over the previous six months, the pause in US military aid cost Ukraine 5,000 square kilometres of territory.

After our unsuccessful counter-offensive in 2023, the Russian army stepped up its offensive. They have not been completely successful either, but they are pleased with their results. They present the capture of each ruined village as a small victory on the way to a big one.

The Ukrainian army is defending the frontlines without enough weapons or ammunition. While American military aid is still on its way to Ukraine, Putin's army will try to achieve its big goals. This will mean hundreds of missiles and drones being fired at Ukrainian communities every day, and ever more vicious attempts to break through Ukrainian lines of defence.

Ukrainians have new hope that the situation at the front will change for the better in the near future. We just need to hold out until the promised help arrives.

The events of the last year and a half have not turned me into a pessimist. I still believe that Ukraine will win. I just don't know how long it will take or how many more times we will be left waiting for help for months on end.

Ukrainians remain steadfast. My village neighbour Tolik is sticking to his promise of not shaving until Victory Day. His wife Nina is less than happy about his long beard which makes him look so old, but she tolerates Tolik's stubbornness. His beard is one more reason to look forward to the victory.

Index

Europe 221–2, 242, 250,
322, 329, 330
see also refugees,
Ukrainian; individual
countries by name
European Union 12, 103,
107, 195, 235, 331
evacuations, mandatory
332
Evdokimova, Nastia 214

F
Facebook 76, 133, 134,
231, 261, 286, 287
fake news/disinformation
53–4, 105, 260, 309–10
see also propaganda,
Russian
Farion, Iryna 85, 262–3
farmers, relocation of 60–1
see also agricultural
industry
"Father Frost" character
117–18, 281
Fedyshyn, Halina 282
film makers 173–4, 176,
191–3
filtration camps, Russian
Federation 18–21, 49
Finland 95
food and drink 23, 24,
27–8, 57–8, 66, 126,
296–300
"Food Train" frontline visit
297
Forbes Ukraine 306
foreign politicians visit the
Ukraine 147–8, 156
"Forgive Us, Dear
Russians" (I. Samarina)
20
France 113, 199
Franko, Ivan 245
F.S.B., Russian 224, 225
see also security services,
Russian
fuel supplies 12, 28–9, 69,
104, 116, 223, 228, 314
see also electricity
supplies
fundraising, war effort 31–3,
76–7, 90, 108, 126,
131–2, 133–4, 169–70,
175, 177, 205–6, 217,
259, 295–6, 339

funerals, Ukrainian 16–18,
88, 97

G
Gagauz people, Ukrainian
96
Ganieva, Daria 52
Gatne, Fastiv district 255–6
Gavrilchenko, Denis 60
Gazprom 223
"General Frost," Russian
belief in 95–6
Geneva Conference speech
(2023), author's 184–7
Georgia 21, 211
Gerasimov, General Valery
222, 251§
Germany 71, 157, 241,
306–7
Gershkovich, Evan 331
Girkin, Igor 213
Glaser, Amelia 164
Gogol, Mykola 214
Golubkov, Taras 176, 177
Google Maps 16
Gorbachev, Mikhail 17
government, Ukrainian
corruption 310–12
dual citizenship bill
305–6, 307–8
military registration
policies 239–40, 286,
317
Ministry of Culture and
Information 22, 175
Ministry of Defence 54,
95, 159, 160, 222, 242,
308–9, 310–12
Ministry of Economics
60
Ministry of Education
242
Ministry of Internal
Affairs 295
and the Moscow
Patriarchate 251–3
National Military
Cemetery 255–6
Parliament 27, 109, 110,
138, 171–2, 239–40,
255–6, 286, 317
payments to
Kyivvmiskbud
Construction Holding
228–9

"presidential bloggers"
136, 137–9
public trust in 247–8
State Property Fund 230
taxes 14–15
traitors and corruption
36, 247
treatment of Russian
P.O.W.s 271
see also Parliament,
Ukrainian; Zelensky,
President Volodymyr
G.P.S. (global positioning
systems) 11–12
grain/wheat industry,
Ukrainian 12, 47, 244
'Gratitude Rallies' 231–2
Grey Bees (A. Kurkov) 94
Gritsenyak, Mykola 282
Groundhog Day, Ukrainian
323
G.R.U., Russian Federation
20
Grushko, Anastasia 208–9
Gryanik, Oleksandr 256–7
Gurskaya, Irina 21

H
hackers, Russian *vs.*
Ukrainian 287–8, 291
Halldór Laxness
International Literature
Prize, author's
acceptance speech
45–50
Halloween festivities 85–6
Hasidic Jews 40–2
Heart Out organisation
255
heating crisis, winter
29–31, 77, 95–6, 250
"Heavenly Hundred"
110
Heroes bookshop,
Vinnytsia 326–7
Hodges, Ben 155
holidaymakers abroad,
Russian 210
holidaymakers abroad,
Ukrainian 210
Holodomor famine and
Remembrance Day 161,
273–4
Holy Vvedensky Convent,
Bukovina 99